Religious Psychology in American Literature

José Porrúa Turanzas, S.A.
EDICIONES

stuðia humanitatis

Directed by
BRUNO M. DAMIANI
The Catholic University of America

ADVISORY BOARD

Religious Psychology in American Literature

A Study in the Relevance of William James

by Victor Strandberg

studia humanitatis

Publisher and distributor
José Porrúa Turanzas S.A.
Cea Bermúdez, 10 - Madrid - 3
España

Distributor for the U.S.A.
Studia Humanitatis
1383 Kersey Lane
Potomac, Maryland 20854

© Victor Strandberg, 1981
I.S.B.N. 0–93–5568–18–2
Library of Congress Catalog Card Number 81–50131

Impreso en Los Estados Unidos
Printed in the United States of America

Cea Bermúdez, 10 - Madrid - 3
Ediciones Jose Porrúa Turanzas, S.A.

---

designed by Richard Kinney

*This book is dedicated
to FRANCES RANSON MANN
in gratitude for her kindness
and in loving remembrance
of her mother and sister.*

Contents

Preface

Perhaps the most useful apology in criticism is that given by Herman Melville at the end of "Hawthorne and His Mosses"—"it is hard to be finite upon an infinite subject, and all subjects are infinite." The subject announced in my title is obviously infinite, and I can not hope to be comprehensive about it. What I have done is to correlate some thirty major American writers with the religious psychology of William James, particularly as expounded in his classic study, *The Varieties of Religious Experience*. By applying James's insights, drawn from a vast amount of documentary testimony, this study hopes to illuminate the work of its selected writers, and at the same time to clarify the larger schools of literary experience which those writers represent: The Sick Soul, the Religion of Healthy-Mindedness, Conversion, Mysticism, and so forth. Admittedly, the intellectual dominance over our age by two avowed atheists, Marx and Freud, seemingly renders James quaint and irrelevant; yet, given the breadth of James's definition of religion, and his insistence on its personal and experiential rather than institutional and dogmatic nature, good reason remains for his view of religion as "the most important of all human functions."[1]

---

[1] William James, *The Varieties of Religious Experience*. Foreword by Jacques Barzun (New York: Mentor Books, 1958), p. 56. Subtitled "A Study in Human Nature: Being the Gifford Lectures on Natural Religion *(continued on page x)*

A secondary apology, growing out of the infinitude of this book's subject matter, concerns the gauntlet of scholars whose terrain one must hope to race across without sustaining the fall of a fatal hatchet. Any writer on a topic such as this book espouses is apt to resemble (to vary the metaphor) a decathlon competitor: each artist he writes about is bound to bring him into an arena wherein that figure's world champion scholar lolls waiting for combat. Compounding this problem are space limitations which, by requiring me to compress this book from a lengthier manuscript version, oblige me to touch only lightly upon some relevant artists and to omit others altogether from the discussion. (For the same reason, I have condensed my footnotes.) I can only hope that the book will be judged mainly by what it contains, rather than by what may be missing.

A final difficulty that could beset this book pertains to the once-vaunted doctrine of the autonomy of art. For my flouting of this doctrine there is no apology, for the evidence overwhelmingly supports my presumption that the artist inhabits his creation. James Joyce's metaphor of the artist paring his nails somewhere outside and above his work does not jibe—to take a famous example—with Richard Ellmann's biographical research showing how Joyce's rage over his supposed cuckoldom or his gratitude over being helped by a Jewish stranger in a brothel figured largely into *Ulysses*. Even that quintessential New Critic Robert Penn Warren has drawn connections of cobweb complexity between the writer's personal life and his art in his excellent studies of Dreiser, Melville, and

(continued from page ix) Delivered at Edinburgh in 1901–1902," this work has been in print since 1902. Having chosen the Mentor Books paperback edition because it is inexpensive and easily available to my readers, I shall hereafter include page references to it within my main text. Other quotations in this Preface are cited from Robert Penn Warren, *Democracy and Poetry* (Cambridge: 1975), p. 71; James E. Miller, Jr., *Theory of Fiction* (Lincoln: 1972), p. 297; and Joseph Conrad, the Author's Note to *Chance*.

Whittier. And in *Democracy and Poetry*, speaking of "the most subtle, complex, and profound relationship in literature," Warren says "It is not only the objective characters that serve as 'models' of selfhood; the work itself represents the author's adventures in selfhood."

So we are free to return to the good sense of the two James brothers: William, whose thought will permeate the following pages; and Henry, whose monumental influence upon modern fiction was perfectly compatible with a sense of the artist's presence in his work. "The great question as to a poet or a novelist is, How does he feel about life?" Henry James wrote. "What, in the last analysis, is his philosophy?" James's devoted admirer, Joseph Conrad, brought that tradition into the high modern period by admitting that in every third sentence, a writer gives his morality away. On this assumption that all serious art is confessional, created indeed for the very purpose of discovering, disclosing, and in some way affirming the innermost being of its maker, we proceed with this Jamesian study of the life and works of our roster of artists with the intent of understanding both life and works better.

*　　　　　м　　　　　*　　　　　*

Several fragments of this text have previously appeared in scholarly journals. The most extensive of these fragments are the pieces on Hart Crane, originally published in *The McNeese Review* (XXXIV, 1975–76), and on Henry James (*The University Review*, June, 1968). I have also re-deployed some shorter excerpts from essays on Poe, Warren, Updike, and Faulkner, appearing respectively in *The University Review* (March, 1969), *Criticism* (Winter, 1968), *Mosaic* (Fall, 1978), and *Faulkner Studies* (I, 1980).

I close with a word of thanks to my typist, Ms. Betty Goodbar, for her good work and good cheer.

William James, courtesy of Manuscript Department of the Perkins Library, Duke University.

Chapter I

Introduction:
Freud, Jung, James

Freud, Jung, and William James represent three dimensions in the study of religious psychology. Freud's dismissal of religion as an infantile regression in *The Future of an Illusion* is done in the name of "science," which takes art, philosophy, and above all religion as its deadly enemies, in Freud's thinking. "Science"—i.e. Freudian psychology—in turn operates in the realm of pure reason, which is the chief weapon Freud enlists in his effort of aiding the conscious mind to cope with disturbances from the unconscious. "The voice of the intellect [also translated as *The voice of reason*] is a soft one, but it does not rest until it has gained a hearing. Finally, after a countless succession of rebuffs, it succeeds This is one of the few points on which one may be optimistic about the future of mankind." Of the emotional or intuitive value of religious experience, Freud cares nothing: "There is no appeal to a court above that of reason . . . . If one man has gained an unshakable conviction of the true reality of religious doctrines from a state of ecstasy which has deeply moved him, of what significance is that to others?"[1]

---

[1] *The Future of an Illusion*, Doubleday Anchor reprint (New York: 1964), pp. 87, 43. Other quotations in this chapter are cited from *(continued on page 2)*

1

Jung's religious psychology, in contradiction to Freud's, elevates the importance of the unconscious while reducing the role of rational consciousness proportionately. The unconscious mind, says Jung in *The Undiscovered Self*, "is the only accessible source of religious experience," and in dealing with both the divine and demonic emanations from the unconscious, "*Reason alone does not suffice*" (emphasis Jung's). As Freud was the advocate of reason, Jung is the advocate of the unconscious, summoned to interpret and defend its symbolic promulgations. Indeed, Jung's lifelong calling to this task was precipitated by just such a mystic vision as Freud, in the above quotation, thought worthless for its lack of "reason" and significance to others. Coming upon Jung in his schoolboy days (at age twelve), the vision disclosed God's displeasure with religious orthodoxy and invested the youth with what became his lifelong mission:

> One fine summer day that same year [1887] I came out of school at noon and went to the cathedral square. The sky was gloriously blue, the day one of radiant sunshine. The roof of the cathedral glittered, the sun sparkling from the new, brightly glazed tiles. I was overwhelmed by the beauty of the sight, and thought: "The world is beautiful and the church is beautiful and God made all this and sits above it far away in the blue sky on his golden throne. . . ."
> . . . I saw before me the cathedral, the blue sky. God sits on his golden throne, high above the world—and from under the throne an enormous turd falls upon the sparkling new roof, shatters it, and breaks the walls of the cathedral asunder.
> So that was it! I felt an enormous, an indescribable relief

(continued from page 1) Carl Gustav Jung, *The Undiscovered Self* (New York: Mentor Books, 1959), pp. 101, 112, and *Memories, Dreams, Reflections* (New York: 1963), pp. 36, 39–40; William James, *The Varieties of Religious Experience* (See Note 1 to Preface), p. 195, *Some Problems in Philosophy* (New York: 1922), pp. 100, 97, and *The Principles of Psychology*, Volume 2 (New York: 1890), p. 297; Gay Wilson Allen, *William James: A Biography* (New York: 1969), p. 415; Andrew Turnbull, *Scott Fitzgerald: A Biography* (New York: 1962), p. 259; *Writers at Work: The Paris Review Interviews* (New York: 1959), p. 282 (Styron) and 146–7 (Simenon); and Wallace Stevens, *The Necessary Angel* (New York: 1951), pp. 120–121.

. . . and an unutterable bliss such as I had never known. I wept for happiness and gratitude. The wisdom and goodness of God had been revealed to me. . . . I had experienced an illumination. From that moment on, when I experienced grace, my true responsibility began.

William James, the predecessor of the other two, remains the largest of the three in his investigative dimensions. Like Freud, James felt that the discovery of the subconscious mind (first made in 1886, he says) was the most important advance made in psychology during his lifetime; and like Jung, James suspected that genuine religious experience draws heavily upon subconscious sources: "If there be higher powers able to impress us, they may get access to us only through the subliminal door." Along with those higher powers, darker forces may also come through that door, James was careful to add—forces of "delusional insanity paranoia" or even "a *diabolical* mysticism, a sort of religious mysticism turned upside down" (p. 326). So James concludes that "that great subliminal . . . region contains every kind of matter: 'seraph and snake' abide there side by side" (326). From "seraph" and "snake" we may extrapolate Jung's and Freud's respective emphases, with James siding more with Jung—naturally enough—in his religious psychology, but at the same time admitting a large element of quasi-Freudian rational skepticism into his fundamentals of judgment. "Once more," he says, "I repeat that non-mystics are under no obligation to acknowledge in mystical states a superior authority conferred on them by their intrinsic nature" (326). To say this, however, was not to say, with Freud, that personal religious experiences had no significance for others; it meant rather that whatever came from the subconscious "must be sifted and tested, and run the gauntlet of confrontation with the total context of experience, just like what comes from the outer world of sense. Its value must be ascertained by empirical methods . . . " (326). As an initial "sifting and testing" process, James

3

chose to limit his source of religious testimony to highly literate and educated people, including many figures of genius like Goethe, Tennyson, and Tolstoy.

Drawing without bias from both "the A-region of personality," or "the level of full sunlit consciousness," and the subconscious "B-region" (366), wherein arise our dreams and "whatever mystical experience we may have," James's religious psychology was thus the most open and empirical of the three, and the most capable of embracing the whole range of religious experiences. For this reason, James's synthesis of psychology, philosophy, and religion, though largely neglected in favor of Freud and Jung and their successors, remains capable of yielding valuable insights into modern literature, far beyond James's acknowledged influence on such literary classics as Nathanael West's *Miss Lonelyhearts* and Robert Penn Warren's *All the King's Men*.

As our pre-eminent pioneer in American psychology, James has particular relevance to American literature, most of all because of the "radical empiricism" which underlies all his thinking. As a Pragmatist, a Pluralist, and an advocate of the Varieties of experience, James shares the affinity of the American artist for immediate experience in preference to any doctrinaire ideology by which experience may be interpreted. Experience, not "reason," is thus the final arbiter of truth, a point that James underscored repeatedly in defining his position as a "radical empiricist" rather than a "rationalist." While admitting, in *Some Problems in Philosophy*, that "concepts [are] . . . a magnificent sketch-map for showing us our bearings," James roundly asserted that "we shall hold fast to this empiricist view [that] . . . concepts . . . can never fitly supersede perception," for "the deeper features of reality are found only in perceptual experience." This latter view had emerged out of his *Principles of Psychology*, that labor of a dozen years, which, published in 1890, had drawn this conclusion among others that would later undergird James's extensive studies in

4

religion and philosophy: "our own reality, that sense of our own life which we at every moment possess, is the ultimate of ultimates for our belief." Concerning his upcoming Gifford lectures, later to be published as *The Varieties of Religious Experience*, James wrote, in the spring of 1900, that his ambition was, "*first*, to defend (against all the prejudices of my 'class') 'experience' against 'philosophy' as being the real backbone of the world's religious life. . . ; and *second*, to make the hearer or reader believe, what I myself invincibly do believe, that, although all the special manifestations of religion may have been absurd (I mean its creeds and theories), yet the life of it as a whole is mankind's most important function."

If we define "the world's religious life" broadly, as James himself did in regarding religion as a psychic phenomenon, we may fairly safely consider James's statement above to reflect the views of a good number of major artists. In fact, James's definition of religion in *The Varieties of Religious Experience* is so broad as to make it difficult for any important writer to escape James's psychic jurisdiction. "At bottom," he says, "the whole concern of both morality and religion is with the manner of our acceptance of the universe" (p. 49). Every serious artist, by having the same concern, serves, by this definition, a religious purpose.

Our main purpose, then, will be to correlate James's masterwork of religious psychology, *The Varieties of Religious Experience*, with a fair number of major American writers. In so doing, we shall reject the doctrine of the autonomy of art, that is, the pretense that characters and personae and other vehicles of meaning in literary works may not be understood as shedding light upon their authors' own psychic condition. It is true, of course, that discretion must be exercised in identifying any writer with his fictional creations; yet all art is ultimately, in one way or another, a confession, a disclosure of the artist himself. A number of first-rate writers have admitted as much: "I sometimes feel that the characters I've created are not much more than . . . projected facts of myself," William Styron said in an interview; "The good writing of any age has always been the product of someone's neurosis." Scott Fitzgerald likewise asserted that "all my characters are Scott Fitzgerald. Even the female characters." George Simenon felt that "if a man has the urge to be an artist, it is because he needs to find himself. Every writer tries to find himself through his characters, through all his writing." Even those two prophets of the High Modern period, T. S. Eliot and Ezra Pound, forsook their masks and their impersonality-of-art doctrines to disburden themselves via personal confession in *Ash-Wednesday* and the *Pisan Cantos*. Wallace Stevens fairly well gave the impersonality-of-art school its death-blow by pointing out the irresistible truth that "the poet manifests his personality, first of all, by his choice of subject . . . . What is the poet's subject? It is his sense of the world."

This "sense of the world"—reminiscent of James's comment that "the whole concern of . . . religion is with the manner of our acceptance of the universe"—is the psychic territory that literature and religion hold in common. In the analyses that fill the rest of this book, while examining each writer's "sense of the world" in the light of William James's religious psychology, we shall draw upon whatever sources may best illuminate that "sense of the world," turning mainly to the creative literature each has written but also to letters, interviews, biographies, and similar background material. If James was right, or even anywhere within the limits of conceivability, in his belief that "the life of it [religion] as a whole is mankind's most important function," the manifestation of religious meaning—in its broadest definition—may similarly be literature's most important function.

For all its complexity of detail and its comprehensiveness of scope, *The Varieties of Religious Experience* manifests a fairly simple structure. The great bulk of the work is given over to a definition and analysis of James's three basic personality types—the "Once-born," the "Sick Soul," and the "Twice-born"—with this central heart of the work being further elucidated by related chapters on "Mysticism" and "Saintliness." Because the relevance of *The Varieties* to American literature lies mainly in the way these three personality types predominate in our literature, and in large measure divide the world among them, we shall in a general way follow James's principle of organization in our present study, classifying and analyzing our artist figures as they happen to fall into one or another of the Jamesian categories.

Some initial definitions of terms are in order. The Once-born, who espouse what James calls "The Religion of Healthy-Mindedness," are those who find the world perfectly satisfactory as it is, and celebrate it accordingly. They are "Once-born" because, having found their world wholly benevolent and their lives entirely satisfying, they have no need to be "born again" into a new and better spiritual perception. Spinoza, Emerson, and, above all, Whitman were to James exemplars of the "feeling that Nature, if you will only trust her sufficiently, is absolutely good" (p. 77). The sick soul, by contrast, is obsessed by the world's evil and suffering to the point of suicidal despair. Within this category of the "Morbid-minded," as James calls such persons, some surprising names are brought forward. James quotes Goethe, for example, as saying in 1824 that "my existence . . . has been nothing but pain and burden, and I can affirm that during the whole of my 75 years, I have not had four weeks of genuine well-being." Not the Romantic Faust but our modern Sisyphus proves Goethe's chosen myth to describe his own life: "It is but the perpetual rolling of a rock that must be raised up again forever" (p. 119). Martin Luther also, when grown old, lines up with James's morbid-minded: "I am utterly weary of life. . . . Rather than live forty years more, I would give up my chance of Paradise" (p. 119).

James's favorite exemplar of the sick soul, however, was

7

his contemporary, Leo Tolstoy, who at about the age of fifty—when rich with good health, fame, and the love and respect of friends and family—was suddenly overcome by "the meaningless absurdity of life—. . . the only incontestable knowledge accessible to man" (p. 132): "Behold me then, a man happy and in good health, hiding the rope in order not to hang myself to the rafters of the room where every night I went to sleep alone; behold me no longer going shooting, lest I should yield to the too easy temptation of putting an end to myself with the gun" (p. 130). Such sickness of soul, according to James, is a radical condition curable only by such a transformation of consciousness as amounts to a change in identity, or being Twice-Born, in James's terminology: "When disillusionment has gone as far as this, there is seldom a *restitutio ad integrum*. One has tasted of the fruit of the tree, and the happiness of Eden never comes again. The happiness that comes, when any does come . . . , is not the simple ignorance of ill, but something vastly more complex, including natural evil as one of its elements, but finding natural evil . . . swallowed up in super-natural good. . . . The sufferer, when saved, is saved by what seems to him a second birth, a deeper kind of conscious being than he could enjoy before" (p. 133).

In thus setting forth his distinction between "the healthy-minded, who need to be born only once, and . . . the sick souls, who must be twice-born in order to be happy," James is not neutral or impartial. He sides strongly with the morbid-minded, feeling "bound to say that healthy-mindedness is inadequate as a philosophical doctrine, because the evil facts which it refuses positively to account for are a genuine portion of reality; and they may after all be the best key to life's significance" (p. 137). To the morbid-minded, James says, "healthy-mindedness pure and simple seems unspeakably blind and shallow" (p. 137), and he cites the predatory design of nature as a type of the radical evil that makes healthy-mindedness untenable (p. 138):

8

The lunatic's visions of horror are all drawn from the material of daily fact. . . . To believe in the carnivorous reptiles of geologic time, is hard for our imagination. . . . Yet there is no tooth in any one of those museum-skulls that did not daily . . . hold fast to the body struggling in despair of some fated living victim. Forms of horror just as dreadful to their victims, if on a smaller spatial scale, fill the world about us today. . . . Crocodiles and rattlesnakes and pythons are at this moment vessels of life just as real as we are; . . . and whenever they or other wild beasts clutch their living prey, the deadly horror which an agitated melancholiac feels is the literally right reaction on the situation.

Because of its lesser degree of complexity, the once-born or healthy-minded personality type inhabits a much smaller area of James's book than does the sick soul or twice-born type of personality. For the same reason, our own study will fix most largely on the sick soul and (where relevant) its Conversion into the Twice-born condition. Perhaps William Styron was right in thinking that good writing always comes from someone's neurosis, or perhaps our own reading bias tends to find the sick soul's torment inherently more interesting than healthy-mindedness—which strikes us as inherently dull or second-rate unless transmuted into art by the highest act of genius. The main substance of this book, then, will be devoted to a discussion of the sick soul and its conversion, but first some comment should be made about the Religion of Healthy-Mindedness, which has sustained a robust tradition in American literature from Colonial times to the present.

Chapter II

The Religion of Healthy-Mindedness

1

What foreigners refer to as the American spirit of optimism thrusts diverse roots down into history. The natural selection process by which only the toughest, most adventurous of Europe's poor became American immigrants; the rapid conquest by these people of an immensely resourceful continent; the shining image of the American Dream as apprehended from the time of Franklin's *Autobiography*; the consummate ease with which the Founding Fathers incorporated the rational self-confidence of the Enlightenment into American political institutions—factors such as these no doubt contributed significantly to the public tradition of positive thinking. But as a phenomenon having genuine religious force, American healthy-mindedness acquired its first true prophet, its figure of Mohammedan or Pauline power, in the person of Ralph Waldo Emerson. Rising to repudiate the Western myth of the Fall by proclaiming that this world *is* the kingdom of God and all men are His incarnations, Emerson became in

William James's phrase "an admirable example" of the healthy-minded individual, one of those who "see God, not as a strict Judge, not as a Glorious Potentate; but as the animating Spirit of a beautiful harmonious world" (p. 78).

For Emerson, it was not always so. At age twenty-six, newly married and recently appointed to his first pastorate, he wrote in his Journal a strange antithesis to these felicitous circumstances: "I know my illdeserts; and the beauty of God makes me feel my own sinfulness the more."[1] An early poem, "Grace," elaborates upon these Puritanical sentiments:

> Example, custom, fear, occasion slow,—
> These scornéd bondmen were my parapet.
> I dare not peep over this parapet
> To gauge with glance the roaring gulf below,
> The depths of sin to which I had descended,
> Had not these me against myself defended.

Yet, even while voicing these sentiments in all apparent sincerity, Emerson was nurturing in his underground religious sensibility directly contradictory feelings. In 1826, several years before either of the above passages was written, Emerson recorded an intuition fully endowed with the true Transcendentalist revelation: "it were fitter to account every moment of the existence of the Universe as a new Creation, and *all* as a revelation proceeding each moment from the Divinity to the mind of the observer." By 1830—still well before his visitation with Wordsworth and Coleridge and Carlyle helped transform his outlook—Emerson's sense of sin was fast succumbing to his perception of humanity's innate divinity: "let [every man] fully trust his own share of God's goodness, that . . . will lead him on to perfection which has

---

[1] *The Heart of Emerson's Journals*, ed. Bliss Perry (Boston: 1926), p. 45. Other quotations are drawn from *Selections from Ralph Waldo Emerson*, ed. Stephen E. Whicher (Boston: 1957), pp. 8–10, 15, 20, 55–56, and from *The Literature of the United States*, Volume I, ed. Walter Blair, Theodore Hornberger, Randall Stewart (New York: 1953), p. 859 (Thoreau).

no type yet in the universe, save only in the Divine Mind."

In these contradictory feelings of Emerson's we see a minor example of what William James, in "The Divided Self, and the Process of Its Unification," called "an incompletely unified moral and intellectual constitution" (p. 141). The unification of Emerson's religious psyche was made possible at last by a changing of the gods, a phenomenon that James defined most cogently in his *Varieties* (p. 257):

> Nothing is more striking than the secular alteration that goes on in the moral and religious tone of men, as their insight into nature and their social arrangements progressively develop. After an interval of a few generations the mental climate proves unfavorable to notions of the deity which at an earlier date were perfectly satisfactory: the older gods have fallen below the common secular level, and can no longer be believed in.

For Emerson the "older gods" turned out to be those of the Christian faith in which he had trained himself for the ministry. Though only feebly Christian by orthodox standards, Emerson's Unitarian heritage retained enough residual worship of the Savior to drive Emerson at last out of the pulpit of his Second Church in Boston, on the grounds that he could no longer in good conscience celebrate the Lord's Supper. When in October, 1832 he broke with the church completely, his Journal portrayed a Christ of greatly shrunken magnitude: "Every teacher, once he finds himself insisting with all his might upon a great truth, turns up the ends of it at last with a cautious showing how it is agreeable to the life and teachings of Jesus, as if that was any recommendation. . . . Well, this cripples his teaching. . . . The truth of truth consists in this, that it is self-evident, self-subsistent. It is light. You don't get a candle to see the sun rise." By 1835 Emerson felt confident enough to checklist Jesus' deficiencies: "I do not see in him cheerfulness: I do not see in him the love of natural science: I see in him no kindness for art; I see in him nothing of Socrates, of Laplace, of Shakespeare." From here it was but a short step to the blasphemies of "The Divinity School Address," proclaiming that God incarnates himself anew in every man and deriding historical Christianity's "noxious exaggeration about the *person* of Jesus." Emerson's summation of Judeo-Christian achievement in this speech—citing as worthwhile only the institutions of the Sabbath and of preaching—must surely be the faintest praise ever rendered the religion.

What lay behind Emerson's dissatisfaction with Jesus was his innate, healthy-minded conviction that men do not need a Savior, for they are already sons of God and heirs to His kingdom by virtue of being born into the natural world. Although capable of expressing a sense of sin, Emerson does not qualify in any way as one of William James's sick souls, because his inner man was not seriously divided or doubt-ridden. Although slow to attain its full definition, the deepest thing in the man was his sense of prophetic mission, unassailably imbedded since childhood: "That which I cannot yet declare has been my angel from childhood until now," Emerson wrote in 1833; "It has separated me from men. It has watered my pillow, it has driven sleep from my bed. . . . It cannot be defeated by my defeats. It cannot be questioned, though all the martyrs apostasize. It is always the glory that shall be revealed; it is the 'open secret' of the universe. . . . It is the soul of religion." Within the decade, in essays like "Nature," "The American Scholar," and "Circles," Emerson formulated the doctrines that would comprise permanent tenets for the religion of healthy-mindedness. Replacing the fallen god of the Christian dispensation would be the Oversoul that animates all men; replacing Original Sin, "the infinitude of the private man"; replacing the heavenly vision, the insistence that we are living in paradise now—there is, and should be, no other; and replacing the Church's evangelical mission, the "conversion of the world" not through repentance or prayer but through the corrected vision of the Transcendental promulgation. "So shall we come to look at the world with new eyes," Emerson declares in concluding "Nature." With those new eyes, we need never look upon evil or suffering again, as sick souls do: "A correspondent revolution in things will attend the influx of the spirit. So fast will disagreeable appearances, swine, spiders, snakes, pests, mad-houses, prisons, enemies, vanish; they are temporary and shall no more be seen. The sordor and filths of nature, the sun shall dry up and the wind exhale."

This total mitigation of the world's suffering simply by looking at it in another way is probably the most recurrent, distinctive, and significant element in the literature of healthy-mindedness, pertaining as much to a Wallace Stevens or Henry Miller as to a Whitman or Thoreau. Totally contrary to the "pity, pain, and fear, and the sentiment of human helplessness" (p. 118) that James identifies as the sick soul's response to suffering, the healthy-minded response is to transform it through the new eyes of an Emerson or a Whitman, or to render it unimportant by ignoring it or bearing it out in an ebullient tough-mindedness. The consummation of Thoreau's great immersion in Nature in *Walden*—at the end of his chapter on "Spring"—involves just such a total mitigation of evil that James thought essential to healthy-mindedness: "We can never have enough of Nature. . . . We are cheered when we observe the vulture feeding on the carrion. . . . I love to see that Nature is so rife with life that myriads can afford to be sacrificed and suffered to prey on one another; that tender organizations can be so serenely squashed out of existence like pulp,—tadpoles which herons gobble up, and tortoises and toads run over in the road; and that sometimes it has rained flesh and blood! . . . Compassion is a very untenable ground."

As against William James's own expression of horror at the world's suffering (quoted earlier in his comment about crocodiles and pythons), this categorical denial of pity enables Thoreau to perceive in Nature a "universal innocence." In

14

addition to divesting the outer world of its horror in this fashion, the other most important purpose of the healthy-minded writer is to free his inner being from pain by divesting it of guilt. Thoreau's deathbed conversation with his aunt Louisa is a fine example of this attitude. To the good lady's question, "Have you made your peace with God?" Thoreau's answer, "I have never quarrelled with Him," measures the bold guiltlessness of the once-born. Similarly effacing guilt, Emerson too made over his God from One who demands repentance for sins to One who sustains man's innate divinity. As a natural corollary, Emerson's Christ in "The Divinity School Address" ceases to be the redeemer of sins and becomes instead the propagator of "a faith like Christ's in the infinitude of man."

2.

In the writings of Walt Whitman, we find James's paramount example of the religion of healthy-mindedness. "The only sentiments he allowed himself to express," James said—his categorical "only" is certainly wrong, but no matter—"were of the expansive order. . . , so that a passionate and mystic ontological emotion suffuses his words, and ends by persuading the reader that men and women, life and death, and all things are divinely good" (p. 81). For this reason, James noted, Whitman has achieved extraordinary power as a religious writer, capable of effecting a true psychological conversion experience in his readers: "many persons today regard Walt Whitman as the restorer of the eternal natural religion. He has infected them . . . with his own gladness that he and they exist. Societies are actually formed for his cult; . . . hymns are written by others in his peculiar prosody; and he is even explicitly compared with the founder of the Christian religion, not altogether to the advantage of the latter" (p. 81).

15

In point of fact, James's rather dour pronouncement has accumulated, apart from James's text, an impressive documentation. Beginning with Emerson's annunciation of Whitman as the new Messiah ("unto us a man is born"), a fair number of Whitman's readers have reacted to Whitman's verse by comparing their reading of it to a religious conversion.[2] "For me the reading of his poems is truly a new birth of the soul," said Anne Gilchrist, an English lady of letters, and her compatriot John Symonds (the poet) testified that Whitman "has revolutionized my conceptions and made another man of me." Robert Louis Stevenson called *Leaves of Grass* "a book which tumbled the world upside down for me," and Richard Maurice Bucke thought of Whitman's poetry as sacred writ: "What the Vedas were to Brahmanism, the Law and the Prophets to Judaism, . . . the Gospels and Pauline writings to Christianity, the Koran to Mohammedanism, will *Leaves of Grass* be to the future of American civilization." A rather surprising presence among this gathering of disciples is William James's brother Henry, that most urbane of highbrows, about whom Edith Wharton reminisced in the following anecdote: "Someone spoke of Whitman, and it was a joy to me to discover that [Henry] James thought him, as I did, the greatest of American poets. *Leaves of Grass* was put into his hands, and all that evening we sat rapt while he wandered from 'The Song of Myself' to 'When Lilacs Last in the Dooryard

---

[2] Emerson's statement is quoted from *The Princeton University Library Chronicle*, Volume 7, Number 3 (April, 1946), p. 101. Other quotations are cited from *The Inner Sanctum Edition of the Poetry and Prose of Walt Whitman*, ed. Louis Untermeyer (New York: 1949), p. 983 (Gilchrist), 1021 (Bucke), 1039–40 (Wharton/James); 1070–1072 (Lawrence); and 517, 519 (Whitman); J. A. Symonds, *Walt Whitman: A Study* (London: 1893), pp. 34–35, 154–160; *Moulton's Library of Literary Criticism of English and American Authors*, Volume IV (New York: 1966), p. 249 (R. L. Stevenson); Gay Wilson Allen, *The Solitary Singer* (New York: 1955), 544 (Ingersoll); *The Letters of Robert Frost to Louis Untermeyer* (New York: 1963), p. 285; *The Nation and Athenaeun* (June 4, 1927), p. 302 (T. S. Eliot); Wallace Stevens, "Like Decorations in a Nigger Cemetery" (Stanza 1); Ezra Pound, "A Pact"; and William Carlos Williams, "Choral: The Pink Church."

Bloom'd'. . . . , and thence let himself be lured on to the mysterious music of 'Out of the Cradle.' "

What Whitman offered these people, in addition to a pantheistically all-inclusive deity, was an annulment of the effects of Man's Fall. Sexual guilt and fear of death, those postlapsarian burdens of knowledge, dissolve to nothing as he advances his themes of sex without guilt and death without horror. Pain does exist in his poetry of love, especially in the homosexual "Songs of Calamus," which evince their genuineness by running the whole gamut of emotions—loneliness, envy, frustration—rather than vaunt the poet's potency as the heterosexual "Children of Adam" poems often do. But in Whitman there is no guilt, sexual or otherwise, a point that William James underscored in citing section 32 of *Song of Myself* to illustrate Whitman's "conscious pride in his freedom": "I could turn and live with animals, they are so placid and self-contain'd,/ . . . They do not sweat and whine about their condition./They do not lie awake in the dark and weep for their sins" (p. 81).

Through such a presumption of innocence, Whitman's children of Adam may partially remedy their fallen condition. Their full reclamation of paradise, however, hangs upon the success of Whitman's master theme, his reconciliation with mortality. By transforming death into a beautiful and welcome fulfillment, as perceived by the "new eyes" of the Transcendentalist revelation, Walt Whitman rendered for his readers the highest achievement of which poetry is capable, thereby fulfilling the purpose he announced for himself in *A Backward Glance*: "I say the profoundest service that poems or any other writings can do for their reader is . . . [to] give him *good heart* as a radical possession and habit" (emphasis Whitman's). And again, in the same essay: "Then still a purpose enclosing all, over and beneath all . . . a desire to attempt some worthy record of that entire faith and acceptance ('to justify the ways of God to man' is Milton's well-known and ambitious phrase)

17

which is the foundation of moral America."

To gauge its magnitude, the Whitman reconciliation with death needs to be set against William James's description of the awareness of death as the supreme cause of soul-sickness: "Back of everything is the great spectre of universal death, the all-encompassing blackness. . . . The fact that we *can* die, that we *can* be ill at all, is what perplexes us. . . . We need a life not correlated with death, a health not liable to illness" (pp. 120–121). In this connection, it is noteworthy that in her reminiscence Miss Wharton identified Whitman's most renowned poems of welcome to death—"Lilacs" and "Out of the Cradle"—as Henry James's favorites, poems that evoked in him something highly analogous to a religious rapture. "Reading, or rather crooning . . . in a mood of subdued ecstasy," James held his audience "rapt" with "Out of the Cradle, Endlessly Rocking" (where Whitman announced his lifelong purpose as "uniter of here and hereafter"); and "when he read 'Lovely and soothing death' "—Whitman's transcendent lyric of welcome to death in "Lilacs"—"his voice filled the hushed room like an organ adagio," according to Miss Wharton's recollection. "Oh yes, a great genius; undoubtedly a very great genius!" was James's judgment. On March 20, 1892, Robert G. Ingersoll ended Whitman's own funeral service with a tribute to precisely this mitigation of mortality in the poet's work: "He has lived, he has died, and death is less terrible than it was before. Thousands and millions will walk down into the 'dark valley of the shadow' holding Walt Whitman by the hand. Long after we are dead the brave words he has spoken will sound like trumpets to the dying."

Robert Frost's dictum, "Great is he who imposes the metaphor," or for that matter Aristotle's statement from two and a half millennia earlier, "the greatest thing by far is to be a master of metaphor" (*Poetics*, XXII), identifies the source of Whitman's persuasive power. His tenure as one of the great poets of the ages derives in no small measure from his gift for striking metaphors both to live by and to die by. D. H. Lawrence's encomium to "Song of the Open Road" nicely illustrates the former category: "Whitman, the great poet, has meant so much to me. Whitman, pioneering into the wilderness of unopened life. Beyond him, none. The Open Road. The great home of the Soul is the open road. . . . Meeting whatever comes down the open road. In company with those that drift in the same measure along the same way. . . . Having no known direction, even. Only the soul remaining true to herself in her going." The other category, metaphors to reconcile us to mortality, ranges across the entire breadth of the Whitman canon. "Whispers of Heavenly Death"—*heavenly* gives the measure of Whitman's healthy-mindedness here— offers a profusion of delicate, healing images:

Whispers of heavenly death murmured I hear,
Labial gossip of night, sibilant chorals,
Footsteps gently ascending, mystical breezes wafted soft and low,
Ripples of unseen rivers, tides of a current flowing, forever
    flowing. . . .

Passage to India also dissolves fear of death, mainly through the metaphorical power of the verbs in the following passage:

Swiftly I shrivel at the thought of God,
At Nature and its wonders, Time and Space and Death,
But that I, turning, call to thee O soul, thou actual Me,
And lo, thou gently masterest the orbs,
Thou matest Time, smilest content at Death,
And fillest, swellest full the vastnesses of Space.
                                        (Section 8)

In this excerpt, as in all his best writing on the subject, we find that Whitman's therapeutic power rests upon his appeal to mankind's most commonplace, routine experience: the fact that we enter eternity every night, and find it perfectly beautiful. So evolves Whitman's master metaphor, our lapse into death being figured as a return to the loving mother who gave us our genesis. Here is the true redemptress of men's souls: death bringing unconsciousness "like some old crone rocking the cradle, swathed in sweet garments, bending aside" at the end of "Out of the Cradle, Endlessly Rocking"; and death the "strong deliveress," the "Dark mother always gliding near with soft feet" with "the sure-enwinding arms of cool-enfolding death" in "When Lilacs Last in the Dooryard Bloom'd." In "The Sleepers," one of the finest poems ever written on the therapy of the unconscious, the night-death-mother coalescence terminates the poem in a mood of perfectly healthy-minded serenity:

> The call of the slave is one with the master's call, and
> the master salutes the slave,
> The felon steps forth from the prison, the insane becomes
> sane, the suffering of sick persons is reliev'd,
> . . . .
> They pass the invigoration of the night and the chemistry of
> the night, and awake.
>
> I too pass from the night,
> I stay a while away O night, but I return to you again and love you.
> . . . .
> I love the rich running day, but I do not desert her in whom
> I lay so long,
> I know not how I came of you and I know not where I go with
> you, but I know I came well and shall go well.
>
> I will stop only a time with the night, and rise betimes,
> I will duly pass the day O my mother, and duly return to you.

In looking at these manifestations of healthy-mindedness in Walt Whitman, we find good reason why the healthy-minded poets of later times often connected themselves with the good gray poet in a tone of high reverence. Wallace Stevens associated his beloved sun with Walt Whitman walking ("His beard is of fire and his staff is a leaping flame"); Ezra Pound made "a pact with you, Walt Whitman," early in his career; William Carlos Williams listed Whitman among "the saints/of this calendar" in his Pink Church; and Allen Ginsberg communed with Whitman ("Ah, dear father, graybeard, lonely old courage-teacher") in "A Supermarket in

California." For the same reason, the sick souls of twentieth century literature displayed small tolerance for him. T. S. Eliot, admitting only that Whitman was "a great versifier," declared that "his political, social, religious, and moral ideas are negligible." Before going on to study our twentieth century specimens of the religion of healthy-mindedness, however, one further specimen from the nineteenth century merits discussion. Emily Dickinson, unlike these others, was evidently not permitted to read Whitman ("I never read his book—but was told that he was disgraceful," she reported to her mentor, T.W. Higginson); but in her own right, she manifests a clear title to representation among William James's innately once-born personality types.

3.

If, as James says, conversion is to be regarded as "in its essence a normal adolescent phenomenon, incidental to the passage from the child's small universe to the wider intellectual and spiritual life of maturity" (p. 164), Emily Dickinson might claim our attention as a typical subject of the Protestant conversion process. At about age fifteen, when several of her intimate friends and relatives were giving over their lives to Christ, Emily felt enormous pressure to follow suit. Her biographer Thomas Johnson quotes a letter to her friend Abiah Root that indicates a real crisis in Emily's spiritual identity:

> I am continually putting off becoming a christian. Evil voices lisp in my ear, There is yet time enough. I feel that every day I live I sin more and more in closing my heart to the offers of mercy which are presented to me freely—Last winter there was a revival here. The meetings were thronged by people old and young. It seemed as if those who sneered loudest at serious things were soonest brought to see their power, and to make Christ their portion. It was really wonderful to see how near heaven came to sinful mortals. [3]

---

[3] *The Letters of Emily Dickinson*, Volume II, ed. Thomas H. Johnson (Cambridge: 1965), p. 404. Other quotations are cited (continued on page 22)

For yet several years, this evangelical dilemma lingered over her without satisfactory resolution. At the Mount Holyoke Female Seminary during her sixteenth and seventeenth years, when the whole student body was classified into three groups—those who were saved, those who "had hope," and those "without hope"—Emily fell haplessly into the latter category, thereby becoming subject to intensely vigorous evangelizing efforts and prayer meetings. These experiences evidently aggravated her guilt and anxiety, as she wrote again to Abiah: "I am not happy, and I regret that last term, when that golden opportunity was mine, that I did not give up, and become a Christian. It is not now too late, so my friends tell me, so my offended conscience whispers, but it is hard for me to give up the world." As late as 1850, in her twentieth year, Emily was still agonizing over her spiritual failure, made all the more unbearable now by the inclusion of all her friends and loved ones—even her dearest sister Lavinia ("Vinnie")—within the circle of the converted:

> Christ is calling everyone here, all my companions have answered, even my darling Vinnie believes she loves, and trusts him, and I am standing alone in rebellion. . . . How strange is this sanctification, that works such a marvellous change, that sows in such corruption, and rises in golden glory, that brings Christ down, and shews him, and lets him select his friends! . . . It *certainly* comes from God— and I think to receive it is blessed—not that I know it from me, but from those on whom *change* has passed. They seem so very tranquil, and their voices are kind, and gentle, and the tears fill their eyes so often, I really think I envy them. . . . You must pray when the rest are sleeping, that the hand may be held to me, and I may be led away.

As it happened, the Saviour's hand never did reach Emily, however, and her inner conflict was resolved instead

---

(continued from page 21) from this book, pp. 392; from Thomas H. Johnson, *Emily Dickinson: An Interpretive Biography* (New York: 1967), pp. 12–15; from H. D. Thoreau, *Walden* ("The Ponds"); and from Ernest Hemingway, *A Farewell to Arms* (New York: 1929), p. 120 and 272.

by a different kind of conversion experience, a gradual coherence of her personality around two centers of passionate intensity that would give thrust and direction to her most significant body of verse. The first such "centre of energy"—to use James's phrase—was her absorption in Nature, a lifelong experience; and the other was her relationship with a succession of male love objects—Benjamin Franklin Newton, the Reverend Charles Wadsworth, and (late in life) Judge Otis Lord. Both of these realms of experience were charged with sacramental meaning in Miss Emily's poetry, indicating that the most significant effect of her teen-age religious crisis was to provide a source of religious symbols that in later years might properly sacralize her secular passions. In hindsight, Emily's apology to Abiah Root—"it is hard for me to give up the world"—contains the key to her anomalous situation. In terms of the Jamesian religious psychology, Emily Dickinson was an innately healthy-minded soul, one who shared absolutely Emerson's and Thoreau's intuition that *this* is the kingdom of God, the world we possess now.

Given her supreme willfulness as an original artist and thinker, it was inevitable that Emily's private healthy-mindedness would clash head-on with the sick soul mentality inherent in her culture's evangelical Christianity, with its insistence that the world is lost and damned without its Savior; and though it tortured her conscience for some years, it was inevitable also that her private intuition would prevail in the end. Thus, just as Thoreau said, "I cannot come nearer to God and Heaven/Than I live to Walden even," so Emily declared that "Nature is Heaven" in "Nature Is What We See," and through her verse she further charged Nature with sacramental meaning in a series of lovely religious metaphors: "In the name of the Bee—/And of the Butterfly—/And of the Breeze—Amen!" ("The Gentian Weaves Her Fringes"); "Oh Sacrament of summer days,/Oh Last Communion in the Haze—/Permit a child to join" ("These Are the Days When

Birds Come Back"); "And Nicodemus' Mystery/Receives its anual reply!" ("An Altered Look about the Hills"); and—one of the half dozen poems published during her lifetime—"My Sabbath";

> Some keep the Sabbath going to Church—
> I keep it, staying at Home—
> With a Bobolink for a Chorister—
> And an Orchard, for a Dome—
> . . . .
> So instead of getting to Heaven, at last—
> I'm going, all along.

Evidently Nature served as Emily's True Church on a lifelong basis, but the experiences that called forth her most intense religious feeling, equivalent to a Jamesian conversion, were linked to her human love objects, especially the Reverend Charles Wadsworth, whose departure to Calvary Church in San Francisco in 1862 marked the high point of Emily's creativity. (More than half of the poems in Thomas Johnson's *Final Harvest*, a 321–page collection of her best work, center on the years 1861–1863.) Not all the religious feeling is joyous; much of it is anguished to the point of psychic breakdown, as in "I Felt a Funeral in My Brain" or when she (thinking of Calvary Church, apparently) keeps referring to herself as Emily Crucified, reciting "Sabachthani" in "I Should Have Been Too Glad, I see" and playing Christ to Wadsworth's Peter in another poem:

> He forgot—and I—remembered
> T'was an everyday affair—
> Long ago as Christ and Peter
> "Warmed them" at the "Temple fire."
>
> "Thou wert with him"—quoth "The Damsel?
> "No"—said Peter—'twasn't me—
> Jesus merely "looked" at Peter—
> Could I do aught else—to thee?

Even with the pain, the sense of betrayal, and the subsequent funeral in her brain, however, Emily's love for Wads-

24

worth provided a psychic coherence expressible only in terms drawn from her orthodox religious upbringing. Wadsworth's last visit to the Dickinson home in Amherst in September, 1861, which Emily would have understood as their last visit together (he unexpectedly returned East at the end of the decade), is apparently the occasion of the most intense expression of her "Religion of Love," complete with its holy communion and acceptance of Calvary:

> There came a day at Summer's full,
> Entirely for me—
> I thought that such were for the Saints,
> Where Resurrections—be—
>
> . . . .
>
> The time was scarce profaned, by speech—
> The symbol of a word
> Was needless, as at Sacrament,
> The Wardrobe—of our Lord—
>
> Each was to each The Sealed Church,
> Permitted to commune this—time—
> Lest we too awkward show
> At supper of the Lamb.
>
> The Hours slid fast—as Hours will,
> Clutched tight by greedy hands
> So faces on two Decks, look back,
> Bound to opposing lands—
>
> And so when all the time had leaked,
> Without external sound
> Each bound the Other's Crucifix—
> We gave no other Bond—
>
> Sufficient troth, that we shall rise—
> Deposed—at length, the Grave—
> To that new Marriage,
> Justified—through Calvaries of Love—

Occasionally, as in "I Never Saw a Moor" and " 'Unto Me?' I Do Not Know You" (where Jesus welcomes her into Paradise), orthodox Christian metaphysics exert some residual power over Miss Emily's religious imagination, but for the most part she seemed to regard Heaven with a disdain like that of Wallace Stevens, thinking that at best the people in Paradise may feel the minor of what earthlings feel. "Master, open your life wide, and take me in forever," she says in one of her Dear Master letters, and then "I shall not want any more—and all Heaven will only disappoint me, because it's not so dear." In "I Cannot Live with You," she claims that she could not rise to the Last Judgment "Because Your Face/Would put out Jesus'," and she likewise downgrades Paradise—

> Because You saturated Sight—
> And I had no more Eyes
> For sordid excellence
> As Paradise

Other writers, like Donne or Hemingway, have spoken of their Religion of Love, saying with Catherine Barkley that "You're my religion" or with Count Greffi, "Do not forget that [love] is a religious feeling" but few have invested their souls into it with the totality that gives the writing of Emily Dickinson its ring of authority. In terms of the Jamesian religious psychology, Miss Dickinson's feelings for both Nature and her human love objects constitute a genuine religious experience, as he defines the term in his chapter on "Circumscription of the Topic": "Religion, therefore, . . . shall mean for us *the feelings, acts, and experiences of individual men in their solitude, so far as they apprehend themselves to stand in relation to whatever they may consider the divine*" (p. 42). If we agree that Emily's religious metaphors and the absolute passion which they represent place her within the circumference of this definition, it must seem all the more regrettable to us that she appeared irreligious in her own eyes, cut off for this reason even from her own family. "They are religious—except me—" she told Higginson in her letter of April 25, 1862, explaining that they "address an Eclipse every morning—whom they call their 'Father.' " No doubt there is some sarcasm in Miss Emily's statement, particularly in her metaphor of God's disappearance (an "Eclipse"); nonetheless, one could wish that she could have drawn directly upon James's description of theology and ecclesiasticism as secondary to personal religious feelings: "it is evident that out of religion in the sense in which we take it, theologies, philosophies, and ecclesiastical organizations may secondarily grow. In these lectures, however, . . . the immediate personal experiences will amply fill our time, and we shall hardly consider theology or ecclesiasticism at all" (p. 42).

Once past her original crisis of religious identity, Miss Emily too hardly considered theology or ecclesiasticism at all, but on the basis of her immediate personal experiences, we may reasonably classify her—like her counterpart in nineteenth-century healthy-mindedness, Walt Whitman—as a true religious poet. Because her occasional dread of death looms larger than Whitman's, hers is not as "pure" a healthy-mindedness as he manifests—and Whitman too is of course not altogether free of doubt and anxiety. But she too mitigates dread through metaphor, death arriving like a courteous gentleman caller in "I Could Not Stop for Death," and the act of dying being nothing more than hanging up "an overcoat of clay" in "Death Is A Dialogue." In her extreme joy in Nature, her preference for this world over any other, her tough-minded faith in her independent spiritual resources, and her rejection of her morbid-minded religious heritage, Miss Emily fills out a profile that we may reasonably classify with the religion of healthy-mindedness.

4.

By the time of Emily Dickinson's death, in 1885, the great luminaries of Transcendentalist healthy-mindedness had had their day, and the rising sun of naturalistic realism was spreading its morbid-minded illuminations across the whole broad vista of American literature. As a serious artistic phenomenon, the literature of healthy-mindedness in effect went off stage while a generation of sick souls took front and center. During the late nineteenth and early twentieth centuries, people like Twain, Crane, Dreiser, Henry Adams, Robinson, and Frost addressed, with varying degrees of morbid-minded intensity, the great crisis of belief precipitated by the recent rise of the natural sciences. Leaving this spectacle for our next chapter, on "The Sick Soul," we may pick up the re-emergent tradition of healthy-mindedness that appeared once this earlier group had finished its task of defining the naturalistic predicament so as to toss it into the laps of post-World War I writers.

Among these newly regenerate apostles of healthy-mindedness, the most important figures seemed to couch their work as an express rejection of *The Waste Land*, that apotheosis of James's "Sick Soul" condition. Hart Crane, for example, declared "I take Eliot as a point of departure towards an almost complete reversal of direction"; and he began work on *The Bridge* to express that reversal only a few months after *The Waste Land* itself appeared in November, 1922.[4] William Carlos Williams, too, pronounced *The Waste Land* a disaster for modern poetry, saying "I had a violent feeling that Eliot had betrayed what I believed in," and he did his best to counteract the damage until his own neo-romantic school achieved post-

---

[4] Philip Horton, Hart Crane (New York: 1937), p. 122. Other quotations are cited from Wallace Stevens, *The Necessary Angel* (New York: 1951), pp. 154–5, 57, 35–36, 30, 148, 17, 138–9, 143, 14–15, 171, 6–7, 12–13, and 23; *The Letters of Wallace Stevens*, ed. Holly Stevens (New York: 1966), pp. 411–412; *Writers at Work: The Paris Review Interviews*, Third Series (New York: 1968), pp. 188 (Saul Bellow) and 29 (William Carlos Williams); William Shakespeare, *Hamlet* (II, ii, 48–49); William Carlos Williams, *I Wanted to Write a Poem* (Boston: 1958), p. 30, *The Selected Letters of William Carlos Williams* ed. John C. Thirlwall (New York: 1957), p. 253, and *Imaginations*, ed. Webster Schott (New York: 1970), p. 314. In this last reference, Williams was actually quoting J. B. Kerfoot while endorsing the latter's "democracy of feeling" concept.

Eliotic ascendancy in the 1950's. Wallace Stevens clearly had T. S. Eliot in mind in claiming "normal love and nomal beauty" as the province of poetry, in opposition to "those that insist on the solitude and misery and terror of the world." As late as 1965, Saul Bellow was describing his recent novel, *Herzog* (1964), as a reaction against "the tone of elegy from the 1920's to the 50's, the atmosphere of Eliot in *The Waste Land.*"

At the same time that these protests against the Waste Land mentality were going forward, each of these writers showed in his own way the inherent difficulty of maintaining the healthy-minded attitude in our modern era. The problem, they all realized, was that which William James had identified in calling healthy-mindedness "inadequate as a philosophical doctrine, because the evil facts which it refuses positively to account for are a genuine portion of reality" (p. 137). Hart Crane came to rely with increasing abjectness—and inefficacy—upon external stimulants, such as alcohol, to keep alive his transcendent vision, which could be jeopardized merely by his reading in Spengler or Eliot; and when his optimism failed, his creativity was stopped dead. Likewise, William Carlos Williams suffered a serious lapse in his creativity as the great negations of the 1930's—depression, fascism, war—assumed prominence. Though admirably deft with his lyric touch while in the role of "the young doctor . . . dancing with happiness" or "the happy genius of my household" in "January Morning" and "Danse Russe," the Williams persona seemed notably unable to assimilate the experience of evil. "Hide it away somewhere/out of the mind," he says in "These," a poem in which "the heart plunges/lower than night" to "an empty, windswept place/without sun, stars, or moon." Thus, while capable of lifting to the verge of sentimentality his healthy-minded affirmations—that the church domes in Weehawken rival the Vatican's, that the man gathering dog lime from the gutter is more majestic than the Episcopal minister, that two gangs fighting over a drunken moll comprise a "Beautiful

Thing"—Williams betrays a hiatus of the imagination when his material may no longer be so rationalized. As in "Death," for example—

> He's nothing at all
> he's dead
> shrunken up to skin
> . . . .
> just bury it
> and hide its face
> for shame.

Quite possibly, this difficulty in handling morbid-minded material may explain the sporadic character of Williams' creativity in *Paterson*, such that "if I hit a low spot and the whole business seems a redundant heap of garbage, the work stops short."

In *Paterson* Williams' epic purpose of lifting a local environment to expression evidently became increasingly difficult to sustain as that environment came to seem increasingly uncongenial to him—an impression objectified in the poem by the increasing pollution of the Passaic River as it nears the sea. That Williams preferred to remain in his state of healthy-minded innocence is indicated in his late poem, "The Visit," where he argues the value of his naivete: "The/naive may be like a sunny day/ . . . and is not to be despised." In a similar vein, Williams ridiculed profundity of thought in "Aigelting-er," another late poem: "They say I am not profound/But where is profundity, Aigeltinger. . . ?/Aigeltinger, you were profound." What remained most worthwhile in Williams' verse, then, according to his own judgment, was not so much his quality of thought as his innovations in form. In an early statement (1925), Williams had described the purpose of his poetry as "the expression of democracy of feeling rebelling against an aristrocracy of form," and late in life, in the 1962 *Paris Review* interview, Williams specified just what he had most valuably contributed to that rebellion:

Interviewer: What do you think you yourself have left of special value to the new poets?
Williams: The variable foot—the division of the line according to a new method that would be satisfactory to an American.

Thus Williams on his own sense of achievement. But, technique aside, for the army of Williams admirers in recent decades perhaps the great charm of his verse is justified by something akin to William James's *Pragmatism*, which holds that any ideology—even if it is naive—is vindicated by good results. In Williams' case the life-affirming tonic of healthy-mindedness is so vindicated.

5.

While it seems regrettable to slight any important members of the healthy-minded camp—E. E. Cummings, for example, the "Now Man" in Tony Tanner's *The Reign of Wonder*—we turn last to a poet whose healthy-mindedness depended upon a prolonged and deliberate assertion of will, and who therefore represents a transition of sorts toward the sick souls of our forthcoming chapter. (Healthy-mindedness, we note in passing, evidently seeks expression mainly in poetry, whereas our sick souls and twice-born tend mostly to be novelists and dramatists.) We turn, that is, to the poetry of Wallace Stevens.

Among the modern celebrators of life, Wallace Stevens is distinguished by his coldly disciplined subordination of the problem of evil. Despising the rampant morbid-mindedness of his time, Stevens condemned Faulkner and Hemingway for their "gross realism" (he otherwise thought them the two best "poets" of the age), affirming instead the poet's "agreement with the radiant and productive world in which he lives." This attitude he defined as "nobility," the greatest missing ingredient of contemporary literature: "For the sensitive poet, conscious of negations, nothing is more difficult than the affirmations of nobility." And he frankly admits that the preservation of this healthy-minded love of the world requires a denial of reality: "The artist transforms us into epicures; . . . he is *un amoureux perpetuel* of the world that he contemplates . . . ; and finally . . . everything like a firm grasp of reality is eliminated from the aesthetic field. With these aphorisms in mind, how is it possible to condemn escapism? The poetic process is psychologically an escapist process."

To be sure, Stevens was not always able to escape his own mind of winter. A poem like "Domination of Black" displays a naturalistic dread—William James's phrase for it was "fear of the universe"—that could easily have emanated out of Eliot's Waste Land:

> Out of the window
> I saw how the planets gathered
> Like the leaves themselves
> Turning in the wind.
> I saw how the night came,
> Came striding like the color of the heavy hemlocks.
> I felt afraid.
> And I remembered the cry of the peacocks.

What kept the peacock's harsh scream out of Stevens' normal tone was the hard-boiled toughness of mind that enabled Stevens to celebrate death at "the mother of beauty" and hence the source of life's greatest fulfillment. Unlike Williams, Stevens thereby enters James's "voluntary" rather than "involuntary" category of healthy-minded individuals:

> . . . we find that we must distinguish between a more involuntary and a more voluntary or systematic way of being healthy-minded. In its involuntary variety, healthy-mindedness is a way of feeling happy about things immediately. In its systematical variety, it is an abstract way of conceiving things as good. . . . Systematic healthy-mindedness, conceiving good as the essential and universal aspect of being, deliberately excludes evil from its field of vision. (p. 83)

Possibly, in Stevens' case, the word *rationalize* might be more exact than *exclude* in that last sentence. The idea of rationalizing evil is in any event what James goes on to define in connection with this voluntary type of healthy-mindedness (p. 83):

> . . . the hushing of it [evil] up may, in a perfectly candid and honest mind, grow into a deliberate religious policy, or *parti pris*. Much of what we call evil is due entirely to the way men take the phenomenon. It can so often be converted into a bracing and tonic good by a simple change of the sufferer's inner attitude. . . .

That this attitude was, for Stevens, a "religious policy"— to use James's phrase—may be inferred from the intolerant and dogmatic way in which he polishes off those Supreme Fictions of the modern world that rivaled and threatened his own. So as to permit no other gods before Beauty, he gunned down Christians, Waste Landers, Romantics, Marxists, and Freudians with indiscriminate avidity, as so many corruptions of the imagination. Thus the following excerpts from Stevens' *The Necessary Angel: Essays on Reality and the Imagination*:

> CHRISTIANS: "The Biblical imagination is one thing and the poetic imagination, inevitably, something else. . . . A poet respects no knowledge except his own and . . . the poet does not yield to the priest."

> WASTE LANDERS: "The instantaneous disclosures of living are disclosures of the normal. This will seem absurd to those that insist on the solitude and misery and terror of the world. . . . But to be able to see the portal of literature . . . as a scene of normal love and normal beauty is, of itself, a feat of great imagination."

> ROMANTICS: "Before going on, we must somehow cleanse the imagination of the romantic. We feel . . . that it is not worthy to survive if it is to be identified with the romantic. The imagination is one of the great human powers. The romantic belittles it. . . . The romantic . . . is to the imagination what sentimentality is to feeling.It is a failure of the imagination. . . . The imagination is the only genius . . . [whose] extreme achievement lies in abstraction. The achievement of the romantic, on the contrary, lies in minor wish-fulfillments and it is incapable of abstraction."

> MARXISTS: "Communism . . . as a phenomenon of the imagination . . . exhibits imagination on its most momentous scale.

33

. . . With the collapse of other beliefs, this grubby faith promises a
practicable earthly paradise."

FREUDIANS: "Boileau's remark that Descartes had cut poetry's
throat is a remark that could have been made . . . of no one more
aptly than of Freud, who . . . repeats it in his *Future of an Illusion*.
The object of that essay was to suggest a surrender to reality. . . .
His conclusion is that man must venture at last into the hostile
world and that this may be called education to reality. There is
much more in that essay inimical to poetry and not least the observation in one of the final pages that 'The voice of the intellect is a soft
one, but it does not rest until it has gained a hearing.' "

Toward the various efforts of these ideologies to combat
the world's sufferings, Stevens held the contempt of one who
understands that pleasure and beauty require the presence of
their opposite numbers, pain and squalor, in order to be
savored in their highest degree of intensity. So in "The
Emperor of Ice Cream" we have the spectacle of the under-
taker's work in stanza two ("Let the lamp affix its beam")
intensifying the sensuous pleasures—at the woman's wake,
we may surmise—in stanza one: the big cigars, concupiscent
curds, and flowers in last month's newspapers. So, too, the
cold eye looking through "Le Monocle de Mon Oncle" succeeds in transforming the loss of sexual power into an aesthetic
blessing. To be a lover, after all, is to resemble that frog who
"boomed from his very belly odious chords," a state not at all
conducive to seeing "a pool of pink,/Clippered with lilies
scudding the bright chromes," or noting how "fluttering
things have so distinct a shade."

In "Esthetique du Mal," as the title discloses, Stevens'
consciously deliberate mode of healthy-mindedness receives
its consummate expression. The first two stanzas make a
classic study in tonal incongruities. "It was pleasant to be
sitting there," "It was almost time for lunch," "There were
roses in the cool cafe"—this airy healthy-mindedness is inter-
spersed with rumblings from Vesuvius in the background that
could overpower with horror a less disciplined imagination:

34

"pain/Audible at noon, pain torturing itself,/Pain killing pain on the very point of pain." What emotional discipline in that word "Audible"!—a remarkable understatement, and perhaps emblematic of this whole process of subordinating evil. Stevens' argument, complete with its attack on the Christian ideal of sympathy, is not particularly novel; Hamlet said it all by declaring "There's nothing either good or bad/But thinking makes it so." What may be novel is the extreme to which Stevens goes in trying to change our thinking. "How red the rose that is the soldier's wound" bespeaks an aesthetic perspective on pain regrettably reminiscent of a comment attributed to Mussolini's son, who allegedly compared a bomb dropped on a group of Ethiopians to a rose unfolding. Of course Stevens was not that type of callous butcher, yet "how red the rose" is surely an odd way to describe torn flesh. That cold eye, once again, behind its monocle, here marks the ultimate degree to which Stevens was willing to go while fulfilling James's definition of healthy-mindedness as "the tendency which looks on all things and sees that they are good" (p. 83). With characteristic stateliness of expression, Stevens spins out his meditations, mourning the birth of Christ and the death of Satan, readily admitting the universal presence of suffering, allowing his tragic sense its say. But he does this only that he may superimpose upon it all the deliberate healthy-mindedness of his conclusion, so similar to that of Whitman and Emerson in its categorical denial of any need for a better world or a transcendent self:

> Perhaps
> After death, the non-physical people in paradise,
> Itself non-physical, may, by chance, observe
> The green corn gleaming and experience
> The minor of what we feel.

Since beauty comes to us mostly through the eye, and secondly through the ear, a panegyric to those two senses rounds off the poem, terminally subordinating evil: "One might have thought of sight, but who could think/Of what it sees, for all the ill it sees?" One arrives at last at a Thoreauvian satisfaction with the gift of life just as it is, "Merely in living as and where we live."

Because so much depends on this capacity to will a healthy-minded attitude, Stevens devoted the bulk of his later writing to the process of re-conceiving reality through the exercise of imagination. Not only his poems, like "The Man with the Blue Guitar" or "Angel Surrounded by Paysans," but his essays deal repetitively, not to say obsessively, with the subject. *The Necessary Angel: Essays on Reality and the Imagination*, defining the imagination as "the next greatest power to faith: the reigning prince," states the outer limitation of this process: "The imagination loses vitality as it ceases to adhere to what is real. . . . It has the strength of reality or none at all." On the face of it, this looks like a potentially fatal limitation in his system: reality, after all, includes much—as his own "Domination of Black" admits—that resists any healthy-minded formulation. But here is where Stevens does a bit of sleight-of-hand with the language. "Reality," it turns out, is a word with split-level meanings. The upper level, that which generates the poet's "pleasure of agreement with the radiant and productive world in which he lives," is what he would guide our eyes to observe as his final achievement in poetry. The bottom level, that realm of "gross realism" that he accused Faulkner and Hemingway of reproducing, is a psychic death-trap whose baleful influence literature must deny, resist, or escape absolutely. In lamenting the modern decline of "nobility" in art, Stevens uses the word "reality" with both meanings in mind—the first use of the word conveying its upper level meaning, the next use referring to "gross realism": "This [loss of nobility] is due to failure in the relation between the imagination and reality . . . —a failure due, in turn, to the pressure of reality. . . . The resistance to this pressure or its evasion in the case of individuals of extraordinary imagination cancels the pressure so far as those individuals are concerned." By thus insisting that "the poetic process is psychologically an escapist process," Stevens advances the rationale that William James identified as crucial in the healthy-minded psychology: "happiness, like every other emotional state, has blindness and insensibility to opposing facts given it as its instinctive weapon for self-protection against disturbance" (p. 83). Perhaps, as our final observation in this chapter, it is appropriate to remark how exactly James prefigures Stevens' master theme, thereby apprehending the permanent basis of the literature of healthy-mindedness (p. 84):

> . . . though the facts [Stevens: Reality] may still exist, their evil character exists no longer. Since you make them good or evil by your thoughts about them, it is the ruling of your thoughts [Stevens: Imagination] which proves to be your principal concern.

Chapter III

The Sick Soul

From the fore-going examples, we may infer that James's once-born type of personality has enjoyed great prominence in American literature, having attracted a large and distinguished following in the Religion of Healthy-Mindedness. Dating from Puritan times, however, James's Religion of Morbid-Mindedness has also had its body of adherents who, beginning with the rise of naturalism in the last century and culminating in the black humor movement of our own age, have pretty largely taken over the American literary kingdom. This fact is what lies behind the wide-ranging phenomena of conversion which will be the topic of Part IV of our discussion, a conversion experience in some form or other being the only release for the sick souls caged within the morbid-minded mentality. Those sick souls who have been unable to achieve conversion will be the special topic of this chapter, along with those whose conversion experience has proved merely nominal, defunctive, or otherwise not efficacious.

1.

Having already designated the Transcendentalist writers as our chief propagators of the Religion of Healthy-Mindedness, perhaps the place to begin is with their great anti-Transcendental adversaries, Hawthorne and Melville. Temperamentally, Hawthorne and Melville each expressed, in his most significant literary art, the psychology of morbid-mindedness that James ascribes to the sick soul. The "prey of a pathological melancholy," as James puts it (p. 124), each fixed his eye, in greater or lesser measure, upon "the vanity of mortal things," "the sense of sin," and "the fear of the universe"—and James goes on to add that "in one or another of these three ways it always is that man's original optimism and self-satisfaction get leveled with the dust" (p. 136). In these two morbid-minded writers, one may also discern the "incompletely unified moral and intellectual constitution" that (James thought) precedes the twice-born condition (p. 141), but neither Hawthorne nor Melville appeared to have the psychic resources necessary for resolving his inner fragmentation through the conversion process.

In his review of *Twice-Told Tales*, Poe said of Hawthorne that "he evinces extraordinary genius, having no rival either in America or elsewhere." What Hawthorne's genius mostly fed upon was a vision of evil of a "radical and general" character, in James's terms, "which no alteration of the environment, or any superficial rearrangement of the inner self, can cure" (p. 117). That is to say, in Hawthorne we are dealing with a mind that needs conversion, but whose "pain-threshold," "fear-threshold," and "misery-threshold"—in James's words—will not permit passage outward: "The sanguine and healthy-minded live habitually on the sunny side of their misery-line, the depressed and melancholy live beyond it, in darkness and apprehension" (p. 117). Hawthorne's habitation among the morbid-minded, evident everywhere in his writing, is confirmed by reminiscences of people who knew him. Bronson Alcott thought him "of the darker temperament and tendencies. . . . There he was in the twilight, there he stayed," and Samuel G. Goodrich portrayed confirmatory physical characteristics: ". . . his eye steel gray, his brow thick, his mouth sarcastic, his complexion stony, his whole aspect cold, moody, distrustful." Perhaps the most telling reminiscence is that of George William Curtis, who, while enjoying a party at Emerson's house, "was for some time scarcely aware of a man who sat upon the edge of the circle, a little withdrawn. . . . As I drifted down the stream of talk, this person, who sat silent as a shadow . . . rose and walked to the window, and stood quietly there for a long time, watching the dead-white landscape. No appeal was made to him, nobody looked after him, the conversation flowed steadily on, as if everyone understood that his silence was to be respected. It was the same thing at table. . . . When he presently rose and went, Emerson . . . said, 'Hawthorne rides well his horse of the night.'"[1]

Beginning with the early sketches that harrow the soil for his later literary harvest, Hawthorne expresses what James called the "pathological melancholy" of the sick soul condition, growing out of the sense of sin, the vanity of mortal things, and the fear of the universe. "You think how the dead are lying in their cold shrouds and narrow coffins, through the drear winter of the grave," says Hawthorne of his insomnia victim in "The Haunted Mind," and then editorializes to us all: "In the depths of every heart there is a tomb and a dungeon,

---

[1] *Moulton's Library of Literary Criticism of English and American Authors,* Volume VI (New York: 1935), 342–345 (Alcott, Goodrich, Curtis). Other quotations are cited from this book, p. 249 (Sophia Hawthorne) and p. 345 (Chorley); from *Nathaniel Hawthorne: Selected Tales and Sketches,* ed. Hyatt H. Waggoner (New York: 1950), pp. 323–4, 331–2; from *The Complete Novels and Selected Tales of Nathaniel Hawthorne* (New York: 1937), pp. 459, 578, 682, 236; from Julian Hawthorne, *Nathaniel Hawthorne and His Wife* Volume I (Boston: 1885), pp. 348, 205, 224; from *The Complete Psychological Works of Sigmund Freud,* ed. James Strachey (London: 1957), Volume 14, p. 301; from James G. Frazer, *The Golden Bough,* Volume I (New York: 1935), p. 236; and from Carl Gustav Jung, *The Undiscovered Self* (New York: Mentor Books, 1959), pp. 107–8. See also the July 4, 1843 entry in Hawthorne's *American Notebooks,* and Randall Stewart's *Nathaniel Hawthorne: A Biography* (New Haven: 1948), p. 259.

though the lights, the music, and revelry above may cause us to forget their existence, and the buried ones, or prisoners, whom they hide." Helpless to fend off an invading army of sorrowful thoughts, Hawthorne's insomniac renders clear the dreadful impotence of the sick soul to help himself out of his morbid-mindedness: "In an hour like this, when the mind has a passive sensibility, but no active strength; when the imagination is a mirror, imparting vividness to all ideas, without the power of selecting or controlling them; then pray that your griefs may slumber. . . . It is too late! A funeral train comes gliding by. . . ." And following the funeral train come fiercer torturers, "the devils of a guilty heart, that holds its hell within itself." So crescendoes what Hawthorne himself calls "this nightmare of the soul; this heavy sinking of the spirits; this wintry gloom about the heart; this indistinct horror of the mind." After thus touching the soul, spirit, heart, and mind he concludes "The Haunted Mind" with a "L'Allegro" type of final upbeat about as convincing as that in "The Procession of Life," whose Chief Marshal turns out to be Death, "immovable, dark rider, waving his truncheon of universal sway," until God makes a token appearance in the tale's very last sentence: "But God . . . will not leave us on our toilsome and doubtful march, either to wander in infinite uncertainty, or perish by the way!"

A similar fear of the universe, tempered by another barely tenable irruption of religious faith, overcame Hawthorne on the occasion of his mother's terminal illness. As cited in Julian Hawthorne's biography, Hawthorne's entry in the family journal for July 29, 1849 describes what is "surely . . . the darkest hour I ever lived." After kneeling a long time by the dying woman and holding her hand, Hawthorne arose and

> . . . stood by the open window and looked through the crevice of the curtain. The shouts, laughter, and cries of the two children had come up into the chamber from the open air, making a strange

41

contrast with the death-bed scene. And now, through the crevice of the curtain, I saw my little Una of the golden locks, looking very beautiful, and so full of spirit and life that she was life itself. And then I looked at my poor dying mother, and seemed to see the whole of human existence at once, standing in the dusty midst of it. Oh, what a mockery, if what I saw were all!,—let the interval between extreme youth and dying age be filled up with what happiness it might! But God would not have made the close so dark and wretched, if there were nothing beyond; for then it would have been a fiend that created us and measured out our existence, and not God. It would be something beyond wrong, it would be insult, to be thrust out of life and annihilated in this miserable way.

Admittedly, even the devoutest soul must be permitted its agony of doubt at a moment like this, yet in Hawthorne this morbid-minded tone kept recurring. Genuine fear of the universe, for example, animates several passages in *The Blithedale Romance* in tones reminiscent of Wallace Stevens' "Domination of Black." Its first victim is Priscilla, in Chapter V ("Until Bedtime"), whom the narrator patronizes: "The sense of vast, undefined space, pressing from the outside against the black panes of our uncurtained windows, was fearful to the poor girl . . . . The house probably seemed to her adrift on the great ocean of the night." Coverdale is not so patronizing, however, about his own response to Zenobia's death by drowning (drawn after a real incident in Hawthorne's experience), an episode provoking dread and doubt and horror:

> She was the marble image of a death-agony. Her arms had grown rigid in the act of struggling, and were bent before her with clenched hands. . . . Ah that rigidity! It is impossible to bear the terror of it. It seemed . . . as if her body must keep the same position in the coffin, and that the skeleton would keep it in the grave. . . . With the last, choking consciousness, her soul, bubbling out through her lips, it may be, had given itself up to the Father, reconciled and penitent. But her arms! They were bent before her, as if she struggled against Providence in never-ending hostility. Her hands! They were clenched in immitigable defiance. Away with the hideous thought!

The thought recurs, however, in Hawthorne's final novel

among other places, and perhaps we may complete our look at this facet of Hawthorne's mobid-mindedness by contemplating (in *The Marble Faun*, Chapter XVIII: "On the Edge of a Precipice")

> . . . that pit of blackness that lies beneath us everywhere. The firmest substance of human happiness is but a thin crust spread over it, with just reality enough to bear up the illusive stage scenery amid which we tread. It needs no earthquake to open the chasm. A footstep, a little heavier than ordinary, will serve; and we must step very daintily, not to break through the crust at any moment. By and by, we inevitably sink.

This same metaphor of the crust over the pit occurs in James's study of "The Sick Soul" as an example of "the worst kind of melancholy," "that which takes the form of panic fear" (p. 135). In this instance, William James himself was the victim of the experience, though in his book he ascribes its description to an anonymous "French correspondent": ". . . suddenly there fell upon me without any warning, just as if it came out of the darkness, a horrible fear of my own existence. . . . After this the universe was changed for me altogether. I awoke morning after morning with a horrible dread at the pit of my stomach, and with a sense of the insecurity of life that I never knew before. . . . I remember wondering how other people could live, how I myself had ever lived, so unconscious of that pit of insecurity beneath the surface of life" (p. 135–6). From this condition James escaped into the twice-born state; Hawthorne evidently was not so fortunate.

On the basis of his fear of the universe alone, Hawthorne might reasonably be classed among the morbid-minded, but his truly personal claim to that status rests upon his world-renowned sense of sin, "that Calvinistic sense of Innate Depravity and Original Sin from whose visitations, in some shape or other, no deeply thinking mind is always and wholly free," as Herman Melville put it in his essay on "Hawthorne and His Mosses." To this way of thinking, actual innocence of foul deeds matters not a whit as measured against the soul's bottomless cesspool of evil motives. "Man must not disclaim his brotherhood, even with the guiltiest," Hawthorne intones in "Fancy's Show Box," "since, though his hand be clean, his heart has surely been polluted by the flitting phantoms of iniquity." As it happens, Hawthorne's status as an oracle of psychological truths has been handsomely confirmed by subsequent study. Freud, Jung, and Sir James Frazer, among others, have put mighty foundations of scholarship beneath similar Hawthornesque sentiments. "Psychoanalysis has concluded . . .that the primitive, savage, and evil impulses of mankind have not vanished in any individual, but continue their existence, although in a repressed state . . . and that they wait for opportunities to display their activity," said Freud in a letter dated December 28, 1914; and Frazer's anthropology did not even require the circumstance of World War I to sustain, in 1913, *The Golden Bough's* prophecy of apocalyptic evil: "The permanent existence of a solid layer of savagery beneath the surface of society . . . [is] a standing menace to civilization. We seem to move on a thin crust which may at any moment be rent by the subterranean forces slumbering below." And Jung, in *The Undiscovered Self*, reinforces the scholarly testimony by asserting, "The evil that dwells in man is of gigantic proportions. . . . Man has done [terrible] things; I am a man, who has his share of human nature; therefore I am guilty with the rest and bear unaltered and indelibly within me the capacity and the inclination to do them again at any time. . . . None of us stands outside humanity's black collective shadow."

With this kind of support for his contentions, one hesitates to question the validity of Hawthorne's sense of sin, but one may nonetheless wonder about the scope and the source of Hawthorne's deeply melancholy propensities. One may, as Frederick Crews does persuasively in *The Sins of the Fathers*, trace them to ancestral crimes in Puritan Salem, whose bloodstains mark even the otherwise light-hearted Customs-House

44

essay. One might also look to theories of racial genesis, as William James does in distinguishing between the Latin and Germanic races: "the Germanic races have tended rather to think of Sin . . . with a capital S, as of something ineradicably ingrained in our nature subjectively . . ." (p. 117). And above all, one looks to cultural influences tracing back to ancient Israel, whose holy writ visits many a dire word upon us: "Behold, God putteth no trust in his saints; yea, the heavens are not clean in his sight./How much more abominable and filthy is man, which drinketh iniquity like water?" (*Job*, 15:15–16). Even St. Paul, whose mighty will fastened Christianity upon the Roman Empire, was unable to conquer his own will to evil: "For the good that I would, I do not: but the evil which I would not, that I do. . . . O wretched man that I am!" (*Romans* 7:19–24).

From ancient writ to modern science, then, much evidence exists that serves to justify Hawthorne's obsession. Yet there is one respect in which he differs from these others: in Jamesian terms, the ultimate source of Hawthorne's melancholy, and the reason why it is pathological, is that his psychology of sin, when most profoundly rendered, negates the possibility of conversion. The trouble with Hawthorne's most desperate characters, that is to say, is that they need conversion but are psychologically powerless to attain it. An interesting case in point is Young Goodman Brown, whose commission of the Unpardonable Sin (seking "to penetrate, in every bosom, the deep mystery of sin") leads to a condition strikingly similar to a case study in James's "The Sick Soul." James's sick soul, a patient in a French asylum, exhibits—like Goodman Brown on his return to the village—"a sort of psychic neuralgia wholly unknown to healthy life. Such anguish may partake of various characters, having sometimes more the quality of loathing [precisely Brown's reaction to the villagers]; sometimes . . . of suspicion, anxiety, trepidation, fear" (p. 126). Just as Brown became "a stern, a sad, a darkly meditative, a distrustful, if not a desperate man," so James's patient, as revealed in a letter James quotes, has "a consciousness . . . so choked with the feeling of evil that the sense of there being any good in the world is lost for him altogether. His attention excludes it, cannot admit it: the sun has left his heaven" (p. 127). Even Brown's final religious despair—"they carved no hopeful verse upon his tombstone, for his dying hour was gloom"—has its counterpart in James's analysis: "And secondly you see how the querulous temper of his misery keeps his mind from taking a religious direction. Querulousness of mind tends in fact rather towards irreligion . . ." (p. 128). The question raised by this comparison is whether a character like Young Goodman Brown is a victim of his own Unpardonable Sin, or more properly a victim of the sick soul mentality in his maker.

Not all Hawthorne's studies in sin, we must concede, raise this question. Some characters, like Hester Prynne, do work out a satisfactory conversion—though we might question whether Hester ever really entered James's Sick Soul condition—and others may deserve their eternal punishment. For an Ethan Brand or a Chillingworth, who in cold blood or malice has violated the innermost soul of another, conversion may be rightly impossible because his Unpardonable Sin has hardened the heart beyond any desire for conversion. Yet there still remain characterizations bespeaking the sick soul state in their author, as though Hawthorne himself were wearing Father Hooper's Black Veil, that gave "a darkened aspect to all living and inanimate things." Sin, in this aspect, works an irreversible chemistry upon the soul such that, though theologically redeemable, a Hollingsworth or Dimmesdale is psychologically damned forever, for lack of the psychic resources that might construe a second birth and thus offer release from an unacceptable identity. It is the psychological damnation that renders *The Scarlet Letter* so powerfully morbid-minded a book, particularly in its portrayal of Dimmesdale as a doomed fly stuck and struggling on the web with no chance of escaping.

As a Christian minister, Dimmesdale knows and preaches the efficacy of the soul's conversion, and he enacts in his own right the ritual of repentance and confession as James himself prescribes it: "For him who confesses, shams are over and realities have begun; he has exteriorized his rottenness. If he has not actually got rid of it, he at least no longer smears it over with a hypocritical show of virtue—he lives at least upon a basis of veracity. . . . One would think that in more men the shell of secrecy would have had to open, the pent-in abscess to burst and gain relief, even though the ear that heard the confession were unworthy" (351). Confessed and contrite at the end, yet is the poor minister crushed to his death in the agony of sin, and without even his death opening a sure salvation:

> "Shall we not meet again?" whispered she. . . . "Surely, surely, we have ransomed one another, with all this woe! Thou lookest far into eternity, with those bright dying eyes! Then tell me what thou seest?"
> "Hush, Hester, hush!" said he. . . . "The law we broke!—the sin here so awfully revealed! let these alone be in thy thoughts! I fear! I fear! It may be that, when we forgot our God,—when we violated our reverence each for the other's soul,—it was thenceforth vain to hope that we could meet hereafter, in an everlasting and pure reunion."

Sharing, as they do, the same matrix of doctrinal beliefs, Hester's is a religion of healthy-mindedness in this scene— "Shall we not spend our immortal life together?"—while Dimmesdale, in shunting her hopes aside, is a sick soul to the end, grateful only for the fact of his torment: "He hath proved his mercy, most of all, in my afflictions. By giving me this burning torture to bear. . . . always at red-heat! By bringing me hither, to die this death. . . . Praised be his name!"

Ironically, the only form of conversion that does seem

47

open to this tortured soul is the malevolent transformation that follows upon his meeting with Hester in the forest, so that upon his return to town (in Chapter 20, "The Minister in a Maze") he has indeed experienced the Jamesian shift in the "hot places" of his consciousness. The "space of a single day," Hawthorne says, "had operated on his consciousness like the lapse of years": "Before Mr. Dimmesdale reached home, his inner man gave him other evidences of a revolution in the sphere of thought and feeling. In truth, nothing short of a total change of dynasty and moral code, in that interior kingdom, was adequate to account for the impulses now communicated to the . . . minister." Up to this point, Hawthorne's language corresponds perfectly to that of James's various testimonies of conversion, but though the *form* of Dimmesdale's inner change is perfectly Jamesian, its substance is altogether destructive, inciting the minister "to do some strange, wild, wicked thing or other, with a sense that it would be at once involuntary and intentional; in spite of himself, yet growing out of a profounder self than that which opposed the impulse." Rather than unifying the man's soul, as the conversion experience purposes (and such conversion can be away from religion into atheism, James concluded), the minister's wild impulses—to utter blasphemy to his deacon or teach foul words to a knot of Puritan children—only rend him further asunder, towards the condition of final, fatal psychic illness.

No one would deny that Hawthorne laid bare real secrets of the soul in his morbid-mindedness, and evidence abounds as to the efficacy of his disclosures. Mrs. Hawthorne recalled, after the writer's death, that "men who had committed great crimes or whose memories held tragic secrets would sometimes write to him or would even come great distances to see him, and unburden their souls. This was after the publication of *The Scarlet Letter*, which made them regard him as the father-confessor for all hidden sins." Yet one must wonder just what Hawthorne, so largely a sick soul himself, found in his heart to tell those people.

Final evidence of something deeply wrong in Hawthorne's psyche might be adduced from the profile of his later writing career, which in his last dozen years produced only one finished novel (his weakest) and a number of abortive fragments about the search for the elixir of life. This subject matter obviously evokes religious meaning, and Hawthorne's failure to deal with it successfully may imply a psychological as well as literary incapacity. It is possible, however, by way of finishing our speculation, to put an opposite interpretation on this matter. If Hawthorne's best work, as seems evident, arose out of the morbid-minded center in his personality, a shift in that center may have removed the subliminal force behind his creativity—leaving his native talent intact but with no true subject to feed upon. Evidence favoring such a shift in his personal center—or conversion, as James calls it—includes the following reminiscence by one Henry F. Chorley, an English gentleman whom Hawthorne visited while consul in Liverpool. "A most genial and original man," Chorley called his guest, "full of humour, in no respect shy. . . . A pleasanter day than the one in question is not in my 'Golden Book.' I think I have never heard any one, save my honoured friend Carlyle, laugh so heartily as did Hawthorne." Devil's laughter, surely, one might suspect in recollecting what Emerson's friends thought of Hawthorne, but possibly by this time Hawthorne had become truly healthy-minded. If so, his conversion, by his own testimony, owed entirely to the effects of his marriage, which may finally have mitigated the long decades of morbid-minded gloom. Certainly, he spoke of his wife as having "saved" him, almost as if in answer to the speaker's need in "The Haunted Mind," a sketch written before Hawthorne met his Sophia: "As your head falls back upon the pillow, you think—in a whisper be it spoken—how pleasant, in these night solitudes, would be the rise and fall of a softer breathing than your own, the slight pressure of a tenderer bosom, the quiet throb of a purer heart, imparting its peacefulness to your troubled one. . . ."

Julian Hawthorne's book about his parents, *Nathaniel Hawthorne and His Wife*, confirms the conversional effect of their courtship upon the previously morbid-minded author. One letter from Hawthorne to his betrothed, dated May 26, 1839, speaks of their relationship as containing a "mystery" which "converts my love into religion." A year and a half later, another letter—dated November 27, 1840—describes the author's inner change in terms directly analogous to James's twice-born psychology:

> Whenever I return to Salem, I feel how dark my life would be without the light that you shed upon it,—how cold, without the warmth of your love. Sitting in this chamber, where my youth wasted itself in vain, I can partly estimate the change that has been wrought. It seems as if the better part of me had been born since then. I had walked those many years in darkness, and might so have walked through life, with only a dreamy notion that there was any light in the universe, if you had not kissed my eyelids and given me to see.

Yet happiness, as John Updike has observed, makes us afraid. Hawthorne's batch of unfinished novels about the search for the elixir of life may betoken such fear, as do his memorable pages, already cited, on the death of his mother or on the black abyss just underfoot in *The Marble Faun*—passages written after his "salvation."

In conclusion, our final judgment of Hawthorne's religious psychology must remain ambiguous. One cannot doubt the reality of the change in him wrought by Sophia Peabody, yet neither can one consider his basic morbid-mindedness to have been fairly overriden by a larger affection. Perhaps we must conclude that Hawthorne's was, in his last decades, a partly converted psyche. His spirit lacked the strength to complete the process of inner unification that James's chapters on conversion talk about.

2.

With Herman Melville we start down the broad highway of naturalistic thinking which, passing through the deserts of Twain and Crane and Robinson and T. S. Eliot, culminates presently in the black humor movement of recent years. James expressly identified philosophic naturalism—the view that nature is all that exists, there being no supernature or spiritual reality—as the key cause of the sick soul's melancholy. "The purely naturalistic look at life," he says, "however enthusiastically it may begin, is sure to end in sadness. This sadness lies at the heart of every merely positivistic, agnostic, or naturalistic scheme of philosophy" (136). In a statement that essentially encompasses Herman Melville's early and later career, James warns, "Let sanguine healthy-mindedness do its best with its strange power of living in the moment and ignoring [*Typee, Omoo*], still the evil background is really there to be thought of, and the skull will grin in at the banquet [*Moby Dick, Pierre, The Confidence Man*]" (p. 136). Melancholy first rises seriously against Melville's essential healthy-mindedness in *Mardi*, whose initial tone is as wholesome as Taji's paeon to fat men (Chapter 95): "For fat men are the salt and savor of the earth, full of good humor, high spirits, fun, and all manner of jollity. . . . Of men, they are the good measures, brimmed, heaped, pressed down, piled up, and running over."[2]

As against the humor, fun, and jollity, a naturalistic vision of reality was already thrusting its tragic note into the book's proceedings. Well before Shakespeare and Hawthorne got into the forefront of Melville's thought—in the fateful summer of 1850—the science of geology was dropping germinous seeds into Melville's soul, producing, in *Mardi* (Chapter

---

[2] Because so many editions of Melville's books exist, and because he so often wrote short chapters, I shall cite chapter references rather than page references, for the benefit of readers using different editions.

132, "Babbalanja Regales the Company with Some Sandwiches"), the ghoulish spectacle of the geological sandwich:

> "My lord, then take another theory—which you will—the celebrated sandwich system. Nature's first condition was a soup wherein the agglomerating solids . . . deposited the primal stratum . . . , sandwiching strange shapes of mollusks and zoophytes, then snails and periwinkles—marmalade to sip and nuts to crack ere the substantials come.
>
> "And next, my lord, we have the fine old time of the Old Red Sandstone sandwich, clapped on the underlying layer and among other dainties embedding the first course of fish. . . . Served up with these were sundry greens—lichens, mosses, ferns, and fungi.
>
> "Now comes the New Red Sandstone sandwich . . . and prodigious lizards, spine-skewered, tails tied in bows. . . .
>
> "Next the Chalk, or Corla, sandwich; but no dry fare for that; made up of rich side courses—Eocene, Miocene, and Pliocene. . . . The third side course, the Pliocene, was goodliest of all—whole roasted elephants, rhinoceroses, and hippopotamuses stuffed with boiled ostriches. . . . Also barbecued mastodons. . . , gallantly served up with fir trees in their mouths, and tails cock-billed."

A couple of belly laughs, years, and books later, we arrive at the human contribution to the whole thing, concerning which, in *Moby Dick*, Ishmael is by no means so merry. The dread heartlessness of nature, that stabs us from behind with thoughts of annihilation, may well serve as the grand theme of the book, with human heartlessness its sorry counterpoint.

As against Whitman's and Emerson's perfect faith in Nature, Melville's "fear of the universe"—to use James's term—gives *Moby Dick* its pervading tone. Whether by virtue of the book's large design (Promethean Ahab crushed like a flea) or by virtue of the small details (Ishmael's ubiquitous anti-Transcendental ruminations), Melville's master novel betrays an essentially morbid-minded mentality. Like Hawthorne describing Zenobia's drowned corpse, Melville sees the inner secret of Nature, and of Nature's putative god, as consisting of a parcel of bones, but unlike Hawthorne, Melville possessed an intellect that could not "Away with the hideous thought." So, in "The Whiteness of the Whale," Ishmael sees that "all deified Nature absolutely paints like the harlot, whose allurements [Nature's vital colors] cover nothing but the charnel-house within"; and again, in "A Bower in the Arsacides," Ishmael finds within the Temple of Nature—the vinetrellised whale-skeleton chapel—"no living thing . . . ; naught was there but bones." Knowledge of nature, or of reality, thus comes to us by way of a dreadful fall from innocence. "Consider, once more, the universal cannibalism of the sea; all whose creatures prey upon each other," says the narrator in "Brit"; ". . . as this appalling ocean surrounds the verdant land, so in the soul of man there lies one insular Tahiti, full of peace and joy, but encompassed by all the horrors of the half known life. God keep thee! Push not off from that isle, thou canst never return!"

That nature evinces joy, majesty, and loveliness is readily conceded, in "The Grand Armada" and "The Symphony" for example, but the book's plot moves inexorably on toward its disclosure of nature as supernal, inhuman power, embodied in Moby Dick. The fear of the universe that drove Pip mad in "The Castaway" here recurs in the figure of Melville's epic hero reduced to the scope of a bubble in the whale's eye—"helpless Ahab's head was seen, like a tossed bubble which the least chance shock might burst" ("The Chase—First Day"). After bestriding the book like a Titan for hundreds of pages, Ahab is so reduced when measured against his adversary as not even to figure in the book's title. For in the end, Melville's subject is not Ahab but Moby Dick: Nature: mindless and heartless cosmic force swallowing up an epic human undertaking in "the great shroud of the sea," which thereupon "rolled on as it rolled five thousand years ago" at the end of the Chase.

In addition to its substantial fear of the universe, *Moby Dick* also expresses a Jamesean "sense of sin," not only in Captain Ahab's much-noted malice, blasphemy, and pride, but also in the general heartlessness of the crew. Ishmael is saved from the final destruction not only because he alone repudiates the evil quest and its sin of malice (in "A Squeeze of the Hand"), but because he alone proves capable of pity. The others all too heartily display the universal cannibalism of the sea, all of whose creatures prey upon each other. Not only in Stubb's Supper, but in numerous other episodes, the Pequod's crew are so guilt-stained with blood that, in one killing ("Stubb Kills a Whale"), the stain symbolically touches every face: "The red tide now poured from all sides like brooks down a hill. His tormented body rolled not in brine but in blood, which bubbled and seethed for furlongs behind in their wake. The slanting sun played upon this crumson pond in the sea, sent back its reflection into every face. . . . At last, gush after gush of clotted red gore . . . shot into the frighted air." With good reason, Ishmael inquires "Cannibals? who is not a cannibal?" (in "The Whale As a Dish") after denoting the "crowds of live bipeds staring up at the long rows of dead quadrupeds" in the meat market. And in "The Pequod Meets the Virgin," "showers of gore" spatter the boatmen who with a singular lack of pity kill a blind and crippled old creature: ". . . from the points which the whale's eyes had once occupied, now protruded blind bulbs, horribly pitiable to see. But pity there was none. For all his old age, and his one arm, and his blind eyes, he must die the death and be murdered, in order to light the gay bridals and other merrymakings of men. . . . It was most piteous, that last expiring spout."

Interestingly, *Moby Dick* expressly develops the four responses to the sick soul condition that William James ascribed to Tolstoy (p. 132). Listed in James's order of appearance, they are:

1.) "mere animal blindness, sucking the honey without seeing the dragon or the mice" (Flask's mindless hedonism, denoted by his name);

2.) "reflective epicureanism, snatching what it can while the day lasts" (precisely Stubb's position, a cheerful fatalism);

3.) "manly suicide" (Ishmael's intention in the novel's first paragraph)
and 4.) "seeing the mice and dragon and yet weakly and plaintively clinging to the bush of life" (Ishmael's final stance, on his coffin-lifebuoy).

Of course, Melville's novel delineates other responses as well: Starbuck's Christian faith, Queequeg's "noble savage" role, and Captain Ahab's negative Transcendentalism; that is, his subscription to Emerson's two paramount beliefs, in "the infinitude of the private man" and in the idea that "behind Nature, throughout Nature, Spirit is present"—with the difference that, for Ahab, that Spirit is evil: "intelligent malignity". But the important thing for our study in religious psychology is that Melville was never able to pull these warring parts of his psyche together. For Melville, the crisis of belief—of not knowing what to believe or what beliefs one might live by—would end only with death, as in Ishmael's meditation in "The Gilder" (Chapter 114):

> There is no steady unretracing progress in this life; we do not advance through fixed gradations, and at the last one pause:— through infancy's unconscious spell, boyhood's thoughtless faith, adolescence's doubt (the common doom), then scepticism, then disbelief, resting at last in manhood's pondering repose of If. But once gone through, we trace the round again; and are infants, boys, and men, and Ifs eternally. . . . Our souls are like those orphans whose unwedded mothers die in bearing them: the secret of our paternity lies in their grave, and we must there to learn it.

In Melville, then, we see a man who underwent the opposite of James's unification of the psyche. A perfectly hearty, healthy-minded man at the start, one who in *Mardi* (Chapter 9) could consel us on the ease of meeting the dark angel ("the inflexible friend, who, even against our wills, from life's evils triumphantly relieves us"), he devolved into the state Hawthorne portrayed in his English Journal (November

20, 1856)—"[he] informed me that he had 'pretty much made up his mind to be annihilated'; but still he does not seem to rest in that anticipation. . . . It is strange how he persists . . . in wandering to-and-fro over these deserts, as dismal and monotonous as the sand hills amid which we were sitting. He can neither believe nor be comfortable in his unbelief. . . ." (Ironically, in "Hawthorne and His Mosses," Melville ascribed his loss of belief to Hawthorne himself, whose general "power of blackness"—particularly poignant in Goodman Brown's cry "My Faith is gone!"—struck Melville with apocalyptic force.) Here we have a true example of the "incompletely unified . . . intellectual constitution" James speaks of in his chapter on "The Divided Self, and the Process of Its Unification," but it is undergoing the opposite process. In *Mardi* and *Moby Dick* Melville had scattered his intellectual fragments throughout the embattled characters he invented, and was never made whole again. Dwelling disjunctively together in his soul, there would always remain an Ahab, a Starbuck, a Stubb and a Pip, and the others, making Ishmael's emergence from the wreckage not at all a second birth but merely a survival.

The most telling birth metaphor in Melville's work is that in "Bartleby the Scrivener," whose title-figure—a burnt-out husk surrounded by concentric rings of walls—gives up the ghost at last in very despair. "Strangely huddled at the base of the wall, his knees drawn up, and lying on his side, his head touching the cold stones," Bartleby obviously lies in the fetal position, but death is the only deliverer. In this final posture of despair, Bartleby turns to the second of what James calls "the only two ways in which it is possible to get rid of anger, worry, fear, despair, or other undesirable affections. One is that an opposite affection should overpoweringly break over us, and the other is by getting so exhausted with the struggle that we have to stop,—so we drop down, give up, and *don't care* any longer" (p. 173). The first way—which in its ultimate degree amounts to conversion—is most strikingly, and if I may say so, movingly rendered in the character of Babbalanja in *Mardi*, whose brilliant intellect and eloquence is unsurpassed in any other Melvillean characterization.

That is to say, Melville's last and greatest example of conversion predates *Moby Dick* and the crisis of the 1850's. Azzageddi, the devil that possesses Babbalanja in his moments of profoundest utterance, is none other than the Jamesian sick soul, ridden nearly to madness by his sense of mortality and fear of the universe. The geological sandwich was just one of his morbid-minded concoctions. There is also Babbalanja's meditation (Chapter 78) in the charnel house of the kings. Shall these bones live?

> "At best, t'is but a hope. But will a longing bring the thing desired? . . . For backward or forward, eternity is the same: already have we been the nothing we dread to be. Icy thought! . . . shall I not be as these bones? To come to this! . . . I do reject your brotherhood, ye libelous remains. But no, no; despise them not, O Babbalanja! Thy own skeleton thou thyself dost carry with thee through this mortal life and aye would view it but for kind nature's screen; thou art death alive; and e'en to what's before thee wilt thou come. Aye, thy children's children will walk over thee. . . ."

Later (Chapters 151 and 185) Babbalanja prophesies, "I say that . . . when I die the universe will perish with me"; later still, he adopts the darker tones of Ecclesiastes. "Nay, nay, death is life's last despair. Hard and horrible is it to die. . . . Yet why, why live? Life is wearisome to all, the same dull round. Day and night, summer and winter, round about us revolving for aye."

The whiteness of the Milky Way thrusts into *Mardi* as well as *Moby Dick* its heartless immensities and thoughts of annihilation, with Babbalanja again the victim of perception (Chapter 175): "Who in Arcturus hath heard of us? They know us not in the Milky Way. . . . We demand eternity for a lifetime when our mortal half hours too often prove tedious. We know not of what we talk. . . ." Moreover, Babbalanja rejects

Taji's religious advice (Chapter 97): "let us hold fast to all we have and stop all leaks in our faith, lest an opening, but of a hand's breadth, should sink our seventy-fours. The wide Atlantic can rush in at one porthole, and if we surrender a plank, we surrender the fleet." Quite the contrary, Babbalanja expressly rejects Alma (Christ) as his personal savior (Chapter 113): "The prophet came to guarantee our eternal felicity; but . . . that felicity rests on so hard a proviso that to a thinking mind but very few of our sinful race may secure it. For one, then, I wholly reject your Alma . . . because of obvious and undeniable things all round us which, to me, seem at war with an unreserved faith in his doctrines. . . . I never was so thorough a disbeliever as now." Yet at the end of the book (Chapter 187) under the gentle persuasions of Serenia, Babbalanja is wholly converted, in terms that might have emerged straight out of Dr. Starbuck's documents:

> "How eloquent he is!" murmured Babbalanja. "Some black cloud sems floating from me. I begin to see. I come out in light. The sharp fang tears me less. The forked flames wane. . . .
> "Oh Alma, Alma! Prince divine!" cried Babbalanja, sinking on his knees. "In *thee*, at last, I find repose. Hope perches in my heart a dove; a thousand rays illume; all heaven's a sun. Gone, gone, are all distracting doubts! Love and Alma now prevail. I see with other eyes. . . . I have been mad. Some things there are we must not think of. . . . All I have said ere this that wars with Alma's precepts, I here recant. . . ."

Following this episode, the mystical vision that befalls Babbalanja—a Dantean tour of the spiritual universe (chapter 188)—effects the grand climax of religious experience in the novel. Now are all the book's characters converted save one— Taji, who would reappear in *Moby Dick* as blaspheming Ahab: "Then, then! My heart grew hard like flint, and black like night, and sounded hollow to the hand I clenched. Hyenas filled me with their laughs; death damps chilled my brow; I prayed not, but blasphemed" (Chapter 189). And with Ahab crushed like an insect in the end, we move at last to Bartleby's abortive fetal posture, "getting so exhausted with the struggle that we have to stop," as James said, "—so we drop down, give up, and *don't care* any longer." Evidence in *Pierre, The Confidence Man, Clarel,* and the vast silence up to his last novella *Billy Budd* implies that Melville himself shared this position.

The development of Melville's intellect in science, philosophy, and theology seems to have caused this morbid-minded cul de sac, abetted by disappointments in his literary life, yet behind all this remains the unfathomable mystery of personality. Walt Whitman, with much the same expansive interest in science, philosophy, and religion, and subject to bitter anathemas in public criticism, remained healthy-minded, productive, and psychically unified through it all. No poet has ever written more largely and beautifully about death, or accepted his own annihilation more serenely. Even the geological sandwich is acclaimed as the source of Whitman's being—

> For it [my embryo] the nebula cohered to an orb,
> The long slow strata piled to rest it on,
> Vast vegetables gave it sustenance,
> Monstrous sauroids transported it in their mouths and
>   deposited it with care. . . .
> Now on this spot I stand with my robust soul.

And he gives his being over to it, as *Song of Myself* ends, in the same spirit, diffusing himself through the soil:

> And as to you Corpse I think you are good manure, but that
>   does not offend me,
> I smell the white roses sweet-scented and growing,
> I reach to the leafy lips, I reach to the polish'd breasts
>   of melons. . . .
> O suns—O grass of graves—O perpetual transfers and promotions.

It may be true that in his final book *Billy Budd* Melville sailed at last into a harbor of mildness, as Auden's poem says, but this book's range of thought is carefully limited. Its theme, as we shall contend in our chapter on "Saintliness," is that men require the inhibiting outer forms of government (Captain Vere's function) and the inner ones of religion (Billy's role) because of "innate depravity" in human nature. As significant and persuasive as this theme is, it does not aspire to the metaphysical profundity of the earlier novels, and so the final harbor of *Billy Budd* seems mild only to the degree that moral tragedy appears preferable to the wild chaos of black laughter where Melville had drifted for decades. Indeed, one of the chief features of black humor is precisely the type of split personality that we see developing in Melville as a result of the "incompletely unified" constitution that James spoke of. The mode of black humor may be traced backward through a succession of such divided personalities from Shrike/Miss Lonelyhearts (representing Nathanael West the cynic and Nathan Weinstein the man of empathetic feeling), through Satan/Joan of Arc (representing Twain the satirist and Clemens the sentimentalist) to Melville, whose only solution to the incompletely unified state appears to have been cathartic laughter like that of Twain or West. Shortly before his conversion, Babbalanja in *Mardi* renders what still remains the essential rationale of black humor (Chapter 183): "We must laugh or we die; to laugh is to live."

Although Babbalanja himself furnishes some fine specimens of black comedy in *Mardi*, Melville's ultimate exercise in perverse laughter is *The Confidence-Man*, his final full-scale novel and the first extended work of black humor in American literature. At the end of this novel, the ultimate con man is unmasked, not surprisingly, to reveal the Biblical deity—"Jehovah shall be thy confidence," Melville quotes from Proverbs (3:26). Behind this sour little parable of theological fraud is an authorial intelligence desperately in need of a belief to live by. Clearly, in Chapter 5, Melville uses the Roman historian Tacitus as a mask for himself when a character declaims, "I hate Tacitus. . . . Without confidence himself, Tacitus destroys it in all his readers." Like T. S. Eliot crying "O my people, what have I done unto thee" in *Ash-Wednesday* (V), Melville evidently felt increasing guilt over leading others into his own desperation, a guilt that contributed to the cessation of his career in fiction while he was yet in his thirties. In this final novel before he turned to his long poem of arid despair, *Clarel*, Melville puts the finishing touches on the portrayal of the sick soul whose features first assumed large definition in the figure of Babbalanja in *Mardi*. But here, manifesting itself among the masks and multiple identities, the composite sick soul is radically incurable and unconvertible. In Chapter 16 we are told that "A sick philosopher is incurable," which truism is ramified in Chapter 17 by the observation that "Some pains cannot be eased but by producing insensibility, and cannot be cured but by producing death." (Consider Bartleby!)

Proceeding apace with his belated intellectual growth, then—a process which began, he told Hawthorne, at age twenty-five—Melville suffered a gradual dissolution of his psychic unity, a loss rather than a shift of the Jamesian "centre of personal energy." For a few years in the 1850's the intellectual growth sufficed in itself to energize his most profound and enduring literary work, but when that period of growth was completed, and the personal energy drained away, there were no "hot and live" ideas around which his deepest being could cohere in a second birth of the spirit; no vital center to rescue the burnt-out husk of Bartleby from the "dead feelings, dead ideas, and cold beliefs" of his maker. As a result, Melville's inspiration died in mid-career, leaving the most profound thinker of 19th century America to live out his last three decades as an unknown customs-officer, his previously prolific creativity reduced to a handful of poems and one late-blooming novella.

In Jamesian terms, Melville underwent the opposite of a conversion experience, which normally is "an adolescent

61

phenomenon, incidental to the passage from the child's small universe to the wider intellectual and spiritual life of maturity" (p. 164). Melville's passage to that wider intellectual life, by fixing his gaze upon the "heartless immensities" of nature with its universal cannibalism close at hand and its thoughts of annihilation among the galaxies, made conversion to healthy-mindedness impossible. In effect, Melville became a hollow man a century ahead of his time, one of those dead souls rendered incapable of any sustaining belief. With much sympathy, William James defined this type of unsaveable soul in his chapter on "Conversion" (pp. 167–168):

> . . . there are objective forms of melancholy also, in which the lack of rational meaning of the universe, and of life anyhow, is the burden that weighs upon one. . . .
> Some persons, for instance, never are, and possibly never under any circumstances could be, converted. . . . They are life-long subjects of 'barrenness' and 'dryness.' Such inaptitude for religious faith may in some cases be intellectual in its origin. Their religious faculties may be checked in their natural tendency to expand, by beliefs about the world that are inhibitive, the pessimistic and materialistic beliefs, for example, within which so many good souls . . . find themselves nowadays, as it were, frozen. . . .

3.

Following Herman Melville's collapse into the sick soul state in the mid-1850's, the Literature of morbid-mindedness advanced, in a sort of Rake's Progress, across some notable stepping stones into the later nineteenth and early twentieth century. In her darker moods, Emily Dickinson was subject to deep morbid-mindedness, especially when thoughts of death worked upon her imagination. With characteristic realism, her spirit withers under the "Jealousy . . . so nearly Infinite" with which the dying woman in "The Last Night That She Lived" looks upon those in the room who will live beyond her, and in "It Was Not Death, For I Stood Up" she shared the experience of being dead as largely as any living being is capable of doing so. "I Heard A Fly Buzz When I Died" goes so far as to undermine the dignity of the deathbed with a sick joke, for how else can we view the approach of a hungry garbage fly as the final sight that the world discloses to the dying speaker? Although essentially a healthy-minded poet, Miss Dickinson anticipated in these darker ruminations the full-blown naturalistic morbidity that characterized Twain's, Crane's, Dreiser's, and Robinson's writings late in the century. Their childhood religious training overmastered by the contradictory revelations of contemporary science, these men could achieve the Jamesian unification of the psyche only around essentially unpalatable beliefs, nihilistic ideas, and morbid feelings.

Twain's *What is Man?*, *The Mysterious Stranger*, and *Letters from the Earth*, as expressions of the sick soul condition, are buttressed by non-fictional statements from his *Notebooks* and *Autobiography*. God's "real character is written in plain words in His real Bible, which is Nature and her history," Twain says in his *Notebook*, and this "Bible of Nature . . . tells us distinctly that God cares not a rap for us—nor for any living creature."[3] Even so, the Bible of Nature is far preferable to that of the Hebrew-Christian heritage, whose pernicious influence drew forth Twain's rage late in his old age. In his "Reflections on Religion," dictated in June of 1906, Twain—thinking no doubt of his own childhood experience—declared that "there has never been a Protestant boy or a Protestant girl whose mind the Bible has not soiled!" "Nothing in all history . . . remotely approaches in atrocity the invention of Hell," he said by way of lodging his ultimate charge against Christian doctrine, and as for Christianity in practice, he can only conclude that "Ours is a terrible religion. The fleets of the world could swim in spacious comfort in the innocent blood it has spilt."

Science, then, is plainly preferable to the Christian re-

---

[3] See *Mark Twain's Notebook*, ed. Albert Bigelow Paine (New York: 1935), pp. 360–362, and *Mark Twain's Autobiography*, Volume II (New York: 1924), p. 7.

ligion but by no means is it to be understood as offering truths that a man can live by. The evolution of mankind, for example, is ground for chagrin rather than pride, as Twain sees it. Man's "working himself up out of the oyster bed to his present position was probably a matter of surprise and regret to the Creator," Twain says in his *Autobiography*, since "his history, in all climes, all ages and all circumstances, furnishes oceans and continents of proof that of all the creatures that were made, he is the most detestable . . . , the only one—the solitary one—that possesses malice." Everything Twain wrote in his last decades confirms that Twain's mind actually cohered around beliefs like these, and as James's study corroborates, the mind possessed of such an outlook can only wish for release in death's oblivion. Not only did Twain look forward to his own death, as the one perfect gift that life has in store; he also refused to wish that his most dearly loved ones—his wife and the two daughters whose deaths preceded his—come back to life again, preferring his own grief to their having to resume the burden of incarnation.[4] Perhaps Twain's waning creative power, once he had completed his memory book trilogy with *Huckleberry Finn* in 1885, may be attributed to the takeover of his mind by these naturalistic truths, ruinous alike to his sense of human worth and his artistic destiny.

In Jamesian terms, we might say that Mark Twain was a man who was never reborn. His soul-sickness, protracted over decades of deepening despair and masked all the while by his public pose as a comedian, found relief only in the psycho-

---

[4] In 1903, the year before his wife Olivia died, Twain called Adam "man's benefactor—he gave him all he ever received that was worth having—Death." After Olivia's death in 1904, Twain's death-wish intensified: "if I live two years more . . . I will kill myself. . . . The country home I need . . . is a cemetery. . . . I have had about enough of this world, and I wish I were out of it." See *Mark Twain's Notebook*, p. 381; and Albert Bigelow Paine's *Mark Twain: A Biography* (New York: Harper and Brothers, 1912), Volume III, p. 1337.

therapy of truth-telling—a truth-telling that often had to be done in private, however. (His fiercest attack upon Christianity, *Letters from the Earth*, was withheld from publication until the 1960's.)

4.

Stephen Crane and Theodore Dreiser, Twain's naturalistic successors, were evidently more perfectly self-unified in their "new birth . . . away from religion and into incredulity," as James described this type of possibility (p. 147). Although his father was a kindly Christian minister, Crane turned away from his family's Methodist heritage as a mere boy, beginning thereupon his path to the fully developed naturalism he would best define in his brilliantly imagistic poetry and in *The Open Boat*.[5] (Crane himself preferred his poetry to his fiction, saying "I like my little book of poems, *The Black Riders*, better than I do *The Red Badge of Courage*. . . . The former is the more ambitious effort. In it I aim to give my ideas of life as a whole.")[6] While still a teen-ager, Crane says, he formulated the theory "that the most artistic and the most enduring literature was that which reflected life accurately." All alone, he thought (until he met Howells and Garland), he had developed the creed that

---

[5] In R. W. Stallman's *Stephen Crane: A Biography* (New York: George Braziller, 1968), Crane recalls his departure from his Protestant heritage (p. 13): "I used to like the church and prayer meetings when I was a kid. . . , but that cooled off and when I was thirteen or about that, my brother Will told me not to believe in Hell after my uncle had been boring me about the lake of fire and the rest of the sideshows." This nonchalance contrasts somewhat with the haunted mind of Mark Twain, who remarked, "I don't believe in it [hell], but I'm afraid of it. When I wake up at night, I think of hell, and I am sure about going there" (Justin Kaplan, *Mr. Clemens and Mark Twain*, New York: 1966, p. 317).

[6] *Stephen Crane: Letters*, ed. R. W. Stallman and Lillian Gilkes (New York: 1960), p. 79. Other quotations are cited from this book, pp. 31, 99; and from *The Portable Stephen Crane*, ed. Joseph Katz (New York: 1969), p. 534.

65

"we are the most successful when we approach the nearest to nature and truth."

But before Crane could reflect life accurately, approaching nearest to nature and truth, the first compelling necessity was to eradicate the major cultural traditions working to the contrary. Like Twain, Crane turned his gift for mockery most savagely upon two traditions in particular, Romance and Religion, the chief source of falsehoods by which men lived, abjuring truth and worsening their suffering. Romance and religion between them had created the false code of respectability that drove poor Maggie to suicide, the false image of war-heroism that deluded Henry Fleming, and the ideological idiocies that rampage through *War Is Kind* and *The Black Riders*. "Ah, what joy!" says a murdered youth in one poem, "To die, thus,/In this medieval fashion,/According to the best legends. . . ." If only Twain's arch-Romantic, Tom Sawyer, could have been so lucky. As for the Christian religion, its Bible is only "A little ink more or less!," its worship service "an ordered walking/Of surpliced numbskulls," and its ministry "a burning candle and an ass."[7] Yet, behind Crane's contempt and sarcasm subsists a genuine religious sensitivity. Of Crane we may say, as Eliot said of Baudelaire, that he "is essentially Christian. . . . Genuine blasphemy is as impossible to the complete atheist as to the perfect Christian. . . . His business was not to practise Christianity, but—what was much more important for his time—to assert its *necessity*" (emphasis Eliot's).[8] In describing contemporary man as a creature in the

---

[7] The four poems quoted in this paragraph appear in *The Work of Stephen Crane*, ed. Wilson Follett (New York: Knopf, 1926), Volume VI, *The Black Riders, War Is Kind and Other Poems*, Introduction by Amy Lowell, pp. 59, 112 and 118, and 35. In her Introduction (p. xi), Amy Lowell recounts the story that "Crane, dining one night with William Dean Howells, to whom he had been introduced by Hamlin Garland, heard the older man read some of Emily Dickinson's poems aloud. The impact of this perfectly fresh and spontaneous poetry shook him profoundly, even to the sudden shooting up in him of a latent poetical urge. So moved, he wrote."

desert, "naked, bestial,/Who, squatting upon the ground,/ Held his heart in his hands,/And ate of it," Crane is coining an image that T. S. Eliot would render into the master metaphor of his age.

In thus portraying his sick soul condition, Crane represents the stage where Eliot too would have ended his quest had he also died before the age of thirty. Although Crane never proceeded to the state of religious conversion, he goes so far as to express—in admirably detailed imagery—the insight that William James called "the core of the religious problem," the cry for help:

> Toward God a mighty hymn
> A song of collisions and cries
> Rumbling wheels, hoof-beats, bells,
> Welcomes, farewells, love-calls, final moans,
> Voices of joy, idiocy, warning, despair,
> The unknown appeal of brutes,
> The chanting of flowers,
> The screams of cut trees,
> The senseless babble of hens and wise men—
> A cluttered incoherency that says at the stars:
> "Oh, God, save us."

So far as any of his biographers have been able to establish, Stephen Crane was a perfectly admirable man—unfailingly honest and gallant with women, including prostitutes; courageous and dedicated as an artist and journalist; and so honorable about money that he hastened his death by doing hack work to pay off debts that were mostly incurred by his spendthrift mistress in England. In short, in terms of ethical character Crane was a Christian gentleman to the end, calling Human Kindness (his capitals) "the final wall of the wise

---

⁸ T. S. Eliot, Introduction to Baudelaire's *Intimate Journals* (1930). Cited from T. S. Eliot: *Selected Prose*, ed. John Hayward (Great Britain: Peregrine Books, 1963), pp. 176–7. In his *Stephen Crane* (New Haven: Twayne Publishers, 1962), Edwin H. Cady remarks on the "intrinsically . . . Christian qualities of Crane's vision," based on Crane's intuitive allegiance to *(continued on page 68)*

man's thought. . . . Therefore do I strive to be as kind and as just as may be to those about me and in my meagre success at it, I find the solitary pleasure of life." In the same letter in which he voiced these sentiments, however—dated January, 1896—Crane also expressed a weariness with life such as to verify William James's assertion that "the purely naturalistic look at life . . . is sure to end in sadness," perhaps even "a pathological melancholy" (pp. 121, 124): "For my own part, I am minded to die in my thirty-fifth year. I think that is all I care to stand." That nature would withhold six years from even this modest an allotment may seem ironic in retrospect, yet Crane had probably lived, at the time of his death, a completed artistic life. Short of conversion into a different personality, it is hard to imagine how he could deepen, not merely repeat, the view of life he had already espoused in his classic exposition of philosophical naturalism. What may have lain ahead could have been the stunted later career endured by his predecessors in the sick soul category: Hawthorne, Melville, Twain. When one has come to a view of life wherein the only legitimate emotion is sorrow—as was nearly true of Hawthorne, in Hyatt Waggoner's observation—then perhaps three decades of being alive is enough.

5.

Dreiser's conversion from Christianity to naturalism took place during his young manhood in three stages. First, in time (his late teens) and importance, came his crucial reading experience in "Huxley and Tyndall and Herbert Spencer,

---

(continued from page 67) "the ideals of the Christian gentleman" (p. 78). Despite the "blasphemies" that contemporary readers found objectionable in Crane's writings, "the first and most essential themes of his thought are religious," Professor Cady observes (p. 74), thus parallelling Eliot's commentary about Baudelaire.

whose . . . *First Principles* quite blew me, intellectually, to bits. Hitherto, until I had read Huxley, I had some lingering filaments of Catholicism trailing about me, faith in the existence of Christ, the soundness of his moral deductions. . . . Now in its place was the definite conviction that spiritually one got nowhere, that there was no hereafter, that one lived and had his being because one had to, and that it was of no importance. Of one's ideals, struggles, sorrows and joys, it could only be said that they were chemic compulsions . . . resulting from the hope of pleasure and the fear of pain."[9] Second came Dreiser's observations of city slums, "unsolved and possibly unsolvable misery and degeneracy, whole streets of degraded, dejected, miserable souls. I . . . suspected even then that man is the victim of forces over which he has no control. . . . Why did nature, when left to itself, devise such astounding slums and human muckheaps?" Finally, Dreiser accredits his newspaper experience for finishing his "conversion" away from Christianity: "This world of newspaper men . . . finally liberated me from moralistic and religionistic qualms." It is true that in his final years, Dreiser got loosely connected with the socialist cause, and even went to a Protestant communion service, but on the whole his naturalistic beliefs remained the center of his world-view and his major achievement lay in applying the insights of philosophic naturalism to human society.

As Robert Penn Warren has said, Dreiser's novels about success (the Cowperwood trilogy) were a failure, whereas his novels about failure (*Sister Carrie, An American Tragedy*) succeeded brilliantly. Because of his sick soul perspective, Dreiser's dream self, depicted in Cowperwood's fantastic success at financial and sexual competition, was never remotely

---

[9] See Dreiser's *A Book About Myself* (New York: 1922), pp. 457–8, 64–66, 70. Robert Penn Warren's "Homage to Theodore Dreiser" is a poem that prefaces his book of the same title, *Homage to Theodore Dreiser* (New York: 1971).

so compelling as Dreiser's nightmare self, depicted in the financial and sexual losses of Hurstwood and Clyde Griffith. And beyond that fear of loss lies yet another nightmare, the knowledge that those naturalistic *summa bona*, sex and money, bring their lucky winner "neither surfeit nor content," as his closing paragraph of *Sister Carrie* editorializes. Certainly Dreiser's biography discloses nothing that might counteract that judgment. Not at all inhibited by Crane's kindly scruples, Dreiser selfishly exploited friends and cruelly abused the women who loved him, yet found no relief from his spiritual torment. "Full of screaming his soul is," Robert Penn Warren writes in "Homage to Theodore Dreiser"; "Nothing could help, nothing, not reading Veblen or even Freud" (writers, respectively, about money and sex, it may be noted). Finally, the case of Theodore Dreiser rests again upon William James's mystery of personality—the unanswerable question as to why one temperament responds to loss and suffering with healthy-minded fortitude, as Emerson did, while another reposes in lifelong melancholy, as did Dreiser.

6.

Numerous other writers affected by the sick soul psychology of naturalism could be mentioned, but as major milestones leading into the twentieth century, it may suffice to mention only two more: Edwin Arlington Robinson and Robert Frost. Robinson's poems, as clearly as any writings of his age, bear out Thomas Carlyle's assertion in *Sartor Resartus* that "Faith is the one thing needful; without it, worldlings, in the midst of plenty, puke up their sick existence."[10] At the

---

[10] *Sartor Resartus*, Chapter VII, "The Everlasting No." In Harrold and Templeman's *English Prose of the Victorian Era* (New York: Oxford Press, 1938), p. 117.

bottom of their malaise, Robinson's gallery of sick souls—
Richard Cory, Flammonde, Minniver Cheevy, Mr. Flood, Cliff
Klingenhagen—have in common the naturalistic sense of fu-
tility that Robinson expresses in his own voice at the end of *The
Man Against the Sky*:

> If after all that we have lived and thought,
> All comes to Nought,—
> If there be nothing after Now,
> And we be nothing anyhow,
> And we know that,—why live?

Like Melville's Bartleby, Robinson here fits James's description of those who cannot be reborn, "getting so exhausted
with the struggle that we have to stop,—so we drop down,
give up, and *don't care* any longer" (p. 173). The death by water
that ends this poem prefigures a number of others in both
literature and real life—Quentin Compson, Phlebas the
Phoenician, Hart Crane, Virginia Woolf:

> 'Twere sure but weaklings' vain distress
> To suffer dungeons where so many doors
> Will open on the cold eternal shores
> That look sheer down
> To the dark tideless floods of Nothingness
> Where all who know may drown.

The only alternative to this sick soul mentality in Robinson's
poems is something even sicker: that is, the black humor
response that Robinson anticipates in a poem like "Cliff
Klingenhagen," where Cliff's act of lightly quaffing off his
glass of wormwood—with a smile—forms a perfect tableau of
the black humor movement.

7.

If any man ever had good reason to be a sick soul, it was
Robert Lee Frost. Having at age eleven lost his father, he lost
his mother to cancer in his mid-twenties, his sister became

71

hopelessly insane, and his wife Elinor, although "the un-spoken half of everything I ever wrote," became embittered and estranged from him to the extent that they had no more sex after her final pregnancy.[11] Of their progeny, he lost his first child, a son, to cholera when the lad was not yet four; an infant daughter died two days after birth; his oldest surviving daughter had to be committed to an insane asylum; another daughter died terribly of illness following childbirth; and his only surviving son, Carol Frost, committed suicide. Culminating it all, Frost's wife died of a heart attack following a cancer operation, making him a widower for a full quarter-century until his own death in 1963. His career, also, for nearly half his long life was a dismal failure; by age 38, he had netted about $200 from twenty years of poetry-writing, and had yet to see a book of his in print. Using a modest inheritance, he finally followed the expatriate trail to England before achieving any fame in his own country.

Yet, for all this frustration and tragedy, it was something else that lay behind Robert Frost's religious crisis, namely the Melvillean problem of knowledge. "Religion," Frost said (in his Introduction to Robinson's *King Jasper*), "is merely consolation for what we don't know." What we don't know, and desperately need to know, Frost thought, is the purpose of nature, from which disclosure the purpose of men as creatures in nature might be inferred. Without such knowledge, Frost's personae—and most notably his Job in *A Masque of Reason*, the poem to which Frost said all his other poems become mere footnotes[12]—are left facing what Tolstoy and James's other sick souls called "the meaningless absurdity of life—the only incontestable knowledge accessible to man" (p. 132). Like

---

[11] *Selected Letters of Robert Frost*, ed. Lawrance Thompson (New York: Holt, Rhinehart and Winston, 1964), p. 450.

[12] Some critics have sharply disagreed with Frost's high opinion of *A Masque of Reason*. Randall Jarrell called it a "frivolous, trivial, and bewilder-

William James himself, Frost was a large-minded type of man, perfectly willing to accept the ultimate truth he sought from either of those deadly adversaries, science or religion. (This openness to both science and religion, I feel sure, is one of the meanings of the "two-hole burrow" in "A Drumlin Woodchuck.") But as it turned out, both of those warring factions proved, for Frost's purposes, defunctive.

Frost's clearest statement about the futility of both science and religion is "Sitting by a Bush in Broad Sunlight," where the defunctive bush and sunlight of today are set against the burning bush of Moses and the life-creating sunlight that once got evolution started: "One impulse persists as our breath;/The other persists as our faith." With neither natural or supernatural power or purpose disclosing itself, both science and religion avail nothing. Neither can answer Job's cry in the *Masque*, "We don't know where we are, or who we are./We don't know one another; don't know you [God];/ Don't know what time it is. . . ." And though Job's wife tells him to stop asking unanswerable questions ("You don't catch women trying to be Plato"), Job cannot cease his intellectual self-torture: "The artist in me cries out for design."

Raised originally in his mother's Swedenborgian religion, Robert Frost was gradually manuevered into the borderland of naturalism by his studies in science.[13] "The Trial by

---

ingly corny affair" (*Poetry and the Age*, New York: 1959, p. 32). But Reuben A. Brower, in *The Poetry of Robert Frost: Constellations of Intentions* (New York: 1963, p. 210), agrees with Frost in calling the *Masque* "a culminating poem in Frost's career, one that refashions forms he had used earlier and that sums up concerns persisting throughout his poetry." Brower discusses William James's *The Varieties of Religious Experience* in connection with *A Masque of Reason* on pages 219–220 of his book.

[13] In his essay "On Emerson," Frost remarks on his mother's religious evolution. Originally his mother was a Scottish Presbyterian; then "Reading Emerson turned her into a Unitarian," but "Reading on into Emerson, that is into 'Representative Men' until she got to Swedenborg, the mystic, made her a Swedenborgian. I was brought up in all three of these religions." See *Selected Prose of Robert Frost*, ed. Hyde Cox and Edward Connery *(continued on page 74)*

Existence" apparently voices Frost's original religious position, something similar to Keats's vision of Earth as a "vale of soul-making" but with an other-worldly dimension (as the source of souls) added. The crisis of insufficient knowledge appears early on, however, with such poems in *A Boy's Will* as "Revelation" (where God has hidden himself too well away in a hide-and-seek game) and "A Prayer in Spring," where the boon prayed for is the power to stop thinking of naturalistic annihilation: "Oh, give us pleasure in the flowers today;/And give us not to think so far away/As the uncertain harvest." The problem of how to sustain losses—or "What to make of a diminished thing" as "The Oven Bird" puts it—has been a crucial issue in most modern literature, but Frost was among the first to tie in the theme of losses with modern physics and its ultimate vision of doom, the theory of entropy. This theory would expand Frost's "Nothing Gold Can Stay" to Nothing *at All* Can Stay, since the whole of nature is destined for icy extinction as the suns and galaxies slowly burn out. In "West-Running Brook," Frost admires the heroism of the life force, which he portrays as white water on the surface trying to resist the black current carrying it deathward ("West-Running"), but there is no doubt that life too is subject to the entropic "stream of everything that runs away":

> It seriously, sadly, runs away
> To fill the abyss' void with emptiness
> . . . .
> And it is time, strength, tone, light, life, and love—
> And even substance lapsing unsubstantial;
> The universal cataract of death
> That spends to nothingness. . . .

In *A Masque of Reason*—where Frost's persona incidentally subscribes to the theory of entropy ("I hold rays

---

(continued from page 73) Lathem (New York: Holt, Rhinehart and Winston, 1966), p. 112. Keats's "vale of soul-making" appears in *John Keats: Selected Poems and Letters*, ed. Douglas Bush (Cambridge: 1959), p. 288.

deteriorate to nothing,/First white, then red, then ultra red, then out")—the poet's crisis of belief reaches its apex in Job's sick soul condition, caused ultimately by man's lack of knowledge about the purpose of being. "Get down into things/It will be found there's no more given there/Than on the surface," Frost-Job declares hopelessly, and adds: "If there ever was,/ The crypt was long since rifled by the Greeks." So "We dance around in a ring and suppose,/But the Secret sits in the middle and knows," as another poem puts it. In the face of this withholding of meaning, Job's answer to the problem of unreason is to extend Robinson's question "why live?" to the whole human project:

> It comes down to a doubt about the wisdom
> Of having children—after having had them,
> So there is nothing we can do about it
> But warn the children they perhaps should have none.

Ironically, for Frost, men know both too much and too little simultaneously. Men lack what might be redeeming knowledge concerning the purpose of nature but at the same time they know too much about the fallen world. So the prayer in "A Prayer in Spring"—"keep us here/All simply in the springing of the year"—goes unanswered, because Frost's persona cannot be innocent enough to escape the oncoming season and mythical Fall. Some of Frost's finest lyrics—"The Oven Bird," "To Earthward," "Nothing Gold Can Stay"— balance precisely upon their transition from paradise remembered to post-lapsarian loss and grief. A few poems like "Birches" render a healthy-minded celebration of life as paradise now ("Earth's the right place for love:/I don't know where it's likely to go better"), but these are greatly overshadowed by the sick soul's dilemma in "The Lesson for Today"—"how to be unhappy yet polite." Knowledge of fall and the Fall in poems like "October," "Reluctance," "The Leaf-Treader," and "The Oven Bird" produces the true Jamesian melancholy.

A large and complex thinker, Frost was not limited to
these pessimistic responses to experience, but there are
enough such negative insights in his poems to sustain an
extended comparison to his fellow spirit in prose, Herman
Melville. ("I was brought up on Melville," Frost wrote in a
letter to John Freeman.)[14] The predatory cannibalism of nature
that so appalled Melville in *Moby Dick* finds a succinct analogue—complete with a depiction of whiteness as the mask of
evil—in "Design," for example. Likewise, Melville's sense (in
Moby Dick, "The Gilder") that the ultimate secret of identity
lies in the grave, "and we must there to learn it," finds its
counterpart in Frost's "There may be little or much beyond the
grave,/But the strong are saying nothing until they see."
Father Mapple's acceptance of his extinction—"I leave eternity
to Thee; for what is man that he should live out the lifetime of
his God?"—similarly finds a counterpart in the last stanza of
"A Prayer in Spring," where Frost defines love as the capacity
to accept one's life as an instrument to be used and discarded
without knowing what its purpose was, according to the
pattern everywhere else in nature:

> For this is love and nothing else is love
> The which it is reserved for God above
> To sanctify to what far ends He will
> But which it only needs that we fulfill.

Most important of all, for our purposes, is the streak of
black humor that arises in both Melville and Frost as a way of
coping with the manifest absurdity of their dilemma. In *Mardi*
(1849), Melville had declared, through his character Babbalanja, that "we must laugh or we die," and Stubb, that cheerful
fatalist who goes to his death with a joke (transmuting
Starbuck's last prayer, "My God, stand by me now!" into
"Stand not by me, but stand under me. . . ."), carries the

---

[14] *Robert Frost on Writing*, ed. Elaine Barry (New Brunswick: 1973), p. 81.

black humor theme in Melville's masterpiece. During his momentary sharing of Stubb's credo that "a laugh's the wisest, easiest answer to all that's queer" (Chapter 39), Ishmael in "The Hyena" gives what might still pass as a reasonable rationale of the mode of black humor:

> "There are certain queer times and occasions in this strange mixed affair we call life when a man takes this whole universe for a vast practical joke, though . . . [he] more than suspects that the joke is at nobody's expense but his own. . . . Prospects of sudden disaster . . . and death itself, seem to him only sly good-natured hits, and jolly punches in the side bestowed by the unseen and unaccountable old joker. That odd sort of wayward mood I am speaking of, comes over a man only in some time of extreme tribulation; it comes in the very midst of his earnestness, so that what just before might have seemed to him a thing most momentous, now seems but a part of the general joke."

Robert Frost's counterpart to this feeling is seen in the tone of wry humor with which he often treats the same topics that were the cause of naturalistic dread in other instances. His concept of entropy, for example—which in "West-Running Brook" causes what James called a genuine "fear of the universe"—appears in the garb of light-hearted humor in "It Bids Pretty Fair"—

> The play seems out for an almost infinite run.
> Don't mind a little thing like the actors fighting.
> The only thing I worry about is the sun.
> We'll be all right if nothing goes wrong with the lighting.

Thus, we have Frost's concept of play, as announced in his tribute to Edwin Arlington Robinson (Introduction to *King Jasper*): "Give us immedicable woes—woes that nothing can be done for—woes flat and final. And then to play. The play's the thing. Play's the thing." This idea that wit, humor, or play is the best defense against psychic pain is closer to Freud than James, yet the heroic spirit of Frost's attitude is something that James would be more likely than Freud to acknowledge. (In fact, Frost acknowledged James as "the most valuable teacher I had at Harvard.")[15] Concerning men's knowing too much, about entropy for example, Frost transmutes fear into play in "Fire and Ice" and "It Bids Pretty Fair." Concerning men's knowing too little, he transmutes frustration into wry humor in "The Bear" (whose "fundamental butt" is really a "but") and "Neither Out Far Nor In Deep," whose people cannot look far or deep, "But when was that ever a bar/To any watch they keep?"

In his final volume, *In the Clearing*—published in 1962, just a few months before the poet's death—Frost makes something of a spiritual comeback, not anything large enough to comprise a conversion into seeing life as clearly meaningful but still enough to imply a repose or reconciliation like Melville's "final harbor" of serenity in *Billy Budd* and *A Rose or Two*. The old dread of losses still persists here, for "waste was of the essence of the [Nature's] scheme" as "Pod of the Milkweed" puts it. "Where have those flowers and butterflies gone?" the poem goes on to ask, and concludes that "the reason why so much/Should come to nothing must be fairly faced" ("And shall be in due course!" the aged poet adds in a footnote). Nonetheless, this final collection includes a "Cluster of Faith" section that rises, or strives to rise, above the sick soul condition. "A Never Naught Song," for example, preaches the Emersonian insight that Mind is an indestructible Reality: "There was never naught,/There was always thought. . . . Everything was there . . . Clear from hydrogen/All the way to men." And "Kitty Hawk," Frost's most ambitious poem of his

---

[15] Lawrance Thompson, *Robert Frost: The Years of Triumph 1915–1938* (New York: Holt, Rhinehart and Winston, 1970), p. 643: "The most valuable teacher I had at Harvard, I never had. . . . He was William James. His books meant a great deal to me." To illustrate this statement of Frost's, Thompson compares some comments made by the two writers; for example, William James said in *The Will to Believe* that "often enough our faith beforehand in an uncertified result is the only thing that makes the result come true," and Robert Frost said in "Education by Poetry" that "the belief in God is a relationship you enter into with Him to bring about the future."

later years, provides a déjà-vu restatement of "The Trial by Existence," the most mystical and visionary poem in Frost's first published volume, *A Boy's Will*. In Part Two of "Kitty Hawk," a breathless tone untypical of Frost—"Then I saw it all;"—ushers in the visionary moment wherein the soul's Fall into the material world is vindicated: "But God's own descent/ Into flesh was meant . . . [to show] That the supreme merit/ Lay in risking spirit/In substantiation." So "Westerners inherit/A design for living/Deeper into matter," and the Wright brothers carried forward man's heroic purpose of "on-penetration/Into earth and skies."

So perhaps this resourceful man came through in the end, after a fashion. As against his immedicable griefs and desert places, he did affirm in his first and final volumes—a round half-century apart—the view of human history as a heroic and meaningful adventure. But history, as William James knew, is seldom sufficient for the truly religious sensibility. Men seek a *personal* redemption or meaning. Over most of his lifespan the crisis of belief was a tragic experience for Frost, which not even the mask of play in *A Masque of Reason* could mitigate. In Jamesian terms, Robert Frost figures as a man who, like Melville, needed conversion to a healthy-minded state but could attain only a stoic endurance lightened now and then by flashes of intuition: his "momentary stay against confusion."

8.

In so far as they exploited humor, in varying degrees of acidity, as the only therapy for the sick soul condition, Melville, Twain, Robinson and Frost were precursors of the black humor literature of the twentieth century. Even Hawthorne, for that matter, remarked on "the fiercer, deeper, more tragic power of laughter . . . when the worst and meanest aspect of life happens to be presented."[16] As the new century elapsed, bringing martial destruction, economic chaos, and ideological fanaticism of hitherto unimaginable proportions, James's causes of the sick soul's affliction—"the vanity of mortal things," "the sense of sin," and "the fear of the universe"— may have come to seem quaintly old-fashioned by reason of understatement. But James's analysis of the core of the religious problem seems, with respect to our recent black humor writers, as relevant as it ever was.

"At bottom" James said, "the whole concern of both morality and religion is with the manner of our acceptance of the universe. Do we accept it only in part and grudgingly, or heartily and altogether? Shall our protests against certain things in it be radical and unforgiving, or shall we think that, even with evil, there are ways of living that must lead to good?" (p. 49). Genuine black humor goes beyond satire in that it postulates no corrective of the evil it envisions; and it lies beyond the realm of tragedy in that it does not grant that "even with evil, there are ways of living that must lead to good." We might say that in its "radical and unforgiving" temper black humor thus denotes the sick soul *in extremis* because of the abject impotence of its condition. If, as James stipulated, the "real core of the religious problem" is the cry "Help! Help!", the black humor writers find any worthwhile help—that is, any redemptive ideology—inconceivable. Though the emotions of pity and fear may sometimes rise from a book like

---

[16] Nathaniel Hawthorne, *The Complete Novels*, p. 341. Other quotations are cited from Joseph Heller, *Catch-22* (New York: Dell, 1962), p. 421; *The Philosophy of William James*, ed. Horace M. Kallen (New York: 1925), p. 156; Jean-Paul Sartre, *Being and Nothingness* (New York: 1966), p. 445; Jay Martin, *Nathanael West: The Art of His Life* (New York: 1970), pp. 201–202 (citing *Contempo* III, 1933); *The Complete Works of Nathanael West* (New York: 1957), pp. 112, 91, 9, 319, 242, 11–12, 25, 5, 18, 34–36, 37–38, 13, 18, 27, 50–51; James Light, *Nathanael West: An Interpretative Study* (Illinois: 1961), p. 30; William Faulkner, *As I Lay Dying* (New York: Vintage, 1964), pp. 39, 203, 244, 196–7, 116; and *The Basic Writings of Sigmund Freud* (New York: 1938) pp. 801–2.

Catch-22 or *Miss Lonelyhearts*, no Aristotelian catharsis of these feelings is possible because no answers to the cry for help—answers analogous to Lear's faithful helpers on the heath or Oedipus' apotheosis at Colonus—are imaginable for such sufferers as West's hapless letter-writers. "What a lousy earth!"—Yossarian's radical and unforgiving protest in *Catch-22*—thus comprises the irremediable essence of our human reality, against which the artist can only invoke the detaching power of laughter.

Violence, decay, or humiliation pertaining to the flesh we are made of seems to be the special focus of the black humorist's dread, reminding us of William James's statement (in *Principles of Psychology*) that "The world experienced—otherwise called the 'field of consciousness'—comes at all times with our body as its center. . . . Everything circles around it, and is felt from its point of view." Sartre, a black humorist of sorts, put the idea more bluntly: "A dull and inescapable nausea perpetually reveals my body to my consciousness. . . . We must realize that it is on the foundation of this nausea that all concrete and empirical nauseas (nausea caused by spoiled meat, fresh blood, excrement, etc.) are produced and make us vomit." In their effort to exorcise this dread or nausea, the black humorists repeatedly mock the desire James identified with religious aspiration, for "a life not correlated with death, a health not liable to sickness" (p. 121). So the pity and fear that connects us with all flesh is converted, mainly by a brilliant mastery of style and technique, into a protective callousness. In its milder manifestations, this stance produces the mechanical lady in Pynchon's *V*, the hero of the tiny penis in *The Sot-Weed Factor*, the numerous dwarfed and deformed in *Miss Lonelyhearts*, and the bloody dismemberments of *Catch-22*, together with that book's stupefying catalogue of illnesses. Its more extreme expression includes a hard-boiled teasing of freaks and cripples, as in John Hawkes' *Second Skin*, which features a belly-bumping contest among grossly obese people, and John Barth's *Lost in the Funhouse*, with its remarkably callous and ingenious treatment of the Siamese twins (joined fore-and-aft) in "Petition."

This correlation between a man's psychic identity and his body not only elevates the ills of the flesh to primary consideration, it also renders psychic rebirth an impossibility in black humorist fiction. Unless flesh heals or is made normal, the soul must remain sick in its carnal prison. But although unable to portray the Jamesian conversion into a new identity, the black humor artist such as Kafka and Beckett and John Barth nonetheless remained interested enough to parody the experience by abruptly changing his protagonist into a beetle or moving him—like Burlingame in Barth's *The Sot-Weed Factor*—through a protean multitude of masks, none of them containing his "real" identity. Beckett also parodies rebirth when the fool in *Waiting for Godot* temporarily—and unhappily—turns into a brilliant and eloquent thinker, but this character is lucky enough to revert to his original mindlessness in the end. And West's Miss Lonelyhearts is reborn as a Christ figure and a "rock" of faith just before his bizarre death by murder.

It is no coincidence that *Miss Lonelyhearts*, our exemplary work of black humor, is enclosed like a sandwich between opening and closing chapters that echo William James. "Miss Lonelyhearts, help me, help me"—the title of Section One—springs from James's definition of religion as a cry for help; and the terminal section as clearly owes its title, "Miss Lonelyhearts has a religious experience" (his death) to *The Varieties of Religious Experience*. In his essay about the book in *Contempo* magazine, West declared that "*Miss Lonelyhearts* . . . is built on all the cases in James's *The Varieties of Religious Experience* and Starbuck's *The Psychology of Religion*." Thus, a succession of states of consciousness would replace narrative plot as West's principle of structure: "Chapter I—maladjustment. Chapter III—the need for taking symbols literally through a dream. Chapter IV—deadness and disorder; see lives of Bunyan and Tolstoy. Chapter VI—self-torture by conscious sinning; see life of any saint. And so on." Indeed, the states of consciousness within West's seventy-odd pages make up a compendium of James's categories. There is Betty the healthy-minded, "greeting the grass and trees with delight"; Shrike the sick soul, his sanity sustained solely by the vampire-grin of black laughter; and Miss Lonelyhearts, the Christian convert, eventually victim of a Christ complex. There is also the appeal to sex, art, work, hedonism, and nature (the dead Pan) as sources of sustenance. And in the end it is the religious ideal of service that puts a period, by violence, to Miss Lonelyhearts' hopeless dilemma. It is appropriate that Doyle the cripple, representing all the book's radically unhelpable sufferers, brings Miss Lonelyhearts the only effective deliverance from suffering by killing him.

Escape through death or madness, for the black humor "hero"; or detachment through laughter, for the observer (Shrike and the reading audience): given the nature of reality, these make up the sum of human choices. A third choice, rebirth into a happier view of life, is, for the black humor writer, mere wishful thinking. Such wishful thinking, how-ever, obviously fascinated Nathanael West with the force of an obsession. Although he was excluded by both his Jewish heritage and his innate scepticism from participation in the Christian communion, he voraciously consumed Christian literature and further cultivated relationships with Roman Catholic girl friends, perhaps the better to pursue this "re-ligious" interest. To two such girls he betrothed himself; the last of them, Eileen McKenney, he married, shortly before their untimely death in an auto accident. To the other, Alice Shepard, he dedicated his first novel, *The Dream Life of Balso Snell*, one of the most bizarre and original works in the history of fiction.

It is a commonplace of West criticism that his four novels

deal with dreams and the violence they engender when the dreamer awakens. These readings seem true enough: in *The Day of the Locust*, victims of the Hollywood dream factory awaken to burn Los Angeles; in *A Cool Million*, the American dream of success, when shattered by the Depression, produces a fascist revolution; in *Miss Lonelyhearts*, the greatest dream of Western civilization, that of a redeeming messiah, ends in the messiah's murder; and in *The Dream Life of Balso Snell*, the energy of the wet dream explodes, as the dreamer awakes, in orgasm. But though *Balso Snell*, like *Miss Lonelyhearts*, devotes much of its bulk to deriding sexual aspirations, its most significant content—again like *Miss Lonelyhearts*—concerns religious aspirations. The book opens with mockery of T. S. Eliot's conversion experience, homing in on *Ash-Wednesday*, his great conversion poem of 1930, in particular (*Balso Snell* appeared in 1931). The periodic style of the following excerpt, bringing the word "Round" to bear upon the "Rust-Laden Holes," also suggests the epic dignity of another religious poet, John Milton, who might have been proud of the original diction—"Entertain" and "Jew-Driven"—in the closing line:

> Round and Full
> Round and Full as
> A Brimming Goblet
> The Dew-Loaded Navel
> Of Mary
> Of Mary Our Mother
>
> Round and Ringing Full
> As the Mouth of a Brimming Goblet
> The Rust-Laden Holes
> In Our Lord's Feet
> Entertain the Jew-Driven Nails.

West goes on to ridicule William James, already his mentor of sorts, by quoting James on the One and the Many ("the eternal wrangle between the advocates of the Singular and those of the Plural"); and he further fuses two of James's references—to "the fountain-head of Christian mysticism, Dionysius the Areopagite," and to the deliberate self-torture of saints with lice (pp. 319, 242)—in his brilliant tour-de-force wherein Maloney the Areopagite canonizes Saint Puce the Flea. One wonders what Alice Shepard, the book's dedicatee, might have made of this use of her Roman Catholic heritage:

"Saint Puce was a flea," Maloney the Areopagite began in a well-trained voice. "A flea who was born, lived, and died, beneath the arm of our Lord. . . ."

"Oh, happy, happy childhood! Playing in the curled brown silk, sheltered from all harm by Christ's arm. Eating the sweet flesh of our Saviour; drinking His blood; bathing in His sweat; partaking, oh how fully! of his Godhead. . . ."

". . . The music of our Lord's skin sliding over His flesh!—more exact than the fugues of Bach. The pattern of His veins!—more intricate than the Maze of Cnossos. The odors of His Body!—more fragrant than the Temple of Solomon. The temperature of His flesh!—more pleasant than the Roman baths to the youth Puce. And, finally, the taste of His blood! In this wine all pleasure, all excitement, was magnified, until with ecstasy Saint Puce's small body roared like a furnace.

"In his prime, Saint Puce wandered far from his birthplace, that hairsilk pocketbook, the armpit of our Lord. He roamed the forest of God's chest and crossed the hill of His abdomen. He measured and sounded that fathomless well, the Navel of our Lord. . . . From notes taken during his travels he later wrote his great work, A Geography of Our Lord.

"After much wandering, tired, he returned at last to his home in the savoury forest. . . . Happy in a church whose walls were the flesh of Christ, whose windows were rose with the blood of Christ, and on whose altars burned golden candles made of the sacred earwax.

"Soon, too soon, alas! the day of martyrdom arived, . . . and the arms of Christ were lifted that His hands might receive the nails. . . ."

"The hot sun of Calvary burnt the flesh beneath Christ's upturned arm. . . . After Christ died, Saint Puce died, refusing to desert to lesser flesh, even to that of Mary who stood close under the cross. . . ."

So perfect in its style and form, this burlesque of the Saints' Lives implies an absorbing study of its subject matter.

So, too, lesser traditions in religious experience caught West's eye as a preparation for his career in literature. Christian Science catches a stray bullet, for example, as a hospital patient, "invoking the aid of Mother Eddy," says " 'I won't die! I am getting better and better. I won't die! The will is master o'er the flesh. I won't die!' Only to have Death answer: 'Oh, yes you will.' " (William James includes "Mind Cures" among his religious phenomena in *The Varieties*.) And the "religous experience" that terminates *Miss Lonelyhearts* is foreshadowed in *Balso Snell* through reference to Baudelaire's prose poem, "Anywhere Out of the World." "This life is a hospital," the French poet wrote, "where each patient wishes for a different bed. . . . Finally, my soul cries out to me, 'It doesn't matter where! it doesn't matter where! Only that it be out of this world.' "

Behind its brilliantly stylized facade of play, *Balso Snell* shares with *Miss Lonelyhearts* and with many other black humor writings the need to exorcise through laughter the irremediable ills of the body; but here, more than in West's later novel, the exorcism employs a fair degree of callousness, possibly even a teasing of freaks and cripples. Two passages from the book imply West's absorption in this theme:

> The only other person living on my floor . . . was an idiot. . . . He was a fat, pink and grey pig of a man. . . . He did not have a skull on the top of his neck, only a face; his head was all face—a face wthout side, back or top, like a mask.
> . . . His Adam's apple was very large and looked as though it might be a soft tumor in his throat. When he swallowed, his neck bulged out and he made a sound like a miniature toilet being flushed. . . .
> The lobby was crowded with the many beautiful girl-cripples who congregate there because Art is their only solace, most men looking upon their strange forms with distaste. But it was otherwise with Balso Snell. He likened their disarranged hips, their short legs, their humps, they splay feet, their wall-eyes, to ornament. Their strange foreshortenings, hanging heads, bulging spinesacks, were a delight. . . .

Spying a beautiful hunchback, he suddenly became sick with
passion. . . .
"No," he answered. "I love only this." As he spoke, he laid
his cool white hands upon her beautiful, hydrocephalic forehead.
Then, bending over her enormous hump, he kissed her. . . .

Here as in *Miss Lonelyhearts*, West confirms James's
judgment (in "The Sick Soul" chapter of *The Varieties*) that
"there are forms of evil so extreme as to enter into no good
system whatsoever," such that "no religious reconciliation
with the absolute totality of things is possible" (p. 138). For
West, the effect was the divided psyche that James had remarked as characteristic of the sick soul—"a certain discordancy or heterogeneity in the native temperament of the
subject, an incompletely unified moral and intellectual constitution" (p. 141). West had evidently hoped to attain in his
writing the self-unification he had, as a student at Brown
University, admired in Euripides, the "fusion of the satirist
and the man of feeling." But in his best work, no such fusion
occurred. The discrepancy that friends—and, later, biographers—noted between Nathan Weinstein, the humiliated,
suffering Jew, and Nathanael West, the black humor artist,
simply extended into the man's fiction. So the morbid-minded
testimonies of all the people Balso meets—this is the book's
principle of structure—are juxtaposed against Balso's impervious healthy-mindedness, evidenced in his response to the
cripples already cited, and in his advice to the sufferers: " 'I
think you're morbid,' he said. 'Don't be morbid. . . . Stop
sniffing mortality. Play games. Don't read so many books.
Take cold showers. Eat more meat.' " And of course the
divided psyche would find its ultimate expression of discord in
Shrike's brilliant mockery of Miss Lonelyheart's unbearable
suffering.
	With the possibility of conversion impacted by his nega-
tive view of reality, and with integration of the psyche therefore beyond attainment, there remained for West only the
recourse to laughter. Not exactly a wholesome laughter, how-

ever, as a character in *Balso Snell* defines it: "People say that it is terrible to hear a man cry. I think it is even worse to hear a man laugh." A bit later in the same book, the rationale for this thought is given, an explanation that exactly describes the role of Shrike in *Miss L.*: "I always find it necessary to burlesque the mystery of feeling at its source; I must laugh at myself, and if the laugh is 'bitter,' I must laugh at the laugh. The ritual of feeling demands burlesque and, whether the burlesque is successful or not, a laugh. . . ." From the sick soul dilemma thus arises the concept of the tragic clown, bent on getting a good laugh from his painful existence even if nothing more may be extracted from it:

> . . . all would agree that 'Life is but the span from womb to tomb; a sigh, a smile; a chill, a fever; a throe of pain, a spasm of volupty: then a gasping for breath, and the comedy is over, the song is ended, ring down the curtain, the clown is dead.'
> The clown is dead. . . . And when I say clown, I mean you. After all, aren't we all. . . clowns? Of course, I know it's old stuff; but what difference does that make? Life *is* a stage; and *we* are clowns. What is more tragic than the role of clown? . . .

While the perfect embodiment of these sentiments would await the appearance of Harry Greener in West's last novel, *The Day of the Locust*, the radical response to pain represented here may fairly be said to infuse West's whole canon. And something similar may be discerned in other black humor writings. Faulkner's closest approximation to a black humor novel, *As I Lay Dying*, ascribes its sick soul temperament to Darl Bundren, who, like West's Shrike, tries to exorcise his own suffering by burlesquing feeling at its source. Like Shrike, too, Darl penetrates with clairvoyant intelligence the inner life of people next to him, so that, for example, the feelings he burlesques are those of his brother Jewel: " 'Jewel,' I say, 'do you know that Addie Bundren is going to die? Addie Bundren is going to die?' "; and *"Jewel, I say, Who was your father, Jewel?"* (*"Goddamn you. Goddamn you."* is Jewel's reply.) In the end, Darl's divided psyche results in clinical schizophrenia and he is carried off to the madhouse, laughing hysterically at the absurdity of his existence. Like *Balso Snell* and *Miss Lonelyhearts*, *As I Lay Dying* focuses on sexuality as a main force behind its characters' afflictions; hence Darl's closing reference to the French spy-glass showing a woman and pig in coition ("Is that why you are laughing, Darl?" "Yes yes yes yes yes yes.") But the book also treats the religious consciousness. The stable, communal life of its comic figures, like Cora Tull and Anse, secure in their conventions of religious faith, is juxtaposed against the angst and loneliness of its tragic people, like Addie and Darl, immobilized in their lack of belief. As West parodied *Ash-Wednesday* to this effect, so Faulkner cites Eliot's *The Hollow Men* to underscore Darl's Sick Soul condition: "How do our lives ravel out into the no-wind, no-sound, the weary gestures wearily recapitulant: . . . in sunset we fall into furious attitudes, dead gestures of dolls." A further variety of religious expression in *As I Lay Dying* is Dewey Dell's "I believe in God, God. God, I believe in God," which is her desperate version of James's dictum that the core of the religious problem is the cry for help. There were good reasons, then, why West and Faulkner singularly enjoyed one another's company during their stint in Hollywood.

If we imagine James's sick soul moving toward a fork in the road, we might say that black humor is the terminus that one of the two paths leads to. The other, and major path, leads to the experience of conversion, a greatly varied and complex phenomenon which is the subject of our next chapter. As we end our look at black humor, however, a final word from James's *Varieties*, together with a confirming extract from Freud's *Wit and the Unconscious*, may best complete the discussion. In *The Varieties*, William James notes with interest how Havelock Ellis "identifies religion with the entire field of the soul's liberation from oppressive moods," and, as a corollary, how "laughter of any sort may be considered a religious exercise, for it bears witness to the soul's emancipation" (pp. 54,

75). Whether Ellis intended his categorical "of any sort" to encompass black humor may be debatable, but his formulation concerning "the soul's liberation from oppressive moods" seems applicable in any case, as Freud confirms when he calls laughter the most effective of the "flight reflexes" whereby the psyche escapes from spiritual pain ("pain from inner sources," he called it, as distinguished from physical pain): "The defense processes are the psychic correlates of the flight reflex, and follow the task of guarding against the origin of pain from inner sources. . . . Humor can now be conceived as the loftiest of these defense functions."

Should that last and greatest defense break down, and should conversion into a happier view of life prove unachievable, there remains only the deathwish as the sick soul's final resort. Albert Camus, in "The Myth of Sisyphus," crystallized the issue in arguing that suicide is the only serious issue in modern philosophy, but our other sick souls have implied as much in their deepening doubt that life is worth living. Melville and Hawthorne, whose careers burned out prematurely; Crane, who wanted to die by age thirty-five; Twain, who would not summon his loved ones back from death if he could; Robinson and Frost, who expressed preference for unconsciousness over conscious life; and our black humor writers—all mark a path of sorts to Camus' focus on suicide, to Baudelaire's "Anywhere Out of This World." This being as far as the Sick Soul mentality can go, we turn to the other of the "only two ways in which it is possible to get rid of anger, worry, fear, despair, or other undesirable affections." namely "that an opposite affection should over-poweringly break over us" (p. 173).

Chapter IV

Conversion

1.

The rise of black humor has probably been the most important innovation in American literature since World War II (West and Faulkner were ahead of their time), but alongside this new development the tradition of "serious" literature has continued to be the mainstream, affirming some measure of existential hope and freedom and dignity. Here the Jamesian system of religious psychology bears most largely upon our discussion, for the conversion of a sick soul into the "twice-born" state, via a wide range of psychic pathways, has been a central feature of American literature, particularly in modern times.

Throughout his *Varieties*, James considers the religious psychology of any individual to be at bottom a function of his inherent personality or "native temperament," as the following description of the twice-born character puts it: "The psychological basis of the twice-born character seems to be a certain discordancy or heterogeneity in the native temperament of the subject, an incompletely unified moral and intellectual constitution" (p. 141). This definition, from Lecture VIII, "The Divided Self, and the Process of Its Unification," has immediate relevance to a number of major artists who have declared some such self-division to be essential to the creative process. William Butler Yeats, for example, described poetry as arising out of a quarrel with oneself, as opposed to mere rhetoric which arises out of a quarrel with other people; and F. Scott Fitzgerald defined a first-rate mind as one which could function effectively while maintaining two opposing ideas at the same time.[1] The conversion experience is a way of achieving psychic unity in such individuals, through—James says—any number of possibilities: "The process of unification, when it occurs, . . . may come gradually, or it may occur abruptly; it may come through altered feelings, or through altered powers of action; or it may come through new intellectual insights, or through experiences which we . . . have to designate as 'mystical' " (p. 146).

Concerning this last pathway to conversion, that of mystical experience, William James found his material so singular and so important to his work as a whole that he gave it a separate chapter, a procedure I have found equally desirable in our present analysis. Though Conversion and Mysticism overlap as interrelated subjects, then, we shall leave the mystic pathway to conversion mainly for our next chapter and focus here on the other main pathway, which we may broadly designate—for lack of a better word—as cultural. The crisis of belief that precipitated the sick soul condition for many of our American writers has been essentially a cultural phenomenon, as Henry Adams realized in marking the distance from the Virgin to the Dynamo. His autobiography specifically cites his religion-less culture as the starting-point of his restless and futile life-long quest for a unifying ideology:

---

[1] Yeats's comment appears in *Major British Writers*, Volume II, ed. G. B. Harrison (New York: 1959), p. 817; Fitzgerald's in *The Stories of F. Scott Fitzgerald*, Volume II (Great Britain: Penguin, 1965), p. 39; and Henry Adams' in *The Education of Henry Adams* (New York: 1931), pp. 34–35.

Of all the conditions of his youth which afterward puzzled the grown-up man, this disappearance of religion puzzled him most. The boy went to church twice every Sunday; he was taught to read hs Bible, and he learned religious poetry by heart; he believed in a mild deism; he prayed; he went through all the forms; but neither to him nor to his brothers or sisters was religion real. . . . That the most powerful emotion of man, next to the sexual, should disappear. . . . seemed to him the most curious social phenomenon he had to account for in a long life.

Yet perhaps Adams' education was better served than he realized by having a void as its beginning. He was now perfectly free—of inherited dogma, of inner conflict, of theologically-based dread and guilt—as he went forth to embrace his concept of blind amoral Force as the innermost reality of the universe that is knowable to man. Although this concept did imply a tragic view of human life, and although Adams may have experienced a divided loyalty between his Virgin and Dynamo, with sentiment running one way and intellect another, he did not display such profound symptoms of inner schism as would betray a need for the Jamesian conversion experience. Other writers have shown such symptoms, for reasons that may be mostly personal in some cases (such as Poe and Nabokov, I suspect) but by reason of reflecting a larger cultural discord in many instances (Eliot's, Pound's, Bellow's, Ellison's, and Updike's, I should say).

Apropos of these latter, Herman Hesse remarked back in the second decade of this century that "Human life is reduced to real suffering, to hell, only when two ages, two cultures and religions overlap." Hesse was thinking in particular of Nietzsche, that shrill prophet of the oncoming crisis in culture resulting from our civilization's transition from a Christian to a naturalistic view of life. But Hesse's remark applies with equal force to a great number of writers both before and after his own time. With the rise of the natural and social sciences, including quasi-sciences like Marxism and Freudian analysis, and with the concomitant erosion of Christianity as a stay against death, a crisis in culture has precipitated most of the conversion experiences we shall examine in this chapter.

However the conversion experience may come, it always involves a basic transformation of the subject's identity, so that he is no longer the man he was earlier. (T. S. Eliot, after his conversion, declared that he considered his earlier poems to be written by someone other than himself, as an engaging example of this changed identity.) The essential fact about conversion is the emotional chemistry that attends a shift in one's guiding ideology: "All we know is that there are dead feelings, dead ideas, and cold beliefs, and there are hot and live ones: and when one grows hot and alive within us, everything has to re-crystallize about it" (p. 162). James defines "the hot place in a man's consciousness, the group of ideas to which he devotes himself," as "*the habitual centre of his personal energy*" (emphasis his), and he explains conversion in terms of a shift in this: "It makes a great difference to a man whether one set of his ideas, or another, be the centre of his energy. . . . To say that a man is 'converted' means, in these terms, that religious ideas, previously peripheral in his consciousness, now take a central place, and that religious aims form the habitual centre of his energy" (p. 162). This "shifting of men's centres of personal energy and the lighting up of new crises of emotion," James further explains, "is partly due to explicitly conscious processes of thought and will," but is "due largely also to the subconscious incubation and maturing of motives deposited by the experiences of life. When ripe, the results hatch out, or burst into flower" (p. 186). The unconscious process of a soul "ripening" towards its conversion is evidently what obtains in most of the cases we shall be looking at. In any case, some large shift with respect to the "hot place" in a writer's sensibility is the common denominator binding the otherwise greatly disparate authors in this chapter. By studying the biographical and literary documents pertaining to these writers in the light of James's formulations, we may better grasp the essential meaning of each writer's life and work. We begin with a sick soul who was remarkably ahead of this time, Edgar Allan Poe.

2.

More than most writers, Edgar Allan Poe has been many things to many people. To any number of general readers, Poe has seemed the Alfred Hitchcock of his time, a master Gothicist with no serious purpose beyond the entertainer's desire to weave a perfect spell. But to Baudelaire, Poe was a beloved fellow spirit on foreign soil, a lonely American nuturing his own flowers of evil with admirable mockery of the philistine moral code during those great heydays of Henry Wadsworth Longfellow. And to another foreign reader, D. H. Lawrence, Poe seemed a courageous pioneer into "the horrible underground passages of the human soul."[2] To Allen Tate, writing in the Modern period, Poe comes across as "Our Cousin, Mr. Poe" because his theme of "inevitable annihilation" and his "lack of a moral center" are more typical of our age than of his. To these major fellow artists, in short, Edgar Allan Poe stands as an example *par excellence* of our Jamesian Sick Soul. Certainly, the sick soul's triad of anxieties—the vanity of mortal things, the sense of sin, and the fear of the universe—are as pronounced in Poe's work as in that of any American writer up until the black humor movement of recent decades.

In so far as James defined this sick soul as a "Divided

---

[2] *The Portable D. H. Lawrence*, ed. Diana Trilling (New York: Viking, 1947), p. 692. Other quotations are cited from Allen Tate, "Our Cousin, Mr. Poe," in *The Partisan Review*, XVI (December, 1949), pp. 1209–1219; Wallace Stevens, *The Necessary Angel* (New York: 1951), pp. 120–121; Joseph Wood Krutch, *Edgar Allan Poe: A Study in Genius* (New York: 1926), pp. 7, 180, 191; and William James, *Pragmatism* (New York: 1955), p. 189. Because most of his tales and poems are short, I have not cited page references to Poe's writings.

Self" rent by "inner discord" (p. 147), Poe foreshadowed Jamesian psychology to perfection. What is more sriking, the fragmentation in Poe's characters, repeated so frequently in the tales as surely to indicate the author's own view of things, remarkably anticipates Freudian psychology, with the Freudian id represented in Poe's Imp of the Perverse, the superego represented in "CONSCIENCE grim/That spectre in my path" (to quote the headnote to "William Wilson"), and the poor embattled ego trying to preserve itself in the middle, loudly insisting "I am not mad."

Poe's criminal monologues, like "William Wilson," "The Imp of the Perverse," "The Black Cat," and "The Tell-Tale Heart," almost always display some such psychical configuration. "The Black Cat," for example, begins with the ego-as-narrator stoutly defending his sanity ("Yet, mad I am not"), just like the narrator in "The Tell-Tale Heart" ("why *will* you say that I am mad?"). The speaker's act of murder, he insists, was not his (the ego's) fault at all, but is totally attributable to "the spirit of PERVERSENESS" which "came . . . to my final and irrevocable overthrow": "I am not more sure that my soul lives, than I am that perverseness is one of the primitive faculties, or sentiments, which give direction to the character of Man." This spirit—objectified into an "Imp" in "The Imp of the Perverse," a raven in Poe's most famous poem, and a gorilla in "Hop-Frog," "The Murders in the Rue Morgue," and elsewhere—incites the speaker's criminal or masochistic behavior despite his conscious will to the contrary. He hangs the black cat "with the tears streaming from my eyes," for example, "and with the bitterest remorse"; whereupon the spirit of perverseness delivers the speaker over to the recoil of the conscience, which sees to it that the speaker is punished— usually by forcing out a compulsive confession of guilt or a revelation of damning evidence. And following confession comes damnation, the speaker at once being "consigned . . . to the hangman and to hell" in "The Imp of the Perverse," or perhaps destroying himself, as in "William Wilson," where the imp of the perverse (who narrates this tale) directly assaults his doppelganger (the spectre of CONSCIENCE in his path) and so learns at the end *"how utterly thou hast murdered thyself."*

That these psychological dynamics represent Poe's own view of things is evident in the rich contempt of his sarcasm in "How to Write a Blackwood Article": "[Maintain] the tone transcendental. . . . Put in something about the Supernal Oneness. Don't say a syllable about the Infernal Twoness." This portrayal of man's radically disunified "moral and intellectual constitution," to use James's phrase, correlates with what James called "the sense of sin" in morbid-minded persons, though Poe's interest in sin was purely psychological, not moral like Hawthorne's. James other two elements of the morbid-minded triad, "the vanity of mortal things" and "the fear of the universe," also find ample expression in Poe's writings. Roderick Usher, for example, who strikingly resembles Poe in looks ("A cadaverousness of complexion; an eye large, liquid, and luminous . . . ; lips somewhat thin and very pallid"), temperament ("alternately vivacious and sullen"), and talent (a poet), has "a mind from which darkness, as if an inherent positive quality, poured forth upon all objects of the moral and physical universe in one unceasing radiation of gloom." (Among his books, Usher's "chief delight" is in his *Vigiliae Mortuorum—The Services for the Dead.*) That this mind also resembles Poe's is evident in the unceasing radiation of gloom emanating from so many tales and poems. At the end of "The Masque of the Red Death," it is not Christ but the Red Death that "had come like a thief in the night," and not God but "Darkness and Decay and the Red Death" that "held illimitable dominion over all."

One might argue that literature is not life, and that Poe's narrator assumes this nihilistic stance only that Poe may deepen the artistic impact of the tale. To whom, however, if not Poe himself, should we ascribe the similar nihilism of "The Coliseum"?—

> Silence! and Desolation! and dim Night!
> I feel ye now—I feel ye in your strength—
> O spells more sure than e'er Judean king
> Taught in the gardens of Gethsemane!

The extreme morbid-mindedness of "The Conqueror Worm" may likewise be ascribed to the characters in "Ligeia," but its sentiments are not at all out of line with Poe's gloomy tone elsewhere, a tone that is all the more confirmed when Ligeia's triumph over the worm via her return from the dead becomes, even for the husband who has pined for her, "a hideous drama of revivication" whereby a vampire spirit occupies another woman's cadaver. A yet more hideous resurrection takes place in "The City in the Sea," where the dead slumber peacefully together—"the good and the bad and the worst and the best"—until the last stanza, where the "stir in the air" and the "redder glow" of the waves signify that Hell has suddenly risen to swallow them all alike, "amid no earthly moans," into eternal damnation.

These ungodly acts of otherworldly powers may be merely Poe's little flowers of evil, fashioned in mockery of the Christian and Transcendentalist philistines of his time, but when the morbid-minded mood persists so largely, it may border upon the "*diabolical* mysticism" James talks about, "a sort of religious mysticism turned upside down" so that "instead of consolations we have desolations; the meanings are dreadful; and the powers are enemies to life" (p. 326). A personality thus influenced may well fall into what James calls "the worst kind of melancholy," that which "takes the form of panic fear" (135). Thinking of the calvalcade of Poe characters, while remembering also Wallace Stevens' dictum that a writer's choice of subject discloses "his sense of the world," we can hardly escape classifying Poe's major personae as extreme versions of the Jamesian sick soul, advanced beyond ordinary unhappiness into "positive and active anguish, a sort of psychical neuralgia wholly unknown to healthy life" (p. 126). Certainly William Wilson, Roderick Usher, the Man of the Crowd, and the narrators of "The Masque of the Red Death" and "The Raven" fit that description; and among them, they touch all the Jamesian specifics pertaining to this psychic illness: "Such anguish may partake of various characters, having sometimes more the quality of loathing; sometimes that of irritation and exasperation; or again of self-mistrust and self-despair; or of suspicion, anxiety, trepidation, fear."

From such a perspective, eternal extinction may seem a boon greatly to be wished, with no hideous drama of revivication or hell-quake to bring back "the lingering illness/ . . . And the fever called 'Living' " to suffering mortals, as the speaker in "For Annie" hopes: "Thank Heaven! . . . the fever called 'Living'/Is conquered at last." Gratefully dead, this speaker captures his satisfaction in a pun: ". . . no muscle I move/As I lie at full length—/But no matter!—I feel/I am better at length." So too, in "The Sleeper," Poe's speaker prays a similar blessing upon his sweetheart: "I pray to God that she may lie/Forever with unopened eye." Even the conquerer worm is a friend here, in a most unromantic touch of realism: "My love, she sleeps! Oh, may her sleep,/As it is lasting, so be deep!/Soft may the worms about her creep!"

In a man who regards death as a boon we may infer a need for conversion out of the morbid-minded condition. Throughout most of his life as a writer, there is no evidence that any such conversion transpired for Poe, but the prose poem *Eureka*, almost the last important thing written in his tragically foreshortened life, discloses at least the rudiments of a conversion possibility. Scholars have disagreed absolutely about the worth and seriousness of this piece—Joseph Wood Krutch, for example, declared it insane—but for our purposes it certainly deserves a careful scrutiny. "There are men anaesthetic on the religious side," James observes, who "can never compass the enthusiasm and peace which those who are temperamentally qualified for faith enjoy. All this may, however, turn out eventually to have been a matter of temporary inhibition. Even late in life some thaw, some release may take place, some bolt be shot back in the barrenest breast . . ." (p. 168). Although described variously as unintelligible or induced by mental derangement, *Eureka* may in fact identify Poe as the beneficiary of just such a late conversion experience. Poe's path to truth here, for one thing—and he does insist *"What I propound here is true"* (emphasis his) in his Preface—disdains both Aristotelian deduction and Baconian induction in favor of the more customary religious path, intuition. "True science," Poe says, "makes its most important advances—as all History will show—by seemingly intuitive *leaps*," for which reason he denounces the rational scientists' "pompous and infatuate proscription of all *other* roads to Truth than the two narrow and crooked paths—the one of creeping and the other of crawling—to which, in their ignorant perversity, they have dared to confine the Soul—the Soul which loves nothing so well as to soar in . . . regions of illimitable intuition."

From intuition, which he defines as *"the conviction arising from those inductions or deductions of which the processes are so shadowy as to escape our consciousness, elude our reason, or defy our capacity of expression,"* Poe derives an assortment of conceptions amazingly ahead of his time. Two notions usually associated with Einstein, for example, show up in these pages: the sameness of space and time (Poe: *"Space and Duration are one"*) and the theory of entropy (Poe: "the plainly inevitable annihilation of . . . the material universe"; and "there must be a continuous diminution of both his [the Sun's] heat and light"). Poe also prefigures our contemporary model of the universe as a closed system, beyond which, entirely inaccessible and unknowable to us, other universes may be functioning. Penetrating, with a mighty effort of imagination, "through the boundary walls of the Universe of Stars, into the illimitable Universe of Vacancy, beyond," Poe glimpses "a limitless succession of Universes," having no relationship or connection whatever, either materially or spiritually, with our own: "it is abundantly clear that, having had no part in our origin, they have no portion in our laws. They neither attract us, nor we them. Their material—their spirit is not ours—is not that which obtains in any part of our Universe. They could not impress our senses or our souls. Among them and us . . . there are no influences in common. Each exists, apart and independently, *in the bosom of its proper and particular God.*" Concerning the universe we live in, Poe infers from Newtonian laws that " 'the tendency to collapse' and 'the attraction of gravitation' are convertible phrases", and on this basis he constructs a Big Bang theory of the cosmic origin and destiny similar to the present-day speculation of astronomers that the universe is expanding from and will ultimately contract into an unimaginably dense central glob:

> . . . there must occur . . . a chaotic or seemingly chaotic precipitation . . . of the planets upon the suns, and of the suns upon the nuclei; and the general result of the precipitation must be the gathering of the myriad now-existing stars of the firmament into an almost infinitely less number of almost infinitely superior spheres. . . . But all this will be merely a climactic magnificence foreboding the great End. . . . While undergoing consolidation, the clusters themselves, with a speed prodigiously accumulative, have been rushing towards their own general centre—and now, with a thousandfold electric velocity, . . . the majestic remnants of the tribe of Stars flash, at length, into a common embrace. The inevitable catastrophe is at hand.

There follows what appears to be the supreme nihilism a sick soul can conceive of, the dissolution of the material universe into nothing: ". . . when, I say, Matter, finally, . . . shall have returned into absolute Unity, . . . it will sink at once into that Nothingness . . . that Material Nihility from which alone we can conceive it to have been evoked."

If Poe's vision of reality terminated here, his philosophy in *Eureka* would align perfectly with the implicit meaning of such tales and poems as "The Masque of the Red Death" and "The Conqueror Worm." As his title *Eureka* implies, however, Poe has found something new and transcendent: an intuitive knowledge concerning what William James considered "the final question of philosophy," that of the "monistic-pluralistic alternative," more commonly known as the problem of the One and the Many. To this question of whether the universe is one thing or many disparate things, Poe addressed his central thesis in *Eureka*: "My general proposition is this: *In the Original Unity of the First Thing lies the Secondary Cause of All Things, with the Germ of their Inevitable Annihilation.*" What this means is that the Many phenomena in existence have sprung from a primordial One which is destined to gather them back into itself (via Newtonian gravitation), thereby dissolving their separate identities. Intuition is the absolute authority that verifies this perception: "I can only declare that with an irresistible intuition, I perceive Unity to have been the source of the observed phaenomena of the Newtonian gravitation. . . . I am not so sure that my heart beats and that my soul lives . . . as I am of the . . . *Fact* that All Things and All Thoughts of Things . . . sprang at once into being from the primordial and irrelative *One*." The multiplicity of phenomena thus represents, for Poe, the fallen condition of the creation, which resulted from "forcing the originally and therefore normally *One* into the abnormal condition of *Many*", indeed "the wrongful condition of *Many.*"

At this point, we may begin to witness the true conversion phenomenon in Poe's consciousness, the moment when the sarcastic, lifelong Transcendentalist-baiter, he who spoke of "Emersonism" as a "pregnant compound indicative of confusion worse confounded," himself espouses the grand Emersonian doctrines:[3] "All things hasten back to Unity";

"Behind Nature, throughout Nature, Spirit is present";
"Mind is the only reality"; "God incarnates himself in man";
"It is one soul that animates all men." Poe's correlatives to
these Transcendental intuitions, occurring in the final pages
of *Eureka*, rest on the conviction that "through the agency of
Matter . . . is *Spirit individualized.* . . . In this view, we are
enabled to perceive Matter as a Means—not as an End." For
this reason, this universe rushing blindly toward "Material
Nihility" is saved from meaninglessness by re-creation in
"the Volition of God": "are we not, indeed, more than justified in entertaining a belief . . . that the processes we have
here ventured to contemplate will be renewed forever, and
forever, and forever; a novel Universe swelling into existence, and then subsiding into nothingness, at every throb of
the Heart Divine?" And Whose is this Heart Divine? Drawing
Transcendentally upon "that cool exercise of consciousness—
that deep tranquillity of self-inspection—through which
alone we can hope to attain the presence of this, the most
sublime of truths," Poe answers that "this Heart Divine . . .
is our own."

Like the Hindu Brahman and the Emersonian Oversoul,
Poe's God in *Eureka* "*now* exists solely in the diffused Matter
and Spirit of the Universe," awaiting "the regathering of this
diffused Matter and Spirit [that] will be but the re-constitu-
tion of the *purely* Spiritual and Individual God." Until then,
"this Divine Being, who thus passes his Eternity in perpetual
variation of Concentrated Self and almost Infinite Self-
Diffusion, . . . feels his life through an infinity of imperfect
pleasures—the partial and pain-intertangled pleasures of

---

³ This attack on Emerson is quoted from "Exordium," in *Selected Writings
of Edgar Allan Poe*, ed. Edward H. Davidson (Boston: Houghton Mifflin Riverside, 1956), p. 434. The five Emersonian precepts quoted here are taken from
"Nature," "The American Scholar," "The Divinity School Address," and
"The Transcendentalist." In the Stephen E. Whicher edition, *Selections from
Ralph Waldo Emerson* (Boston: Houghton Mifflin Riverside, 1960), these five
quotations appear on pages 40, 50, 194, 105, and 76.

those inconceivably numerous things which you designate as his creatures, but which are really infinite individualizations of Himself."

Following upon this perception is the reconciliation with the world's evil that James considered the hallmark of the conversion process, providing a salvation of the sick soul from his morbid-minded melancholy. "In this view alone," Poe says of his *Eureka* vision, "we comprehend the riddle of Divine Injustice. . . . In this view alone the existence of Evil becomes intelligible; but in this view it becomes something more—it becomes endurable." So too yields the Infernal Twoness of old to the Supernal Oneness once targeted for mockery. Now, in the closing lines of *Eureka*, that Oneness summons its whole creation to "an identity with the Divine Being, . . . an identity with God," and the speaker's soul hungers for that time when "these myriads of individual Intelligences become blended— when the bright stars become blended—into One," so that "Man will at length attain that awfully triumphant epoch when he shall recognise his existence as that of Jehovah." With this apotheosis pending, certain that the Many shall be One, the author of "The Conqueror Worm" has some words of cheer to help us through the waiting period: "In the meantime bear in mind that all is Life—Life—Life within Life—the less within the greater, and all within the *Spirit Divine*."

3.

In 1948, T. S. Eliot delivered a lecture later published under the title "From Poe to Valéry." A better title might have been "From Poe to T. S. Eliot," since Eliot's greatest debt during his formative years traces back to Poe through the French Symbolist poets whom he admired and emulated: Valéry, Mallarmé, Baudelaire, and Laforge. Even during his college years, according to Eliot's friend and biographer, Robert Sencourt, Arthur Symons' *The Symbolist Movement in Poetry* had immense influence upon the author of "Prufrock," and late in his career Eliot declared that he owed more to Jules Laforge than to any other poet, living or dead—which is saying a great deal in light of Shakespeare's and Dante's pervasive influence.[4]

By way of the Symbolist movement, then, Poe's work touched Eliot's to at least some extent; "one cannot be sure one's own writing has *not* been influenced by Poe," was the Anglican proselyte's gingerly way of putting it. For our study, however, the Symbolist technique of even so brilliant a poem as "The City in the Sea" may be less significant than the affinity Poe and Eliot shared as fellow exemplars of the Sick Soul condition. Although their conversion experience differed markedly in many ways, no such distinction marks the record with respect to their profoundly affecting sojourn among the morbid-minded.

If, as William James contended, "the two main phenomena of religion" are "melancholy and conversion" (p. 28), our most orthodox example of both phenomena rightly should be T. S. Eliot. A sick soul in *extremis* during the years when he struck off the master metaphors of his age, Eliot astounded his following with the announcement, in 1928, that he had become an Anglo-Catholic in religion, a Royalist in politics, and a Classicist in literature. Ezra Pound spoke for many when, thinking Eliot had turned chicken at last, he reproached his old friend in the Pisan Cantos—"Tell Possum [the world ends] with a bang not a whimper,/With a bang not a whimper."

[4] Robert Sencourt, *T. S. Eliot: A Memoir* (New York: 1971), pp. 27–30. Other quotations are cited from this book, p. 132 (Eliot and Buddhism); T. S. Eliot, *To Criticize the Critic* (London: Faber, 1965), p. 22 (Laforgue), and p. 27 (Poe); *T. S. Eliot: Selected Prose*, ed. John Hayward (Great Britain: Peregrine, 1963), p. 81; Grover Smith, *T. S. Eliot's Poetry and Plays* (Chicago: 1974), pp. 180–195; and Wallace Fowlie, *Journal of Rehearsals* (Durham: 1977), p. 138.

Unlike Tolstoy, who suddenly experienced the sick soul state at about the age of fifty, Eliot was a sick soul from the beginning, finding his defense against pain solely in the exercise of cathartic sarcasm in the black humorist fashion. Behind his brilliant verbal armor, one finds in Eliot the full Jamesian catalogue of causes for the pathological melancholy that James identified with the religious temperament. The vanity of mortal things is nicely captured at the end of his early poem "Rhapsody on a Windy Night"—

> "The bed is open; the tooth-brush hangs on the wall,
> Put your shoes at the door, sleep, prepare for life."
> The last twist of the knife.

Likewise the fear of the universe turns up in a series of skeleton images, the "chuckle spread from ear to ear" in *The Waste Land* (III) and the "breastless creatures under ground/ [who] Leaned backward with a lipless grin" in "Whispers of Immortality." And the Easter message is correspondently inverted—"He who was living is now dead"—in *The Waste Land* (V), having been supplanted by the naturalistic resurrections at the end of "The Burial of the Dead" (frost heaving the corpse to the surface, or a dog digging up its bones). Finally, the sense of sin seems remarkably active in Eliot's temperament, producing the accusatory eyes fixed upon Prufrock ("eyes that fix you in a formulated phrase") and the Hollow Men ("Eyes I dare not meet in dreams") as well as the guilt that makes the young man feel like a dog in "Portrait of a Lady": "I mount the stairs and turn the handle of the door/And feel as if I had mounted on my hands and knees."

Intimations of a profound need for conversion—a change of identity—occur in scenes where Eliot's people desperately scramble to hide their real identity. Prufrock must strive to "prepare a face to meet the faces that you meet." The young man must "borrow every changing shape" in "Portrait of a Lady"—"dance/Like a dancing bear,/Cry like a parrot, chatter like an ape." And the Hollow Men must "also wear/

Such deliberate disguises" as would suit a scarecrow: "crossed staves/In a field/Behaving as the wind behaves."

Eliot's search for an overbelief or form of life that might sustain its meaning—the Jamesian "hot place" in one's consciousness—attains its maximum degree of futility in "Gerontion," the 1920 precursor to (and originally part of) *The Waste Land*. In "Gerontion," Eliot examines and discards in turn four "centers of belief" around which people have traditionally organized their life's meaning: adventurous action, religious faith, participation in history, and personal intimacy. For Gerontion, the circumstance of being read to by a boy betrays a life in which nothing heroic or even adventurous has happened: "I was neither at the hot gates/Nor fought in the warm rain . . . heaving a cutlass." In his sick soul state, like Poe's, Christianity has lost its credibility as a form of salvation ("We would see a sign!") while ironically and irrationally retaining some force of damnation ("Came Christ the tiger"). Unable to believe in the supernatural ("I have no ghosts"), Gerontion derives from his scornful/envious contemplation of the international Christian communion (Mr. Silvero, Hawkagawa, Madame de Tornquist) only a deepening of his dread—in his despair, he may be committing the Unpardonable Sin of the Gospels: "After such knowledge, what forgiveness?" There remains only the meaning of history, a labyrinth of "cunning passages, contrived corridors" which "Guides us by vanities" (in both meanings of "vanity"); and the memory of personal love, made inaccessible now by marital discord and by the dessication of the old man's sensory apparatus. In the end, the sole prospect that awaits him is the imminence of dying, a thought that brings him full circle to imagining adventurous action. In that trip around Cape Horn, he may at last experience something interesting: "Gull against the wind, in the windy straits/Of Belle Isle, or running on the Horn. . . ."

The upshot of all this fear, guilt, and impotence is the Sybil's death-wish in the headnote to *The Waste Land*, but in

Eliot's case psychic death is the preparation for a reborn identity. "The securest way to the rapturous sorts of happiness of which the twice-born make report has as an historic matter of fact been through a . . . radical pessimism," James asserts (p. 124), in turning to his case studies of "The Sick Soul." Such pessimism, as expressed in the black nihilism of a West or a Beckett, carries the danger of permanent enclosures with no conversion possible. What made conversion possible for Eliot, as opposed to these others, was a lack of psychic coherence, which, as James said, "connects itself with the life of the subconscious self-so-called." The result is that "the man's interior is a battle-ground for what he feels to be two deadly hostile selves, one actual, the other ideal" (p. 143).

For Eliot, the warring factions within his divided self consisted of his rational consciousness on one side, leading to the despairing Hollow Man condition, and his subliminal religious desire on the other. The latter would eventually irrupt through his intellectual repression to seize command of the man's psyche. In hindsight, we may now perceive the configuration of that conflict to be the most dramatic and meaningful element in his poetry, thematically speaking. The opening shot in this inner warfare appears to date back to "Preludes," which juxtaposes its prevailing naturalistic hopelessness against an intruding religious desire—"The notion of some infinitely gentle/Infinitely suffering thing" (ultimately Christ) in its closing passage. That notion is wiped away sarcastically ("Wipe your hand across your mouth and laugh") in this poem, only to return more strongly in Eliot's later, still predominantly naturalistic poems: in Gerontion's envy of Christian worship, for example (the eucharist "To be eaten, to be divided, to be drunk/Among whispers"), and in the intensively imagined oasis in *The Waste Land* ("water over a rock/Where the hermit-thrush sings in the pine trees"). Most spectacularly, the conflict recurs in his most overtly atheistic

108

work, *The Hollow Men,* where the opposing voices of intellectual despair and subliminal religious desire are placed in stunning proximity:

> This is the dead land
> This is cactus land
> Here the stone images are raised
> Here they receive the supplication of a dead man's hand
> Under the twinkle of a fading star.
> . . . .
> Waking alone
> At the hour when we are
> Trembling with tenderness
> Lips that would kiss
> Form prayers to broken stone.

In this latter stanza, Eliot displays the "melancholy . . . in a more melting mood" (p. 128) that distinguishes his essentially religious temperament from James's non-religious pessimists: "melancholy . . . forfeits all title to be called religious when, in Marcus Aurelius's racy words, the sufferer simply lies kicking and screaming after the fashion of a sacrificed pig. The mood of a Schopenhauer or a Nietzsche . . . reminds one, half the time, of the sick shriekings of two dying rats" (p. 47).

Eliot also appears to exemplify the process of "unconscious cerebration" which, after a long incubation period, may hatch forth the twice-born personality. This "involuntary and unconscious" way to conversion, which is classified as "the type by self-surrender" (p. 169), requires that "The personal will . . . must be given up" (pp. 170–1), for "In the extreme of melancholy the self that consciously *is* can do absolutely nothing. It is completely bankrupt and without resource, and no works it can accomplish will avail" (p. 196). *Ash-Wednesday* speaks practically like a case history for James's study on this point. Section I shows Eliot resigning his will absolutely with regard to what was most important to him in this world, his artistic status. Renouncing "the blessèd face/And . . . the voice" of the Muse, giving up "the one veritable transitory power" of drinking "There, where trees flower, and springs flow" (the garden of the Muses), Eliot declares the permanence of his conversion: "Because I do not hope to turn again . . ./Desiring this man's gift and that man's scope/I no longer strive to strive towards such things." Once the eagle of modern poetry, he cannot help but give one last parenthetical twitch of pride implying that everyone knows his past achievements—"(Why should the agèd eagle stretch its wings?)"—but henceforth the eagle is grounded, "these wings . . . no longer wings to fly/But merely vans to beat the air." The same vestigial pride also suffices to produce a royal "we"—the King of Poetry having abdicated—in Eliot's prayer for forgiveness of his secular poetry: "For what is done, not to be done again/May the judgement not be too heavy upon us." Giving up his will also means giving up his intellectual judgment, for the vision of world-wide suffering that produced *The Waste Land* is subsumed under the claim that "I rejoice that things are as they are," buttressed by the supplication "Teach us to care and not to care" (i.e. to care about the world's sufferings), and "Teach us to sit still."

In Section II of *Ash-Wednesday* Eliot likewise accepts his physical annihilation, his earlier dismay about "the chuckle spread from ear" replaced now by a calm prevision of his bones (including "the hollow round of my skull") lying "scattered and shining . . ./In the quiet of the desert. This is the land which ye/Shall inherit by lot." Death might now be compared to waiting in darkness for the next act in a theater to begin, or the next station in a subway tunnel to appear; so "East Coker" (III) tells us, in *Four Quartets*, and here the resignation is complete: "I said to my soul, be still, and let the dark come upon you. . . . /I said to my soul, be still, and wait without hope. . . ./Wait without thought." Here Eliot largely fills the definition of the "self-surrender type" James speaks of, wherein "when the will has done its uttermost towards bringing one close to the complete unification aspired after, it

110

seems that the very last step must be left to other forces and performed without the help of its activity" (p. 170).

Eliot's move toward Christianity thus was his version of that cry for help which William James considered the essence of the religious attitude: "Here is the real core of the religious problem: Help! help!" (p. 137). Eliot's cry for help, though muted in his earlier poems in deference to his rational consciousness, visibly gains strength as the time of his conversion draws near. In "Gerontion," it lurks half-concealed by the objectivity of a Biblical quotation: "We would see a sign!"; in *The Waste Land*, it assumes a more appropriately subjective expression in a series of "If" clauses—"If there were water/ . . . . If there were the sound of water only"; and in *The Hollow Men*, written just prior to the conversion experience, the cry for help assumes its most overt and maximal appeal in one of the cathartic utterances of the age: "the supplication of a dead man's hand." It is true that at the end of *The Hollow Men*, Eliot sardonically classifies his upwelling of religious desire in the poem, including this cry for help, as a "whimper," but this was to be the last time that this long-term conflict within his divided self would be resolved in favor of his naturalistic intellect. At the end of his next poem, *Ash-Wednesday*, his cry for help would be offered openly and without shame, in the spirit of his discovery that humility is the only wisdom: "And let my cry come unto Thee."

Appropriately, Eliot's conversion is rendered in an elaborate sequence of images of rebirth. Unlike his death-foreseeing aged speakers like Tiresias and Gerontion (whose end will shortly be to "Stiffen in a rented house"), the speaker in *Ash-Wednesday* sees his life as "the time of tension between dying and birth," and the four Ariel Poems bring on the second birth of the psyche, with each of the four poems serving a separate function with respect to the rebirth metaphor. "Journey of the Magi" essentially retells the death of the old self in Eliot's journey to the Christ child. "With the voices

111

singing in our ears, saying/That this was all folly," the Magus as yet can not be sure of his future deliverance: "were we led all that way for/Birth or Death?" But although the new birth "was/Hard and bitter agony for us, like Death, our death," he is sure that he welcomes the death of the old self in its Waste Land setting: "We returned to our places, these Kingdoms,/ But no longer at ease here, in the old dispensation,/With an alien people clutching their gods./I should be glad of another death." "A Song for Simeon" moves even closer to the death of the old man, with Simeon feeling his life to be "light, waiting for the death wind,/Like a feather on the back of my hand," and wanting it to come, "Having seen thy salvation." "Animula" brings the new birth to its imminent moment with its closing prayer, "Pray for us now and at the hour of our birth," and "Marina" actually delivers the twice-born soul into our presence. The old king's twice-born state in "Marina" is indicated for one thing by the nine-month duration of his voyage ("Between one June and another September"). It is implied also by the king's reunion with his long-lost daughter: "This form, this face, this life . . . ; let me/Resign my life for this life, . . ./The awakened, lips parted, the hope, the new ships." And it is imaged above all in the lush new land looming ahead in lieu of the Waste Land:

> What seas what shores what granite islands towards my timbers
> And woodthrush calling through the fog
> My daughter.

There is nothing in Eliot's later writing to contradict James's conclusion (here he quotes Dr. Starbuck, his collaborator) that "the effect of conversion is to bring with it 'a changed attitude towards life, which is fairly constant and permanent, although the feelings fluctuate' " (p. 206). Nonetheless, Eliot never got wholly free of his earlier naturalistic outlook, thereby resembling Bunyan and Tolstoy in James's study, who even after their conversion could never "become what we have called healthy-minded. They had drunk too

112

deeply of the cup of bitterness ever to forget its taste" (p. 155). Thus *Ash-Wednesday* (V) speaks of naturalism and Christianity having to co-exist together in his consciousness ("The desert in the garden the garden in the desert"), and repeats his earlier prayer with the Waste Land setting added: "Teach us to sit still/Even among these rocks" (VI). Though stripped of its one-time bitterness, the mournfully melancholy tone of old also intrudes upon *Four Quartets* in many places, like "The Dry Salvages" (II) where Eliot hears "the soundless wailing,/The silent withering of autumn flowers" and the "barely prayable . . . prayer of the bone on the beach." There are a few mystic glimpses in *Ash-Wednesday* (IV), followed by a collapse into ordinary reality ("And after this our exile"); and *Four Quartets* ("Burnt Norton," II) describes a visit to "the still point of the turning world" ("I can only say, *there* we have been"). According to Wallace Fowlie's reminiscence, T. S. Eliot did in fact have an authentic mystic experience to which Fowlie, assisting the priest at mass, was a witness.

> Eliot was a daily communicant at the mass and on Tuesdays he and I were often the only ones with the priest in the chapel. . . . One of those Tuesdays has remained memorable for me. Only three of us were present. At the time of communion Eliot had risen and come up to the altar to receive. The priest and I had turned back to the altar, and I could hear Eliot rise and return to his place. At that moment there was such a loud thud, as if Eliot had fallen, that the priest and I turned around. Eliot was flat on his face in the aisle, with his arms stretched out. It was obvious at a glance he had not fallen.
>
> Under his breath, and as if speaking to himself, the priest said, 'What should we do?'
>
> I suggested, 'Let's finish here first.' So, we turned to the altar. . . .
>
> The priest finally said to me, 'I think you should help him up. Something may be wrong.' I went on ahead and put my arm under his shoulder. He came up with me easily. Almost no physical effort was required on my part to help him back to his seat. As I preceded the priest into the small room at the end of the aisle, I realized that Eliot had just undergone a mystical experience.

An interesting interlude, surely, but the fact remains that, for the most part, Eliot's religious portion is that of "A Song for Simeon": "Not for me the martyrdom, the ecstasy of thought and prayer,/Not for me the ultimate vision." Accepting his spiritual mediocrity. Eliot, in some ultimate degree of religious modesty, asks only that after his death ("our temporal reversion") his body may become good manure: "We, content at the last,/If our temporal reversion nourish . . ./The life of significant soil" ("The Dry Salvages," V).

So we may say of Eliot what James said of Bunyan, that "the full flood of ecstatic liberation seems never to have poured over poor John Bunyan's soul" (p. 156). But James also pointed out that "the completest religions would . . . seem to be those in which the pessimistic elements are best developed," and he goes on to add that "Buddhism, of course, and Christianity are the best known to us of these" (p. 139). It is interesting that these are precisely the two religions that most deeply attracted Mr. Eliot. He seriously considered becoming a Buddhist about the time he was writing *The Waste Land* (hence, Buddha's Fire Sermon turns up in the title of the poem's third section), and he evidently found both Buddhism and Christianity to be, as James described them, "religions of deliverance: the man must die to an unreal life before he can be born into the real life" (p. 139). So the two exits out of the Waste Land are Buddhist and Christian: the Buddhist Nirvana in "Death by Water" set against the Christian ordeal of purgatorial suffering and discipline in "What the Thunder Said."

After the second birth Eliot received, if not pentecostal glory, at least inner peace and endurance. Religious conversion did for him what he claimed literature, at its highest, should do for everybody, bringing us ultimately "to a condition of serenity, stillness, and reconciliation," according to his essay on "Poetry and Drama." This mood of serenity, stillness, and reconciliation dominates the *Four Quartets*, coming to bear with extra emphasis on the poem's conclusion ("Little

114

Gidding," V), where "A condition of complete simplicity/ (Costing not less than everything)" delivers the assurance that "all shall be well and/All manner of thing shall be well."

With these words Mr. Eliot has reached the final "state of assurance," as James calls it, whose "central [characteristic] is the loss of all the worry, the sense that all is ultimately well with one, the peace, the harmony, *the willingness to be . . .*" (emphasis his, p. 198). It bespeaks "a state of mind, known to religious men, but to no others, in which the will to assert ourselves and hold our own has been displaced by a willingness to close our mouths and be as nothing in the floods and waterspouts of God. . . . Fear is not merely held in abeyance, . . . it is positively expunged and washed away" (p. 53). And it signifies, to James, the culmination of the conversion experience (p. 229):

> The transition from tenseness, self-responsibility, and worry, to equanimity, receptivity, and peace, is the most wonderful of all those shiftings of inner equilibrium, those changes of the personal centre of energy, which I have analyzed so often; and the chief wonder of it is that it so often comes about, not by doing, but by simply relaxing and throwing the burden down. This abandonment of self-responsibility seems to be the fundamental act in specifically religious, as distinguished from moral practice. . . . Christians who have it . . . are never anxious about the future, nor worry over the outcome of the day.

That the poet of "Gerontion" and *The Hollow Men* could come to illustrate these Jamesian precepts is indeed a remarkable fact. In his long journey from the Waste Land to this new-found land, with each part of the way on record in his unrivalled powers of articulation, Mr. Eliot must stand out as our chief modern example of the Jamesian twice-born man.

4.

A conversion with somewhat regrettable consequence befell T. S. Eliot's friend Ezra Pound, whose *Hugh Selwyn*

Mauberly records one of the Jamesian shifts in the "hot places" of the author's consciousness, in this case signifying a change in Pound's identity from a hedonist or "medallion" poet to a moral, political, and ideological crusader. Pound's hedonist identity shone through many of the earlier masks or personae through whom he spoke: Cino, who sings of women and the sun; Bertrans de Born, whose art alone can save Lady Audiart's beauty from bent and wrinkled age; and the ancient Chinese counterparts to these troubadours who captured fragments of Cathay in perfect amber. His classical Roman personae, who are often too Pound-like to conceal the American poet's own features, propagate a veritable religion of pleasure. "Blandula, Tenulla, Vagula" explicitly rejects "paradise" in favor of "apostles of terrene delight," whose "cult" will "be founded on the waves" and "on triune azures" seen in earth, sea, and sky. "Erat Hora"—a love poem—also puts beauty and pleasure at the top of everything: "Nay, whatever comes,/One hour was sunlit and the most high gods/May not make boast of any better thing/Than to have watched that hour as it passed."

It is a good thing for Mr. Pound that he was able to have his paradise in these poems, because in the first dozen lines of his *Cantos* he descends into hell, "the Kimmerian lands" whose "close-webbed mist, unpierced ever/With glitter of sun-rays" suspiciously resembles T. S. Eliot's London. And while there are Purgatorial passages—especially in the Pisan Cantos—and even a few glimpses of paradise scattered here and there in the Cantos, the novel substance that the *Cantos* add to Pound's poetry comes largely under the category of "Pound's Inferno," his consignment of usurers, munitions-makers, corrupt politicians, and other devil figures to verbal hellfire.

Two milestones stand out in Pound's transformation from the poet of hedonism and the maker of medallions (like Mauberly) engaged in the artist's eternal battle to preserve beauty against time. One is Pound's own citation of 1918 as the year in which he "began investigation of causes of war, to oppose same."[5] The ravages of World War I—and particularly their cost to the artistic world—pulled Pound out of the palace of art and into the modern world, just as the Easter Uprising of 1916 affected Yeats, with the regrettable difference that Pound's investigation of the causes of war led him into the treacherous grounds of conspiratorial theory. The other landmark was his reading, in 1919, of C. H. Douglas's *Economic Democracy*. Here is where Pound's mind really began to crack, by conventional definitions, or where he underwent a conversion process, in Jamesian terminology. The brilliant theorist, lyricist, and "translator" of the Imagist and Vorticist periods now receded gradually into the area of "dead feelings, dead ideas, and cold beliefs" of the past, while the ideological propagandist advanced to take over, Douglas's Social Credit theory being the "hot and live" idea James speak of, around which "everything has to re-crystallize."

Canto XXXVIII shows the typical effects of Pound's transformation. Here, after scathing abuse of the bankers, arms-manufacturers, and politicians Pound held responsible for causing the war, the poet pauses to transmit Douglas's theories—"and the power to purchase can never/(under the present system) catch up with/prices at large"—and abruptly associates this learning with a heavenly epiphany of mind-expansion: "and the light became so bright and so blindin'/in this layer of paradise/that the mind of man was bewildered." This passage—which is followed immediately by an attack on the Krupp armaments empire—may lend itself to an ironic interpretation, but I believe it is most profitably understood as an honest rendering of praise to Pound's mentor.

---

[5] *Selected Poems of Ezra Pound* (New York: 1957), p. viii. The "Biography'" on this page was obviously written by Pound himself.

To Pound, paradise was a state of consciousness, and in his new role as investigator and crusader, truth had replaced beauty as the proper stimulant of the highest, most heavenly consciousness. In this passage, as elsewhere in the Cantos (the Rock-Drill Cantos, especially), the image of light breaking from above is the figure for the experience of divine reason illuminating one's mental landscape. As we know, tragic consequences resulted from Pound's delusions, and it was perhaps fortunate that his trial for treason was forestalled by his incarceration for insanity. For our own judgment, it would be best, I think, to consider Pound's conversion in the light of Faulkner's preference for "truth" rather than "fact." Objective fact, as brought out in court (and Faulkner's lifelong aversion to Law resulted from its preference for fact rather than truth), showed that Pound was a vicious anti-Semite and a possibly treasonous political crackpot. The truth of the soul, however, which is subjective and often contradictory to objective fact, is that Pound really believed that the treason in this case took place in the White House, not in Rapallo, and that his broadcasts in Italy were the efforts of a persecuted patriot "in support of the U. S. Constitution." Patriot or traitor, from the moment he began investigating the causes of war in 1918, Pound pursued a mental voyage as bizarre as that of his favorite persona, Odysseus, a voyage that began with a Jamesian conversion experience and ended in a martyrdom unique among American writers.

5.

In the November 27, 1976, number of the *Saturday Review* magazine, Vladimir Nabokov answered an interviewer's question:

Q. What surprises you in life?
A. Its complete unreality; the marvel of consciousness—that

sudden window swinging open on a sunlit landscape amidst the night of non-being; the mind's hopeless inability to cope with its own essence and sense.

In its assertion of the "complete unreality" of life, the art of Vladimir Nabokov represents a type of conversion experience exactly contrary to that of T. S. Eliot, Saul Bellow, and Ralph Ellison, for whereas these latter moved from a sense of the world's absurdity into a faith in its meaning, Nabokov unified his psyche around his belief in the essential lunacy of the world. Nabokov's early novel, *The Eye* (1930), remarks upon the implications of such a world-view: "A thing I had long suspected—the world's absurdity—became obvious to me. I suddenly felt unbelievably free. . . . If I wished, I could, at that moment, run out into the street and, with vulgar expletives of lust, embrace any woman I chose, . . . or smash a store window."[6] James's *Varieties* again takes account of this mentality in "The Divided Self, and the Process of Its Unification," where James observes that "the process of remedying inner incompleteness and reducing inner discord . . . need not necessarily asume the religious form. . . . For example, the new birth may be away from religion and into incredulity; or it may be from moral scrupulosity into freedom and license. . . . In these non-religious cases the new man may also be born either gradually or suddenly" (p. 147).

It is this freedom and license, perhaps combined with some inherent aristocratic toughness, that distinguishes Nabokov from the sick souls in the black humor movement whose laughter is a flight from pain. Nabokov had more reason than most to reject the world as absurd, having lost his

---

[6] *The Eye* (London: Panther Books, 1968), p. 27. Other quotations are cited from this book, pp. 7, 9, 36, 75; *Bend Sinister* (London: 1947), p. 152; and *Speak, Memory* (New York: Pyramid, 1968), pp. 103, 209, 219. See also *Playboy Interviews* (Chicago: 1967), p. 253: "We shall never know the origin of life, or the meaning of life, or the nature of space and time, or the nature of nature, or the nature of thought."

father—a widely revered libertarian whom the Tsar once imprisoned—to an assassin's bullet in Berlin in 1922, and having been cut off for life from the fabulously rich personal and cultural patrimony of his fatherland by the Bolshevik takeover. In addition, he shares the metaphysical prospect, so disturbing to some others, that "our existence is but a brief crack of light between two eternities of darkness," as the first sentence of his autobiography, *Speak, Memory*, tells us. But unlike most others, Nabokov seized upon his conception of the world's absurdity as an opportunity to free himself of its claims and impositions. Proudly he proclaims his books "blessed by a total lack of social significance," and he rejects categorically the two leading prophets of our age, Marx ("that crabbed bourgeois . . . author of *Das Kapital*") and Freud (variously "the Viennese quack" and "that figure of fun").

Nabokov's belief that literature should have nothing to do with conventional reality may owe something to the Russian Formalist Movement that flourished among Russian emigré artists with whom Nabokov associated. In his Preface to *Russian Formalism* (1965), Victor Erlich defines the tenets of this movement in terms that describe Nabokov's work perfectly, at the same time evoking analogies with the New Criticism movement in America: "Russian Formalism—which arose around 1914 and was suppressed around 1930—keeps the work of art itself in the center of attention: it sharply emphasizes the difference between literature and life, it rejects the usual biographical, psychological, and sociological explanations of literature." Here certainly is a key to Nabokov's literary ethos that may be as well stated as is possible in a single sentence. Yet, behind Nabokov's seemingly capricious disdain for ordinary realism is a perspective much more personal and profound than any literary movement can explain. The explanation may rather come—and it does, brilliantly, I think—from the Jamesian religious psychology.

120

No correlation in our entire study exceeds in significance the affinity between William James and Vladimir Nabokov concerning the subjective and objective views of reality. For Nabokov, the subjective is the essence of art; for James, it is the essence of religion. For both men, nothing can be more important. Nabokov's central formulation of this all-important issue takes the shape of a rhetorical question in an early novel, *Bend Sinister*: "Now let us have this quite clear. What is more important to solve: the 'outer' problem (space, time, matter, the unknown without) or the 'inner' one (life, thought, love, the unknown within . . .)?" James's parallel formulation occurs in his "Conclusions" chapter, at the end of *The Varieties* (pp. 376–377):

> In spite of the appeal which this impersonality of the scientist makes . . . , I believe it to be shallow. . . . The reason is that, so long as we deal with the cosmic and the general, we deal only with the symbols of reality, but *as soon as we deal with private and personal phnomena as such, we deal with realities in the completest sense of the term.* [emphasis James]
> The world of our experience consists at all times of two parts, an objective and a subjective part, of which the former may be incalculably more extensive than the latter. . . . Yet the cosmic objects, so far as the experience yields them, are but ideal pictures of something whose existence we do not inwardly possess but only point at outwardly, while the inner state is our very experience itself . . .

From this hypothesis ensues, in James's discussion, a perfect rationale for Nabokov's incomparable parade of ego-maniac crackpots and dreamers, irretrievably absorbed within their vital inscape: "If this [the foregoing hypothesis] be true, it is absurd for science to say that the egotistic elements of experience should be suppressed. The axis of reality runs solely through the egotistic places,—they are strung upon it like so many beads" (p. 377). And again, to cement the Nabokov-James connection (the impassioned visage of a Humbert or Charles Kinbote is surely discernable here): "Individuality is founded in feeling; and the recesses of feeling, the darker, blinder strata of character, are the only places in the world in which we catch real fact in the making. . . . Compared with this world of living individualized feelings, the world of generalized objects which the intellect contemplates is without solidity or life" (p. 379). To conclude, James says, "Let us agree, then, that Religion [Nabokov: Art], occupying herself with personal destinies and keeping thus in contact with the only absolute realities which we know, must necessarily play an eternal part in human history."

Freed from the "outer problem" by his sense of the world's absurdity, Nabokov found himself divinely free to furnish his inner world with all the power and beauty and magic his imagination could muster, along the lines of such favorite classics as *Alice in Wonderland, Ulysses,* and *Remembrance of Things Past.* Time, reason, morality and the other enslavements of the outer world become powerless within this inner kingdom, and a man may give over his soul totally to love or lust or the pursuit of beauty, whatever is most real within the core of his being, thereby experiencing the secular type of new birth that James spoke of ("the new birth . . . may be produced by the irruption into the individual's life of some new stimulus or passion, such as love . . ."—p. 147). The world knows what this mentality produced in *Lolita,* but it is interesting to see this "hot place" in Nabokov's consciousness shaping up towards the creation of Lolita decades earlier in *The Eye:*

> . . . at the merest thought of her, a moaning, awful, salty night would well up within me. . . . What difference did it make to me whether she were stupid or intelligent . . . or what she thought about the universe? I really knew nothing about her, blinded as I was by that burning loveliness which replaces everything else and justifies everything, and which, unlike a human soul (often accessible and possessable), can in no way be appropriated, just as one cannot include among one's belongings the colors of ragged sunset clouds . . . or a flower's smell.

122

Here Nabokov made his one concession to the "outer" world, by acknowledging (as he would again in *Lolita*) that beauty is not possessable through sexual intercourse (it is possessable only through art). But no matter! Morality submits to *Lolita*'s joyous "incest," reason submits to *Pale Fire*'s splendidly mad footnotes, time submits to *Ada*'s twisted anachronisms, and Nabokov has personally claimed victory of the inner world over the outer in *Speak, Memory*, first in the name of beauty and then of love:

> I confess I do not believe in time. . . . And the highest enjoyment of timelessness—in a landscape selected at random—is when I stand among rare butterflies and their food plants. This is ecstasy, and behind the ecstasy is something else, which is hard to explain. It is like a momentary vacuum into which rushes all that I love. A sense of oneness with sun and stone.

and:

> Whenever I start thinking of my love for a person, I am in the habit of immediately drawing radii from my love—from my heart, from the tender nucleus of a personal matter—to monstrously remote points of the universe. Something impels me to measure the consciousness of my love against such unimaginable and incalculable things as the behavior of nebulae (whose very remoteness seems a form of insanity), the dreadful pitfalls of eternity, . . . the helplessness, the cold, the sickening involutions and interpenetrations of space and time. . . . It cannot be helped. . . . that slow-motion, silent explosion of love, . . . unfolding its melting fringes and overwhelming me with the sense of something much vaster, much more enduring and powerful than the accumulation of matter or energy in any imaginable cosmos. . . .

This is the language of the twice-born, one knowledgeable about "the helplessness, the cold, the sickening involutions and interpenetrations of space and time" but able, in James's formulation, "to get rid of . . . worry, fear, despair, or other undesirable affections" by having "an opposite affection . . . over-poweringly break over" him (p. 173).

6.

Saul Bellow and Ralph Ellison represent interesting specimens of twice-born deliverance through recourse to ethnic "soul-words." Soul-words are terms that refer to the innermost spiritual values that an ethnic or cultural group lives by. For American blacks, the soul-word is "soul" itself: that man or woman is most to be admired who has the most "soul," or emotional sensibility. For Finns, the soul-word is *sissu*, which means—so far as soul-words are definable—the ability to withstand great pain without showing it. (I personally witnessed an impressive example of *sissu* in Finland a few years ago when, after presenting half of a fifty-page lecture, I offered to stop there, but—without displaying pain—the audience elected to hear the whole lecture.) For the Japanese culture, the soul word is "yamato-damashi," or "Have manhood. Don't come back till the job is done"—which helps to explain the kamikaze pilots and the jungle fighters still waging World War II in the 1970's. For the predominant white society in America, the soul-word is "class"—he is most admired who has "got class" in the eyes of his peer group, and having class normally implies a competitive ethos: standing out above the ordinary.

For Saul Bellow, rebirth has come through recourse to the soul-word of the Jewish sub-culture: the Hebrew "L'Chaim," or "to Life!" In his early novels, Bellow's "hot place" in the consciousness seemed largely fixed upon the figure of the suffering Jewish victim—swindled, cuckolded, outcast, totally betrayed by friends and family. In his first novel, *Dangling Man* (1944), Bellow's persona remarks that "I was still an apprentice in suffering and humiliation,"[7] but in

---

[7] *Dangling Man* (New York: Meridian, 1960), p. 47. Other quotations are cited from *The Adventures of Augie March* (New York: Compass, 1960), p. 536;

The Victim (1947) and *Seize the Day* the apprentice moved into full possession of the sick soul condition, which culminates in the scene at the end of *Seize the Day* where Tommy Wilhelm seizes the pretext of a stranger's funeral to weep for himself abjectly. But as early as *The Adventures of Augie March* (1953), published three years before *Seize the Day*, a conversion experience is in gestation, finding expression through the hero's *"animal ridens* in me, the laughing creature, forever rising up." In an interview in *Show* magazine (September, 1964) the interviewer elicited an explanation of that conversion experience:

> *Interviewer:* You are quoted as saying that you started your third novel, "Augie March," as comic relief from a more somber novel you were working on [*Seize the Day,* apparently].
>
> *Bellow:* Well, I am a melancholic—a depressive temperament. But I long ago stopped enjoying melancholy—I got heartily sick of my own character.

From a reminiscence of a decade earlier, in *The Saturday Review* (September 19, 1953), we excerpt a more detailed account of that shift in the author's center of gravity. While in Paris in 1948 on a Guggenheim grant, Bellow says, he "wrote 100,000 words of a novel. It was a grim book, in the spirit of the first two, when I suddenly decided, 'No.' Actually, my feeling wasn't as mild as I'm describing it. I felt a great revulsion."

Augie March and *Seize the Day* thus represent the two halves of Bellow's divided psyche finding separate expression during the early 1950's. By the late 50's, in *Henderson the Rain King,* those warring parts of the author's psyche were fighting out their battle within the same pair of book covers. In an engaging exercise of what Henry James called the alchemy of

---

Show (September, 1964), 36–38; *The Saturday Review* (September 19, 1953), p. 13; *Henderson the Rain King* (New York: Viking, 1965), pp. 33, 304, 267, 274, 297, 272, 283, 328, 269, 271; *Mr. Sammler's Planet* (New York: Viking, 1973), pp. 303, 209, 236; *Herzog* (New York: Fawcett, 1965), pp. 107, 93, 118; and *Writers at Work: The Paris Review Interviews,* Third Series (New York: Viking, 1968), pp. 188, 192.

art, Bellow transmits his theme by way of some pseudo-African anthropology (a subject in which he had earned a degree at Northwestern University), but that tactic scarcely suffices to conceal the Jewish "L'Chaim" hiding behind the African "Grun-tu-molani" ("I want to live!"). Nor does Henderson's WASP background conceal his identity as, initially, one of Bellow's suffering Jewish victims. "Gene," his wife tells him, "when you suffer you suffer harder than any person I ever saw." And later, he admits, "I *was* monstrously proud of my suffering. I thought there was nobody in the world that could suffer quite like me."

The self that suffers is precisely what he proceeds to exorcise when he is called upon to achieve grun-tu-molani through impersonation of a lion in the native rituals: "And so I was the beast. I gave myself to it, and all my sorrow came out in the roaring. My lungs supplied the air but the note came from my soul." Although characterized by Bellow as a Gentile, Henderson compresses the whole Jewish tradition of lamentations into his roars, so that the king suspects some malingering in this state: "But what the king called pathos was actually (I couldn't help myself) a cry which summarized my entire course on this earth, from birth to Africa; and certain words crept into my roars, like 'God,' 'Help,' 'Lord have mercy,' . . . and also 'De profooooondis,' plus snatches from the 'Messiah' (He was despised and rejected, a man of sorrows, etcetera)."

But in the classic Jamesian pattern of conversion, the sick soul begins to see a path to deliverance opening up—"Yes, I thought, I believed I could change; I was willing to overcome my old self"—and a shift in the "hot place" of Henderson's consciousness seems underway: "Maybe my mind, beginning to change sponsors, so to speak, was stimulating the growth of a different man." At the climax of the conversion experience an irruption of cosmic consciousness from his childhood overcomes him, and the priestess proceeds to interpret the vision for him:

It is very early in life, and I am out in the grass. The sun flames and swells; the heat it emits is its love, too. I have this self-same vividness in my heart. There are dandelions. I try to gather up this green. I put my love-swollen cheek to the yellow of the dandelions. I try to enter into the green.

Then she told me I had grun-tu-molani, which is a native term hard to explain but on the whole it indicates that you want to live, not die.

The consciousness of achieving an illumination, which James calls "the essential mark of 'mystical' states" (p. 313), affects Henderson as well. "Because the sleep is burst, and I've come to myself," he says, he may come to share the king's religious position—so curiously identical to that of William James himself—that after its enlightenment, "the mind of the human may associate with the All-Intelligent to perform certain work. . . . All human accomplishment has this same origin. . . . What Homo sapiens imagines, he may slowly convert himself to."

Herzog and *Mr. Sammler's Planet* carry forward the twice-born psychology. Mr. Sammler, physically twice-born after climbing out of the ditch where murdered Jews, including Sammler's wife, have been left for dead, has undergone a chance of identity as a result. "Till forty or so I was simply an Anglophile intellectual Polish Jew and person of culture—relatively useless," he says, but now, in contrast to a world which has come to live by Schopenhauer's notion that "the organs of sex are the seat of the Will," Mr. Sammler lives by his higher insight—"The spirit knows that its growth is the real aim of existence."

Herzog, like Henderson, is initially presented as a man proud of his capacity for suffering. Sandor Himmelstein types him for us—"when you suffer, you really suffer. You're a real, genuine old Jewish type that digs the emotions." Herzog's suffering, however, includes an extra dimension: besides being swindled, betrayed, and cuckolded by friends and family, he carries the added burden of intellectual masochism. A "prisoner of perception," much like those sick souls whom James describes as the "prey of a pathological melancholy" (p. 124), Herzog spends most of the novel struggling, via his letters, with the Waste Land mentality of the modern intellectual tradition, which holds that "truth is true only as it brings down more disgrace and dreariness upon human beings, so that if it shows anything except evil it is illusion and not truth."

Herzog is lifted out of both personal and intellectual suffering at last by the revelations of *real* sufferings in the courtroom episode, defining life's real victims—the hermaphroditic Aleck-Alice trapped going drag, or the three-year-old boy beaten to death by his parents. Herzog's final rejection of the nay-sayers is confirmed by Saul Bellow himself in interviews. In the *Atlantic Monthly* of March, 1963, Bellow asserts that "we have had our bellyful of a species of wretchedness which is thoroughly pleased with itself. . . . Either we want life to continue, or we do not. If not, why write books?" In his *Paris Review* interview (1965), Bellow further identifies *Herzog* with this reaction: "The tone of elegy from the 1920's to the 50's, the atmosphere of Eliot in *The Waste Land* . . . is the essence of much modern realism. . . . I think a good deal of *Herzog* can be explained simply by the implicit assumption that existence . . . has value, that existence is worth-ful." And in his *Show* magazine interview of September, 1964, Bellow relates this reaction against the nay-sayers directly to the influence of his Jewish subculture:

> Romantic thought in the 20th Century has been apocalyptic nihilism—a conviction that the world is evil, that it must be destroyed and rise again. This one finds in D. H. Lawrence and one sees it also in writers like Ezra Pound. . . .
> I've a nagging sense that the human situation is not as described by these late romantic writers. I may be disappointed in

existence—but I feel I have a right to demand something other than romantic disappointment. I think the Jewish feeling resists romanticism and insists on an older set of facts.

The fact that Bellow's inner conflict between "L'Chaim" and the suffering Jewish victim recurs from book to book does not invalidate this conversion. Rather, it places Bellow alongside such twice-born writers as John Bunyan and Leo Tolstoy, of whom Professor James makes the following observation (p. 155):

> Neither Bunyan nor Tolstoy could become what we have called healthy-minded. They had drunk too deeply of the cup of bitterness ever to forget its taste. . . . The fact of interest for us is that as a matter of fact they could and did find *something* welling up in the inner reaches of their consciousness, by which such extreme sadness could be overcome. Tolstoy does well to talk of it as *that by which men live*; for that is exactly what it is, a stimulus, an excitement, a faith, a force that re-infuses the positive willingness to live, even in full presence of the evil perceptions that erewhile made life seem unbearable.

7.

If the "*something* welling up" in Bellow's inner consciousness is the magic of "L'Chaim," for Ellison's black hero deliverance comes through recourse to "soul" traditions. Amidst the succession of false identities forced upon the narrator, usually couched in terms of rebirth (he is told "You're a new man" after his brain operation, for example, and the brotherhood's code term for revolution is "Hurry, Doctor, she's already in labor!"),[8] a genuine rebirth comes upon him via the midwifery of soul-food and soul-music. Initially, the

---

[8] *Invisible Man* (New York: Signet, 1952), p. 214. Other quotations are cited from this book, pp. 249, 224, 330, 229–231, 11–12, 15, 63, 105, 381, 498; from *Shadow and Act* (New York: Signet, 1966), pp. xi-xii; and from William James, *Pragmatism* (New York, Meridian, 1955), p. 190.

129

Invisible Man's ideal social self resembled that of Artur Sammler's Anglophile years, his highest hope being to become like the crowd in the Men's House who carried the *Wall Street Journal* in one "always manicured and gloved" hand while "the other hand whipped a tightly rolled umbrella back and forth at a calculated angle; with their homburgs and Chesterfields, their polo coats and Tyrolean hats worn strictly as fashion demanded." But his role as orator for the Brotherhood brings an awareness "that there were two of me: the old self that slept a few hours a night and dreamed sometimes of my grandfather . . . ; and the new public self that spoke for the Brotherhood and was becoming so much more important than the other that I seemed to run a foot race against myself."

In this Jamesian "divided self" condition, the self that prevails is the yam-eater of yore who had been "suddenly overcome by an intense feeling of freedom" just by eating soul-food publicly: " 'They're my birthmark,' I said. 'I yam what I am' " And if eating yams on the street is a way of telling the public, "I am a Negro," soul-music is the means of impressing this fact into his own deepest consciousness. In a scene notably reminiscent of Hart Crane's flights of mysticism, the Invisible Man experiences a profound shift in the "hot place" in his consciousness while under the combined influence of drugs and Louis Armstrong's music: "Once when I asked for a cigarette, some jokers gave me a reefer, which I lighted when I got home and sat listening to my phonograph. . . . So under the spell of the reefer I discovered a new analytical way of listening to music. The unheard sounds came through. . . . That night I found myself hearing not only in time, but in space as well. I not only entered the music, but descended, like Dante, into its depths." There follows the jazz sermon, on the text of the "Blackness of Blackness," which in effect calls the whole book into being. "Then somehow I came out of it," he says, "ascending hastily from this underworld of sound to hear Louis Armstrong innocently asking, *What did I*

do/To be so black/And blue?" The immediate effect of the experience is similar to that recounted in many of James's case
studies on Mysticism: "At first I was afraid. . . . Nevertheless,
I know now that few really listen to music. I sat on the chair's
edge in a soaking sweat. . . . It was exhausting—as though I
had held my breath continuously for an hour under the terrify-
ing serenity that comes from days of intense hunger. . . . I
had discovered unrecognized compulsions of my being."

Music being the essential art-form in which *soul* finds
expression, other black folk also find the twice-born release in
this fashion. Trueblood, after committing incest, is cast out by
his family, condemned by his preacher as "the most wicked
man he's ever seen," and too guilt-ridden to pray for God's
forgiveness. But "finally, one night, way early in the mornin', I
looks up and sees the stars and I starts singin'. I don't mean to,
I didn't think 'bout it, just start singin' . . . . I sings me some
blues that night ain't never been sung before, and while I'm
singin' them blues I makes up my mind that I ain't nobody but
myself . . . ." The soloist in the college choir also reaches the
mystic depths of being through her singing—"She began
softly, as though singing to herself of emotions of utmost
privacy. . . . Gradually she increased its volume, until at last
the voice seemed to become a disembodied force that sought to
enter her, to violate her, shaking her, rocking her rhythmi-
cally, as though it had become the source of her being. . . ."

For Ellison himself, a trumpeter since youth and a
member of the Jazz Institute, the long term effect of black
music has been to imply freedom, creating open possibilities
as against the restrictive forms—musical and otherwise—of
the larger American society. In his Introduction to *Shadow and
Act*, he draws the analogy between musical and social emancipation thusly: ". . . while these [black] musicians and their
fellows were busy creating . . . a freer, more complex and
driving form of jazz, my friends and I were exploring an idea of
human versatility and possibility which went against the barbs

or over the palings of almost every fence which those who controlled social and political power had erected to restrict our roles in the life of the country."

In *Invisible Man*, this sense of freedom is what finally arises out of the twice-born identity. A Jamesian Pluralism is the narrator's resulting ideology, with James's "really dangerous and adventurous" universe replacing the Brotherhood's Marxist dogmas: "What if Brother Jack were wrong? What if history was a gambler, instead of a force in a laboratory experiment?" The book's Epilogue accordingly stresses what James called "altered powers of action" (p. 146), one of the standard modes of conversion: ". . . my world has become one of infinite possibilities. What a phrase—still, it's a good phrase and a good view of life, and a man shouldn't accept any other; that much I've learned underground." In terms of the Jamesian system, Ellison's conversion-psychology thus fits the "conscious and voluntary" as opposed to the "involuntary and unconscious" mode of transformation. "In the volitional type the regenerative change is usually gradual," James says, "and consists in the building up, piece by piece, of a new set of moral and spiritual habits. But there are always critical points here at which the movement forward seems much more rapid" (p. 169). In *Invisible Man*, these critical points make up a rebirth into black culture, its rites of passage marked by the eating of yams, the absorption into soul-music, the example of Rhinehart's multiple identities. Reborn as a Negro, the Invisible Man finally emerges in possession of the most healthy-minded of all American ideologies, the sense of "infinite possibilities" associated with the Transcendentalist promulgation.

8.

Up to this point, the Jamesian psychology of conversion appears solidly verified by the artist-changelings we have studied: Eliot the poet of naturalism becoming a neo-Christian, Poe the sick soul becoming a neo-Transcendentalist, Bellow the "melancholiac" becoming a yea-sayer. By way of conclusion, some additional testimony may be useful for clarifying James's system. The essential fact behind the conversion process is the imperative which Robert Penn Warren identified in the work of Joseph Conrad, that "The lowest and the most vile creature must, in some way, idealize his existence."[9] When the terms of that idealization change, undergoing what James called "the shifting of men's centres of personal energy within them," we have the situation so admirably described by Ralph Waldo Emerson's helm metaphor in "Circles": 'The key to every man is his thought. Sturdy and defying though he look, he has a helm which he obeys, which is the idea after which all his facts are classified. He can only be reformed by showing him a new idea which commands his own."

Given sufficient passion, as occurs with Nat Turner's fixation upon Margaret or Humbert's upon Lolita, this commanding idea can assume the daimonic force which Rollo May describes in *Love and Will*, wherein the idea and its objective embodiment (a love object, a political or religious movement, an aesthetic artifact, or whatever) becomes a sort of magnetic core around which the whole personality is galvanized. Dr. May defines the daimonic as *"any natural function which has the power to take over the whole person"* (emphasis his). Although "The daimonic can be either creative or destructive," May holds that "It is shown particularly in creativity." "The daimonic arises from the ground of being rather than the self as such," May adds, which parallels James's "subconscious incubation" of integrating powers; and he cites Aristotle's

[9] Robert Penn Warren, *Selected Essays* (New York: Vintage, 1966), p. 43. Other quotations are cited from *Selections from Ralph Waldo Emerson*, ed. Stephen E. Whicher (Boston: 1957), p. 169; and Rollo May, *Love and Will* (New York: Delta, 1969), pp. 123–5.

"eudaimonism" (good-daimonism) in a way that resembles the end of James's conversion process: "Happiness is to live in harmony with one's daimon. Nowadays, we would relate 'eudaimonism' to the state of integration of potentialities and other aspects of one's being. . . ."

To live in harmony with one's daimon, in Rollo May's phrase, or to reconcile conflicting parts of the self, in James's way of thinking, is the final stage of the conversion process. There is no doubt that the subject of conversion could be greatly expanded beyond the above examples, for it is one of the grand themes in American literature. For our purposes, however, enough has been said to confirm the relevance of James's religious psychology to yet another cluster of important American writers. We turn next to what William James considered the most crucial of all religious phenomena, Mysticism.

Chapter V

Mysticism

1.

"Over and over again," James says in beginning his chapter on Mysticism, "I have raised points and left them open and unfinished until we should have come to the subject of Mysticism." Now at last, James felt, he might unify his work as a whole by taking up this subject of paramount importance: "One may say truly, I think, that personal religious experience has its root and centre in mystical states of consciousness; so for us . . . such states of consciousness ought to form the vital chapter from which the other chapters get their light" (p. 292). So too in our present study, a thread of mystic consciousness obviously may be traced through our exemplars of The Religion of Healthy-Mindedness and of Conversion. Bellow's and Ellison's depiction of profoundly changed consciousness; T. S. Eliot's grand epiphany of the still point in *Four Quartets* ("I can only say, *there* we have been"); Poe's suddenly altered views of life; Emerson's and Whitman's spontaneous connection with the universal current of Being—all these elements of our previous discussion properly converge upon this chapter.

By the same token, some of our forthcoming exemplars

of mystic consciousness might have figured into our discussion of Conversion had not the issue of Mysticism taken precedence. Among these writers concerned with Mysticism/Conversion, the writers of the South occupy a place of such importance as to merit a separate consideration before we go on to our chief and "purest" example of mysticism, the writings of Hart Crane. Even though leaving practicing Roman Catholics like Walker Percy and Flannery O'Connor out of our discussion, and fixing solely upon the vaguely—and for the most part lapsed—Protestant representatives of Southern culture, we find ourselves engaged with a pervasive religious consciousness not to be found outside the region, possibly excepting the small enclave of Jewish writers whose rise to eminence culminated in Saul Bellow's capture of the Nobel Prize in 1976. However irregular or unorthodox their system of beliefs, our great writers of the South—Wolfe, Faulkner, Styron, Warren, McCullers, and even Twain—have not shared Henry Adams' experience of living in a religionless culture.

Among the reasons for the persistence of religious consciousness in writers of the South, William James touches upon an important one while observing the cultural basis of conversion. "In Catholic lands," he says, "and in our own Episcopalean sects, no such anxiety and conviction of sin is usual as in sects that encourage revivals. The sacraments being more relied on in these more strictly ecclesiastical bodies, the individual's personal acceptance of salvation needs less to be accentuated and led up to" (p. 165). Owing to the Protestant fundamentalism that is the majority religion in the area, the South remains the pre-eminent religious culture of the nation in which one achieves salvation through a personal crisis; and though "getting saved" may not be the Southern writer's overt subject, it forms his paradigm for whatever struggle for identity preoccupies his imagination. However varied the terms of their "salvation" may be, an Ike McCaslin (*The Bear*), a

Jack Burden (*All the King's Men*), and a Biff Brannon (*The Heart Is a Lonely Hunter*) share the Protestant burden of unmediated responsibility for their own soul. The intensely private and personal experience of conversion or mystic consciousness is much more compatible with this tradition than with, for example, the literature of protest popularized by Steinbeck and Joseph Heller.

Its Protestant heritage also makes the South the last great reserve of Bible-readers in American culture, people who regard the Book as a sacred text rather than an aesthetic artifact. This fact, one of Styron's characters notes, establishes a link between the Southerner and the Jew: "I've often thought there's more kinship deep down between a southern Methodist and a Jew from Brookline, Mass. than there is between two Pennsylvanians, and no doubt two people who have known Isaiah or Job 38 are more likely to feel some strange and persuasive bond than a couple of mackerel-snappers who have never known anything but the New York Journal in their life."[1] To Styron's Isaiah or Job 38 we might add his own use of the Gospels and the Book of Revelations in *The Confessions of Nat Turner*, as well as Faulkner's two haunting Biblical titles, *Absalom, Absalom!* and *If I Forget Thee, O Jerusalem* (the latter, quoted from Psalm 137, regrettably was changed to *The Wild Palms*).

Beyond his random uses of scripture the Southern writer also expresses the religious consciousness of his region by re-conceptualizing the primal Biblical myth of the Fall in terms

[1] William Styron, *Set This House on Fire* (New York: Signet, 1961), p. 346. Other quotations are cited from this book, pp. 16–18; Joseph Blotner, *Faulkner: A Biography* (New York: 1974), p. 1002; Dixon Wecter, *Sam Clemens of Hannibal* (Boston: 1952), pp. 63–64; *Writers at Work: The Paris Review Interviews* (New York: 1959), p. 282 (Styron) and Second Series (1965), p. 239 (Hemingway); Carson McCullers, *The Heart Is a Lonely Hunter* (New York: Bantam, 1961), pp. 254–6; William Faulkner, *The Hamlet* (New York: Vintage, 1956), pp. 219–220; Isaiah 55:12.

of local history—somewhat as the black slaves reconceptualized the myth of the Exodus in terms of their life situation. Unlike his countrymen in any other region, the white Southerner of any intelligence and sensitivity has had to regard his native land in terms of Biblical déjà-vu: an Original Sin, slavery, precipitating the Fall, or Civil War, followed by the forced exit from paradise—the *Gone With the Wind* view of things. Certainly a Fall from grace has entered the personal psychology of our major Southern writers, leading to titles like *Look Homeward, Angel* and *All the King's Men*. About half of Robert Penn Warren's poetry (which totals fourteen volumes) fastens upon this theme, as do Mark Twain's greatest books. Thus Twain speaks of Hannibal (fictionalized as St. Petersburg, meaning "heavenly place") as his Paradise Lost: "the town of my boyhood—. . . we see now that we were in heaven then and there was no one able to make us know it. . . ." And Faulkner constructed his favorite among his own novels upon the same insight, mythologizing that day when the Compson children first tasted the forbidden knowledge of sex and death (Caddy's muddy drawers and Damuddy's funeral) by supplying a snake and a tree and a "Voice that breathed o'er Eden."

Related to his Protestant heritage—and to our theme of conversion/mysticism—is the exacerbated conscience of the white Southern author. Hemingway's dictum that great writing comes out of a sense of injustice is nowhere more verified than in this region where social beliefs have clashed so appallingly with the Biblical imperatives enjoining a just society. *Huckleberry Finn* remains our most celebrated classic on this theme, but other works have been no less powerful. Faulkner's most tragically embittered trio of novels, *Sanctuary*, *Light in August*, and *Absalom, Absalom!*, sprang out of a similar depth of guilt and shame concerning his society's scapegoats, such that Quentin Compson's great outcry about not hating the South ("*I dont hate it! I dont hate it!*") surely reveals his author's profound emotional discord. Even second rate talents like Erskine Caldwell and journalists like James Agee and W. J. Cash, when confronting the spectacle of economic and racial inequity in the South, may be said to demonstrate William Styron's observation that "The good writing of any age has always been the product of someone's neurosis." In this respect, the white Southern writer has been lucky: thanks to the peculiar history of his region and its Biblical culture, his neurosis is built-in and ready-made at birth. Guilt, rage, and shame together with pride and love toward his native land render the Southern white, assuming that he have some moral integrity and intelligence, a prime candidate for William James's "Divided Self" condition, marked by "a certain discordancy or heterogeneity in the native temperament . . . , an incompletely unified moral and intellectual constitution."

In the best Southern writers, this "neurosis" produces a tone comparable to that of the Old Testament prophet summoning damnation upon his beloved but wayward people. Here is Carson McCullers' jeremiad, for example, a fictionalized account yet factual enough to be verifiable in the statistics of W. J. Cash (in *The Mind of the South*):

". . . if you was to ask me to point out the most uncivilized area on the face of the globe I would point here . . . . Here. These thirteen states. . . . In my life I seen things that would make a man go crazy. At least one third of all Southerners live and die no better off than the lowest peasant in any European Fascist state. The average wage of a worker on a tenant farm is only seventy-three dollars per year. And mind you, that's the average! . . . just about ten cents for a full day's work. Everywhere there's pellagra and hookworm and anaemia. And just plain, pure starvation. . . .

". . . Absentee ownership. In the village is one huge brick mill and maybe four or five hundred shanties. The houses aren't fit for human beings to live in. . . . Built with far less attention to needs than sties for pigs. . . . A young linthead begins working . . . at such times as he can get himself employed. He marries. After the first child the woman must work in the mill also. . . . They buy food and clothes at a company-owned or dominated store. . . . With three or four younguns they are held down the same as if they had on chains. That is the whole principle of serfdom. Yet here in America we call ourselves free."

There is much more of the same in Carson McCullers' writing, but let us set the above passage alongside Faulkner's portrait of the Southern tenant farmer, here typified by Mink Snopes in *The Hamlet*:

It was dusk. He emerged from the bottom and looked up the slope of his meagre and sorry corn and saw it—the paintless two-room cabin with an open hallway between and a lean-to kitchen, which was not his, on which he paid rent but no taxes, paying almost as much in rent in one year as the house had cost to build; not old, yet the roof of which already leaked and the weather-stripping had already begun to rot away from the wall planks and which was just like the one he had been born in which had not belonged to his father either, and just like the one he would die in if he died indoors . . . and it was just like the more than six others he had lived in since his marriage and like the twice that many more he knew he would live in before he did die and though he paid rent on this one he was unalterably convinced that his cousin [Flem Snopes] owned it and he knew that this was as near as he would ever come to owning the roof over his head. . . . He . . . mounted through the yellow and stunted stand of his corn, yellow and stunted because he had had no money to buy fertilizer to put beneath it and owned neither the stock nor the tools to work it properly with and had had no one to help him with what he did own in order to gamble his physical strength and endurance against his body's livelihood. . . .

And finally, we have William Styron's version of the exacerbated conscience of the white South. The following excerpt, from *Set This House on Fire* (1959), expresses a contemplation of racial injustice that would culminate in *The Confessions of Nat Turner*:

". . . These are miserable times. . . . You can almost sniff the rot in the air. . . . So on the state level they'll still vote in year after year this millionaire apple farmer [Harry Byrd] who guarantees them good roads and miserable schools and above all that the negro will never get an even break. . . . Look out there, son. That's where they came in, in the year 1619. It was one of the saddest days in the history of man. We're still paying for that day, and we'll be paying for it from here on out. . . .

"What this country needs is for something to happen to it. Something ferocious and tragic, like what happened to Jericho or the cities of the plain—something terrible, I mean, son, so that when the people have been through hellfire and crucible, and have suffered agony enough and grief, they'll be men again, human beings, not a bunch of smug contented hogs rooting at the trough. Ciphers without mind or soul or heart. Soap peddlers! I mean it, son, these are miserable times. . . . What has happened to this country would shame the Roman Empire at its lowest ebb."

To sum up, we may say that writers of the South, in general, have drawn their view of life from a culture in which the Jamesian religious psychology may thrive. Informed by a deeply ingrained knowledge of the Bible, and precipitated perhaps by the "neurosis" Styron sees as inherent in all good writing—a neurosis compounded of love and pride warring with guilt and despair, the phenomenon of conversion occupies a central place in the region's literature, as our exemplary figures—Warren, Styron, and McCullers—demonstrate. And like the phenomenon of conversion, mysticism enters the literature of the South in a big way because of the region's cultural predispositions. The solidarity of the Southern family and its long-rooted presence in a local environment may well have imparted to our Southern writers a greater sense of consanguinity with others than is typical elsewhere. Even during his alienation from community and family—a standard theme in Southern writing—the Southern persona at least has once known deeply the sense of blood-membership in a larger organism than himself, and has felt a personal relationship with history. In addition, the Southerner's deeply imbibed knowledge of the Bible would have made him familiar with numerous expressions of mystic consciousness, ranging from the ecstasies of Isaiah—"the mountains and the hills shall break forth before you into singing, and all the trees of the field shall clap their hands"—to the apocalyptic visions of Saint John.

141

2.

By way of defining our subject, two modes of mystic experience may properly claim our attention, one Christian and the other pantheistic. The Christian mode, that of glossolalia or "speaking in tongues," refers to the infilling of the Holy Spirit by which Christ's disciples at Pentecost experienced personal contact with the Divine Presence. A recurrence of this phenomenon in recent decades, which has generated wide interest in all branches of Christianity, provides material by which American literary attitudes towards mystic consciousness may be measured. Here, to start, are the testimonies of two practitioners of glossolalia whose intellectual and emotional integrity are indisputable, Charles G. Finney and James Baldwin. (Though non-Southerners, they represent Protestant fundamentalism as well as does any Southerner.) In James's *Varieties*, the Reverend Mr. Finney felt the descent of the Holy Spirit "in a manner that seemed to go through me, body and soul. . . . Indeed, it seemed to come in waves and waves of liquid love. . . . It seemed like the very breath of God. I can recall distinctly that it seemed to fan me, like immense wings./No words can express the wonderful love that was shed abroad in my heart. I wept aloud with joy and love; and I do not know but I should say I literally bellowed out the unutterable gushings of my heart" (p. 204). And James Baldwin, in *Go Tell It on the Mountain*, struggles for imagery in which to describe his Pentecostal seizure:

> And something moved in John's body which was not John. He was invaded, set at naught, possessed. This power had struck John, . . . had opened him up; had cracked him open, as wood beneath the axe cracks down the middle, as rocks break up; had ripped him and felled him in a moment. . . . Then John saw the Lord—for a moment only; and the darkness, for a moment only, was filled with a light he could not bear. Then, in a moment, he was set free; his tears sprang as from a fountain; his heart, like a fountain of waters,

burst. . . . And he wanted to rise up, singing, singing in that great morning, the morning of his new life.[2]

It is interesting to compare these first-hand descriptions of a mystical experience with treatments of glossolalia recorded by three other writers, two of them low- and middle-brow authors of enormously popular best-sellers, the other a high-brow aesthetician greatly admired in Academe. First, the low-brow version, from Grace Metalious's *Peyton Place*:

> When he finally reached the steps of the building, he fancied that he heard singing, but he did not notice the black, gilt-lettered sign next to the entrance which proclaimed this as The Peyton Place Pentecostal Full Gospel Church. . . . He took one step forward into the aisle between the wooden pews, and fell flat on his face with a resounding thud.
> Well, I'll be a dirty sonofabitch, thought Kenny, if some bastard didn't push me.
> He did not realize it, but his thought formed itself on his lips and left them in a low, indistinguishable whisper. . . .
> "The unknown tongue!" screamed a hysterical woman. "He speaks the unknown tongue!" and at once, the congregation went into an uproar. . . .
> For two hours, Kenny lay on the floor of the church and raved drunkenly in unintelligible words. . . . Exactly what words, Kenny was never absolutely sure, but that did not bother him. The members of the Peyton Place Pentecostal Full Gospel Church accepted him as a man of holiness, and before too many years had passed Kenny was baptized and ordained as a minister in the sect.

John Steinbeck, being much more generously disposed toward his "Holiness people" in *The Grapes of Wrath*, refrained from the drunken minister gambit. But even to his kindly understanding the Pentecostal experience produced nothing more than a cacophony of animal noises:

---

[2] *Go Tell It on the Mountain* (New York: Dell, 1965), pp. 193, 204. Other quotations are cited from *Peyton Place* (New York: 1956), pp. 302–304; *The Grapes of Wrath* (New York: 1958), pp. 288–289; *Lost in the Funhouse* (New York: 1969), p. 112; *The Heart Is a Lonely Hunter*, p. 42; *The Sound and the Fury* (New York: 1961), p. 310; *Brother to Dragons* (New York: 1953), p. 118.

> From some little distance there came the sound of the begin-
> ning meeting, a sing-song chant of exhortation. . . . It swelled and
> paused, and a growl came into the response. . . . The rhythm
> quickened. Male and female voices had been one tone, but now in
> the middle of a response one woman's voice went up and up in a
> wailing cry, wild and fierce, like the cry of a beast; and a deeper
> woman's voice rose up beside it, a baying voice, and a man's voice
> traveled up the scale in the howl of a wolf. The exhortation stopped,
> and only the feral howling came from the tent, and with it a
> thudding sound on the earth. Ma shivered. Rose of Sharon's breath
> was panting and short, and the chorus of howls went on so long it
> seemed that lungs must burst. . . .
>
> Now the high voice broke into hysteria, the gabbling screams
> of a hyena, . . . and the sobbing changed to a little whining, like
> that of a litter of puppies at a food dish.

Our high-brow observer, John Barth in "Glossolalia" (a sketch
in *Lost in the Funhouse*), takes the phenomenon seriously
enough to attempt reproducing the unknown tongue, but his
subsequent commentary may be the most pejorative of the
three, linking glossolalia with his own sick soul's nihilism:

> Ombo té scelé te, beré te kúre kúre. Sinté te lúté sinte kúru, te
> ruméte tau ruméte. Onkó kerre scéte, tere lúte, ilee léte leel' lúto.
> Scélé.
> Ill fortune, constraint and terror, generate guileful art; despair
> inspires. The laureled clairvoyants tell our doom in riddles. Sewn in
> our robes are horrid tales, and the speakers-in-tongues enounce
> atrocious tidings. The prophet-birds seem to speak sagely, but are
> shrieking their frustration. The senselessest babble, could we ken
> it, might disclose a dark message, or prayer.

Our Southern writers have been much more knowledgeable about this form of mysticism, and therefore much
more receptive, in the spirit of William James. Not that James is
entirely uncritical. "It is odd," he says concerning mystical
theology, "that Protestantism, especially evangelical Protestantism, should seemingly have abandoned everything me-
thodical in this line. Apart from what prayer may lead to,
Protestant mystical experience appears to have been almost
entirely sporadic" (p. 312). Carson McCullers' Portia murmurs
an analogous misgiving in *The Heart Is a Lonely Hunter*:

"Now, I not a big shouter. I belongs to the Presbyterian Church and us don't hold with all this rolling on the floor and talking in tongues. Us don't get santified ever week and wallow around together. In our church we sings and lets the preacher do the preaching. . . .

"Now Highboy he were Holiness boy before us were married. He loved to get the spirit ever Sunday and shout and sanctify hisself. But after us were married I got him to join with me. . . ."

But Faulkner converts a similar episode into the emotional climax of *The Sound and the Fury*, whereof the two protagonists sit "in the midst of the voices and the hands"—a splendid understatement!—listening to the Reverend Shegog give utterance: "With his body he seemed to feed the voice that, succubus like, had fleshed its teeth in him. . . . while the voice consumed him, until he was nothing and they were nothing and there was not even a voice but instead their hearts were speaking to one another in chanting measures beyond the need for words. . . ." And Robert Penn Warren, in *Brother to Dragons* (1953), speaks as one who would know inwardly what Baldwin and Finney experienced—the "Truth-dazzled hour when the heart shall burst/In gouts of glory hallelujah! . . . the hour of the Pentecostal intuition."

3.

This openness toward a kind of mysticism conventionally associated with the evangelical Protestantism of the South may partly explain a similar openness toward a different form of mysticism that is crucially important to our study: the pantheistic illumination that William James called Cosmic Consciousness. Defined, variously, as "a monistic insight, in which the *other* in its various forms appears absorbed into the One" (p. 299), and "a return from the solitude of individuation into the consciousness of unity with all that is" (p. 304), cosmic consciousness may evince enough power, in James's religious

145

psychology, to effect the conversion of a divided psyche into the twice-born state: "We pass into mystical states from out of ordinary consciousness as from a less into a more, as from a smallness into a vastness, and at the same time as from an unrest into a rest. We feel them as reconciling, unifying states" (p. 319). And again: "The keynote . . . is invariably a reconciliation. It is as if the opposites of the world, whose contradictoriness and conflict make all our difficulties and troubles, were melted into unity" (p. 298).

We have already observed such irruptions of mystic feeling in a number of non-Southern writers, from Emerson and Whitman to Bellow and Nabokov—whose butterfly hunting, he said, produced "ecstasy, and behind the ecstasy . . . a sense of oneness with sun and stone."[3] But our Southern writers have shared a capacity for cosmic consciousness to a remarkable degree. To begin, we may cite William Faulkner's vision of death, in *The Bear*, as a passage into a unified, collective identity, gathering hunter and hunted, flesh and foliage, into a larger process that goes on and on:

> . . . the knoll which was no abode of the dead because there was no death, not Lion and not Sam: not held fast in earth but free in earth and not in earth but of earth, myriad yet undiffused of every myriad part, leaf and twig and particle, air and sun and rain and dew and night, acorn oak and leaf and acorn again, dark and dawn and dark and dawn again in their immutable progression and, being myriad, one: and Old Ben too, Old Ben too. . . .

In the Blotner biography, Faulkner rendered a strikingly original conception of death as passage into a larger cosmos, musing that maybe when he died, he would turn into a radio wave. In any case, we may say that for Faulkner, cosmic

---

[3] *Speak, Memory* (New York: 1968), p. 103. Other quotations are cited from *The Bear* in *Go Down, Moses* (New York: 1942), pp. 328–9; Joseph Blotner, *Faulkner: A Biography*, p. 1764 ("radio wave"); *Soldiers' Pay* (final page of any edition); *The Mansion* (final page of any edition); *From Death to Morning* (New York: 1935), pp. 33, 68–70; *The Portable Thomas Wolfe* (New York: 1946), p. 557.

consciousness formed a sort of parentheses enclosing his literary canon. His first novel, *Soldiers' Pay*, ends in the heart's yearning for self-transcendence: "Feed Thy Sheep, O Jesus. All the longing of mankind for a Oneness with Something, somewhere." His last novel—apart from *The Reivers*, a minor enterprise—ends with Mink Snopes experiencing just such an absorption, simply through yielding up his separate consciousness in sleep:

> . . . he could feel the Mink Snopes that had had to spend so much of his life just having unnecessary bother and trouble, beginning to crep, seep, flow easy as sleeping; he could almost watch it, following all the little grass blades and tiny roots, the little holes the worms made, down and down into the ground already full of the folks that had had the trouble but were free now, so that it was just the ground and the dirt that had to bother and worry and anguish with the passions and hopes and skeers, the justice and the injustice and the griefs, leaving the folks themselves easy now, all mixed and jumbled up comfortable and easy so wouldn't nobody even know or even care who was which any more, himself among them, equal to any, good as any, brave as any, being inextricable from, anonymous with all of them: the beautiful, the splendid, the proud and the brave, right on up to the very top itself among the shining phantoms and dreams which are the milestones of the long human recording—Helen and the bishops, the kings and the unhomed angels, the scornful and graceful seraphim.

That reference to Thomas Wolfe's "unhomed angels" evokes comparison with another prose poet whose sense of union with the whole of reality sometimes attained religious intensity. "I thought . . . how our lives touch every other life that ever lived," Wolfe writes in "Death the Proud Brother," and he thinks also, like Faulkner, and like Whitman in "The Sleepers," how men attain psychic healing during the nightly release from a separate, conscious identity:

> In Sleep we lie all naked and alone, in Sleep we are united at the heart of night and darkness, and we are strange and beautiful asleep; for we are dying in the darkness, and we know no death, there is no death, there is no life, no joy, no sorrow and no glory on the earth but Sleep.

147

> Come mild and magnificent Sleep, . . . bringer of peace and dark forgetfulness, healer and redeemer, dear enchantress, hear us. . . . Seal up the porches of our memory, tenderly, gently, steal our lives away from us, blot out the vision of lost love, lost days, and all our ancient hungers; great Transformer, heal us!

To a mind that thus welcomes Sleep as healer and redeemer, death too may be similarly accommodated: St. Francis' little Sister Death becoming Wolfe's Proud Brother. As a "reconciling, unifying" vision, to use James's description of mystic consciousness, Wolfe's apostrophe to Death in "Death the Proud Brother" rivals Whitman's "Lilacs" and "Whispers of Heavenly Death" in its power to reconcile the living consciousness to its mortality:

> . . . what have you ever touched that you have not touched with love and pity, Death? Proud Death, wherever we have seen your face, you came with mercy, love, and pity, Death, and brought to all of us your compassionate sentences of pardon and release. For have you not retrieved from exile the desperate lives of men who never found their home? Have you not opened your dark door for us who never yet found doors to enter, and given us a room who, roomless, doorless, unassuaged, were driven on forever through the streets of life? Have you not offered us your stern provender, Death, with which to stay the hunger that grew to madness from the food it fed upon, and given all of us the goal for which we sought but never found, the certitude, the peace, for which our ever-laden hearts contended, and made for us, in your dark house, an end of all the tortured wandering and unrest that lashed us on forever?

And in *You Can't Go Home Again*, which preoccupied Wolfe as hs death was coming near, an irruption of mystical consciousness comes with the force of a final testament. Famous as the passage has become, it deserves requoting here as a supreme example of James's principle that in mystical consciousness "the keynote . . . is invariably a reconciliation." Herewith the reconciliation of a man to his imminent mortality:

> Dear Fox, old friend, thus we have come to the end of the road that we were to go together. . . .
> But before I go, I have just one more thing to tell you:

148

Something has spoken to me in the night . . . and told me I shall die, I know not where. Saying:

"To lose the earth you know, for greater knowing; to lose the life you have, for greater life; to leave the friends you love, for greater loving; to find a land more kind than home, more large than earth—

"—Whereon the pillars of this earth are founded, towards which the conscience of the world is tending—a wind is rising, and the rivers flow."

4.

From these fragmentary expressions of mystical insight, we turn to our three Southern writers who combine the Conversion/Mysticism phenomena in an artistically organized fashion. William Styron is the most orthodox of the three, and the only one who has stated flatly, "I am a Christian," so that his portrayal of the twice-born experience takes on a strongly Christian coloring. Robert Penn Warren portrays conversion through what James called "altered feelings, or altered powers of action," and Carson McCullers through James's "new intellectual insights" (p. 146). All three enounce some experience of cosmic consciousness at the heart of the conversion process.

Styron's rendering of the twice-born experience is best seen as an attentuated delivery, covering his first three large novels. *Lie Down In Darkness*, published in 1951, renders the sick soul in its terminal stages, seeking release in alcoholism and suicide, portrayed respectively in Milton Loftis and his daughter Peyton. Ostensibly, the cause of this soul-sickness is the Oedipal rivalry between Peyton and her mother that tangles them all in a web of poisonous hatred, and there is in addition the universal guilt implied in Peyton's suicide on the same day the atomic bomb hits Hiroshima. But the book's sub-plot, which climaxes in a Negro revival meeting on the day of Peyton's funeral, suggests a deeper malaise in the Loftis family: their defunctive religious faith. Unlike the "dead feelings, dead ideas, and cold beliefs" of their Anglican confession, which terminates in Peyton Loftis exclaiming "There is no God,"[4] the book's Negro revivalism really touches the "hot place" in the worshippers' consciousness, their center of energy. It makes no difference that Daddy Faith is a swindling con man, because religious experience is an internal thing, not subject to the censorship of reason. As James put it, in defending his subordination of intellect to feeling in *The Varieties*, "Individuality is founded in feeling; and the recesses of feeling, the darker, blinder strata of character, are the only places in the world in which we catch real fact in the making . . ." (p. 379). Elsewhere he agrees that "to the medical mind these ecstasies signify nothing but suggested and imitated hypnoid states, on an intellectual basis of superstition, and a corporeal one of degeneration and hysteria," but while admitting that "these pathological conditions have existed in many and possibly all the cases," he adds that "that fact tells us nothing about the value for knowledge of the consciousness which they induce. To pass a spiritual judgment upon these states, we must . . . inquire into their fruits for life" (p. 316–7). In Styron's first novel, there is no mistaking that the fruits for life of the Negroes' faith are efficacious, a point that Styron underscores by counterpointing the Negro revival service against the pathetic funeral in the Loftis family.

Styron's second novel, *Set This House on Fire* (1959), again treats a sick soul in need of conversion, as the book's title (from a Donne sermon) implies. The outward manifestation of soul-sickness is again alcoholism and suicide (at one point the

---

[4] *Lie Down in Darkness* (New York: 1951), p. 342. Other quotations are cited from *Set This House on Fire*, pp. 55–56, 246–8; *The Confessions of Nat Turner* (New York: 1968), pp. 401, 403; *William Styron's Nat Turner: Ten Black Writers Respond*, ed. John Henrik Clarke (Boston: 1968), p. 16. See also Styron interview in *Yale Literary Magazine* (Fall, 1968), pp. 27, 33.

protagonist determines to slaughter himself, his wife, and children), but the cause here is not only despair but guilt—guilt arising from that neurosis which any white Southerner of intelligence and conscience must have felt until recently about the Negro. Adrift in Italy, Styron's hero manages to deal with his guilt, which focuses on his wrecking a Negro's cabin back home in Virginia, by ministering to a dying Italian peasant, a member of that country's oppressed "nigger" class. His metaphysical despair, however, calls forth a genuine religious conversion. Originally, Cass Kinsolving followed the pattern of Tolstoy's crisis. "A man cannot live without a focus," he (Cass) said. "Without some kind of faith. I didn't have any more faith than a tomcat. Nothing! Nothing! . . . I was sick as a dog inside my soul, and for the life of me I couldn't figure out where that sickness came from."

What heals his soul is a sudden irruption of what James calls the cosmic consciousness, or an intuition of connection with the whole of life. James recorded an account of one such "lifting of the veil" which befell a man observing a single flower: "I felt all the happiness destined for man. This unutterable harmony of souls, the phantom of the ideal world, arose in me complete. I never felt anything so great or instantaneous. I know not what . . . secret relation it was that made me see in this flower a limitless beauty" (p. 361). Styron's account begins with some ladybugs, observed beside a hotel window:

> I remember going to the window. It was a spring afternoon, warm, full of pollen. . . . Then there were these elephant vines, huge and green and tropical. These shiny harmless little ladybugs . . . were swarming all over the leaves, . . . [with] spotted black backs and ruset-colored glossy wings. . . . I stood there for a long while looking at the leaves and the ladybugs, . . . and then I looked up. And I'll swear at the moment as I looked up it was as if I were gazing into the kingdom of heaven. I don't know quite how to describe it—this *bone-breaking* moment of loveliness. . . . Ah my God, how can I describe it! It wasn't just the *scene*, you see—it was the sense, the bleeding *essence* of the thing. . . . It was no longer a street that I was

watching; the street was inside my very flesh and bones, you see, and for a moment I was released from my own self, embracing all that was within the street and partaking of all that happened there in time gone by, and now, and in time to come. And it filled me with the craziest sort of joy.

Thus the delivery of a sick soul into the twice-born state. In *The Confessions of Nat Turner* (1967), Styron's hero is again in the sick soul condition, owing this time to a sense of total alienation from that God whose command to rise up in bloody rebellion has brought Nat—at the book's outset—to the eve of his execution. Nat's conversion into final serenity comes in two stages, the first being his revulsion at the bloodbath which he himself has ordained and yearned for, and the second being the feeling of love that flows between him and his victim: "And as I think of her, the desire swells within me and I am stirred by a longing so great that like those memories of time past and long-ago voices, flowing waters, rushing winds, it seems more than my heart can abide. *Beloved, let us love one another: for love is of God; and everyone that loveth is born of God, and knoweth God."*

It is most regrettable that the black critics who assaulted this book as the product of Styron's while racist prejudice failed to see that the book's real prejudice is not racial but religious: Styron made over his Nat Turner into a Christian, a man who repented his violence not due to sexual love for a white woman nor due to weakness of resolve but owing to his soul's conversion: "*Yes*, I think . . . *I would have done it all again. I would have destroyed them all. Yet I would have spared one. I would have spared her that showed me Him whose presence I had not fathomed or maybe never even known."* Most regrettable of all have been the attacks on Nat's—and Styron's—manhood as a result of this portrayal. "The prophet . . . of the Black Resurrection still awaits a literary interpreter worthy of his sacrifice," said one such critic; "you have to bring a man to find a man." What such a critique fails to see is that Nat Turner is most largely a "man" at precisely that moment when he crawls off in the midst of the bloodshed to puke up his guts into the bushes, and Styron is most imaginatively a "man" when, transcending race hatred, he envisions Nat's twice-born state of religious experience.

5.

Robert Penn Warren, in his 1953 Introduction to *All the King's Men*, identified Machiavelli, Dante, and Spenser as "figures that stood in the shadows of imagination" behind his book.[5] "Another one of that company," he says, "was the scholarly and benign figure of William James." Direct Jamesian influence finds a twofold expression in the novel: in the political pragmatism of Willie Stark, the governor, and in the pluralism of Jack Burden's final religious outlook. In his Introduction, Warren defined one of his themes as "the problem of naturalistic determinism," which translates into Jack Burden's allegiance to The Great Twitch through most of the novel. James's Pluralism hypothesis was constructed precisely to counteract the deterministic implications of contemporary science and philosophy. Rather than adopt the view of man as a hapless microbe within the stypefying magnitude of nature, James insisted that men's choices make a real and permanent difference in the universal scheme of things. "Who knows whether the faithfulness of individuals here below to their own poor over-beliefs may not actually help God in turn to be more effectively faithful to his own greater tasks?" James

---

[5] *All the King's Men* (New York: Modern Library, 1953), p. vi. Other quotations are cited from this book, pp. 463, 11–12, 376, iv, 201; *Robert Penn Warren: A Collection of Critical Essays*, ed. John L. Longley, Jr. (New York: 1965), p. 241 (the "osmosis of being"); William James, *Pragmatism* (New York: 1955), p. 187; *Flood* (New York: 1965), p. 353; Robert Penn Warren, *Selected Essays* (New York: 1966), p. 197 (Melville).

153

queries in his "Conclusions" to *The Varieties* (p. 391); and elsewhere he writes,

> The belief in free will is not in the least incompatible with the belief in Providence, if you allow him to provide possibilities as well as actualities to the universe. . . . Suppose that the world's author put the case to you before creation, saying: "I am going to make a world not certain to be saved, a world the perfection of which shall be conditional merely, the condition being that each several agent does its own level best. I offer you the chance of taking part in such a world. Its safety, you see, is unwarranted. It is a real adventure, with real danger. . . ."

Intellectually speaking, the substance of Jack Burden's conversion in *All the King's Men* consists in his moving away from the Great Twitch philosophy into this Jamesian position, denoted by the book's closing sentence about accepting "the awful responsibility of Time." The Scholarly Attorney's pamphlet a page or two from the end of the book also confirms the Jamesian position, in justifying the real and permanent evil in the universe as evidence of God's seriousness in permitting men to create their own destiny freely: "The creation of evil is therefore the index of God's glory and his power. That had to be, so that the creation of good might be the index of man's glory and power."

Conversion is not solely a matter of intellectual change, however. As William James repeatedly demonstrated, it is most likely to spring from deeply subconscious processes, and to hatch out or burst into flower after long incubation. In Jack Burden's case, the incubation period is intimated throughout the novel in a long series of foetus images, like the "clammy, sad little foetus which is you" early in Jack's narrative and which "wants to lie in the dark and not know, and be warm in its not-knowing." The twice-born state in Jack's case comes appropriately with his waking to his mother's scream, for a new Jack Burden is born in the knowledge that he has caused the suicide of his father. Dropping the wise-guy sarcasm that has characterised his narrative to date—similar to the corrosive

154

irony of T. S. Eliot or (Styron's) Cass Kinsolving before *his* conversion—Jack describes the usual effects of such a shift in the hot place in one's consciousness: "I found that I was not laughing at all but was weeping. . . . It was like the ice breaking up after a long winter. And the winter had been long."

A clue to Warren's own conversion, if we may use that term to describe a shift in "the group of ideas to which [a man] devotes himself," may be found in Warren's casual comment, also in the Introduction to *All the King's Men*, that the novel was "interrupted . . . by the study for and writing of a long essay on Coleridge." Jack Burden's feeling, during his Great Twitch and Great Sleep periods, that "one thing had nothing to do, in the end, with anything else" seems to have afflicted Warren himself in his earlier fiction and especially in his poetry, where, in one instance, he watches some soldiers marching and remarks—

> And I am I, and they are they,
> And *this* is *this*, and *that* is *that*,
> . . . .
> And the wind has neither home nor hope
> And cause is cause, effect, effect. . . .

As against this sense of fragmentation and loneliness, Coleridge's sense of "the One Life we all live" (as Warren's essay on Coleridge described it) must have arisen from *The Ancient Mariner* with redeeming force, to judge by Warren's subsequent use of the idea. Such an irruption of "cosmic consciousness," as James called it, enters *All the King's Men* by way of the "judgment of the cows," who—together with an occasional negro chopping cotton or a woman throwing out water—stand and observe the vehicles of the book's important people hurtle by throughout the narrative. Such intuitions of the "One Life" are sustained with increased conviction in Warren's later writing, culminating in Warren's concept of an osmosis of being in a 1955 essay: "[Man is] in the world with continual and intimate interpenetration, an inevitable osmosis of being, which in the end . . . [merges] the ugly with the beautiful, the slayer with the slain, [evoking] such a sublimation that the world which once provoked . . . fear and disgust may now be totally loved." In *Flood*, his "Romance" published in 1964, Warren adds the word *mystic* to this formulation: "There's some spooky interpenetration of things, a mystic osmosis of being, you might say." And in his "Ballad of a Sweet Dream of Peace," in *Promises* (1957), Warren distills his intuition of cosmic unity into what I believe to be the single most important line in his fourteen volumes of poetry: ". . . all Time is a dream, and we're all one Flesh, at last."

Warren's lengthy journey toward this monistic insight occupied approximately the first third of his nearly sixty years as a man of letters. His first book, about John Brown the abolitionist, and his first couple of novels, *Night Rider* and *At Heaven's Gate*, portray a world broken into solipsistic fragments, with the Warren persona, behind his social mask, typically living out some incommunicably private dream from which he might emerge abruptly to do violence to some other actor. Warren's poetry during those first two decades of his career comprises a gallery of *isolatos*: the passing stranger in "To a Face in a Crowd," the runaway murderer in "Pondy Woods," the bereft son in "The Return: An Elegy," the disenchanted lovers in "Love's Parable," "Bearded Oaks," "Picnic Remembered," and—most solipsistic of all—"Monologue at Midnight." Finally, in the "Mexico Is a Foreign Country" sequence, the narrator raises his complaint to the highest level:

—Each pours his tale into the Great Schismatic's ear.

For God works well the Roman plan,
Divide and rule, mango and man,
And on hate's axis the great globe grinds in its span.

His conversion from this outlook by means of an irruption of cosmic consciousness precipitated, in the middle

156

1940's, Warren's finest work in the two genres that he has mastered: in fiction, *All the King's Men*; in poetry, "The Ballad of Billie Potts." In a slightly earlier poem, "Pursuit," the incubation—as James might call it—of the new outlook might be witnessed in the definition of love as "a groping Godward, though blind,/No matter what crevice, cranny, chink, bright in dark, the pale tentacle find," and in a foreglimpse of the osmotic vision: "Solution, perhaps, is public, despair personal/ . . . There are many states, and towns in them, and faces." But the full flowering of Warren's cosmic consciousness first entered Warren's creative literature at the end of "The Ballad of Billie Potts."

Here the osmosis of being becomes manifest in the vast spectacle of the world's creatures coming "home," to their source in eternity. Bankrupt and without resource in his surface existence, the human wanderer in this poem finds significance at last only through his participation in that subconscious purpose shared by even the lowliest creatures:

> The bee knows, and the eel's cold ganglia burn,
> And the sad head lifting to the long return,
> Through brumal deeps, in the great unsolsticed coil,
> Carries its knowledge, navigator without star,
> And under the stars, pure in its clamorous toil,
> The goose hoots north where the starlit marshes are.
> The salmon heaves at the fall, and, wanderer, you
> Heave at the great fall of Time, and gorgeous, gleam
> . . . .
> In your plunge, fling, and plunge to the thunderous stream:
> Back to the silence, back to the pool, back
> To the high pool, motionless, and the unmurmuring dream.

In language charged with religious diction, Warren displays the "reconciling, unifying" effect of cosmic consciousness in that his formerly isolated persona now becomes "Brother to pinion and the pious fin" in that grand odyssey, and in that he may now accept his mortality:

> And you, wanderer, back

157

After the striving and the wind's word,
To kneel
Here in the evening empty of wind or bird,
To kneel in the sacramental silence of evening. . . .

Like James's other converts from the sick soul condition, as distinct from the innately healthy-minded, Warren backslides from his monistic optimism periodically. Often he contemplates the darker implications of his osmotic insight, as seen in the universal sharing of guilt in *Brother to Dragons* and *You, Emperors, and Others*. But once attained, the moment of cosmic consciousness proves tenacious enough to recur repeatedly in Warren's later writings. It produces the metaphor of "The Human Fabric" in "Fall Comes to Back-Country Vermont" (in *Tale of Time*, 1966), where a death in the community tears the human fabric but "in the act/Of rending irreparably the human fabric,/Death affirms the fact of that fabric." And it even impinges with great force upon Warren's criticism, as in this excerpt from his essay on Herman Melville (1945): "Melville's act was toward humanity, not away from it. He renounced all the prerogatives of individuality in order to enter into the destiny that binds all human beings in one great spiritual and emotional organism. He abdicated his independence so as to be incorporated into the mystical body of humanity."

Eventually, after a quarter-century of working at it, Warren completed his most elaborate expression of mystic insight, *Audubon: A Vision* (1969). Wholly immersed in nature among his birds, impassioned nearly to orgasm by the magnificence of the woman being hanged, Audubon is one of Warren's figures of grace who has learned "How thin is the membrance between himself and the world." After relating the events of his poem and rendering the obituary of its hero ("He died, and was mourned, who had loved the world"), Warren terminates his "Vision" of Audubon with a short lyric that surprisingly resembles one of James's testimonies in his

158

chapter on Mysticism. Warren's lyric, "Love and Knowledge," puts the question, "What is love?" and answers, "One name for it is knowledge." That Love and Knowledge disclose a sacrifice of every life to the One Flesh that goes on and on, and that they sustain a sacramental acceptance of mortality, is implied in the scene from "Billie Potts" we have looked at. Here in *Audubon* that theme is rendered in Warren's final vignette of the great French naturalist: "He slew them, at surprising distances, with his gun./Over a body held in his hand, his head was bowed low. . . ."

Much more could be said about Warren's recurrent expressions of cosmic consciousness, and about the dialectical tension that obtains in his work from the counterpoint between the ultimate reality of One Flesh and the immediate reality of individual identity. In William James's terminology, Warren is here confronting the dilemma of the monistic-pluralistic alternative, or the question of the One and the Many. Characteristically, Warren has sought, since attaining his monistic insight in "Billie Potts," to maintain both perspectives. As a religious philosopher, he has found redemptive meaning in the vision of One Flesh; as a literary artist, he has cared too much for individual beings to subsume them within a larger synthesis. In his "Osmosis of Being" speech of 1955, Warren himself declares the discrepancy: "Despite this osmosis of being to which I have referred, man's process of self-definition means that he distinguishes himself from other men. He disintegrates his primal instinctive sense of unity, he discovers separateness." Like our other Southern writers, then, Robert Penn Warren renders that paradox of community/isolation which seems so peculiarly extended within his native region: cosmic consciousness sufficient to disclose a "mystic osmosis of being," that "we're all one Flesh, at last," coexisting with a tragically profound sense of any individual's separateness from other beings. For our perhaps most pronounced example of this paradox, we turn to our final writer of

159

the South, again illustrative of conversion through cosmic consciousness, Carson McCullers.

6.

For Carson McCullers, cosmic consciousness is defined within the Spinozan tradition that "the highest good is the knowledge of the mind's union with the whole of nature."[6] Spinoza is mentioned by name several times in *The Heart Is a Lonely Hunter* (Dr. Copeland likes to read Spinoza, for example), and Spinozan pantheism is the actual religion of the book's original central character, Harry Minowitz, a Jew by descent—"Harry believed that after you were dead and buried you changed to plants and fire and dirt and clouds and water. It took thousands of years and then finally you were a part of all the world."

What James called "new intellectual insights" characterize the conversion experience in McCullers' fiction, because the intellect—"the *mind's* union" with nature—is paramount. Without that governance, feelings and emotions are untrustworthy, leading to a kind of love that produces only deeper loneliness for most McCullers characters. Love that focuses upon a single individual is the deadliest trap for these people, as the followers of John Singer in *The Heart* and the victims of the love triangle in *The Ballad of the Sad Cafe* learn. Also unavailing is the effort to join oneself to some idealized community,

---

[6] See B. A. G. Fuller, *A History of Philosophy, Part Two: Modern Philosophy* (New York: 1938), 118–119, and John Herman Randall, *The Career of Philosophy: From the Middle Ages to the Enlightenment* (New York: 1962), p. 453. Other quotations are cited from Johann Eduard Erdmann, *A History of Philosophy*, Volume II (London: 1889), p. 86; *The Heart Is a Lonely Hunter*, pp. 228, 114, 26–27, 193, 304–5, 113, 306–7; *The Ballad of the Sad Cafe and Other Stories* (New York: 1964), pp. 147, 149, 151; *Clock Without Hands* (New York: 1963), pp. 134, 211, 213, 208–9; Carson McCullers, *The Mortgaged Heart* (New York: 1972), pp. 311, 319; T. S. Eliot, "The Dry Salvages," Part III, in *Four Quartets*.

like the socialist society envisioned by Jake Blount and Dr. Copeland or the wedding party that eventually leaves Frankie Adams forlorn in *The Member of the Wedding*.

The conversion from "spiritual isolation," which McCullers called "the basis of most of my themes," to the mind's union with the whole of reality, her answer to the problem, is effected by means of a secondary tenet of the Spinozan philosophy, one greatly admired by Goethe: "He who loves God truly cannot desire that God should love him in return." It is no coincidence that the most admirable exponents of spiritual love in modern literature have been sexless creatures: Faulkner's Dilsey, Hemingway's Jake Barnes, Eliot's Tiresias, Updike's George Caldwell, McCullers' Biff Brannon. So Carson McCullers defines the contrast between erotic love, which yearns for responsive love from its object of passion, and agape love, which wants nothing in return. "The passionate, individual love—the old Tristan-Isolde love, the Eros love—is inferior to the love of God, to fellowship, to the love of Agape—the Greek god of the feast, the God of brotherly love—and of man." Carried to its ultimate degree, this agape love for the whole of reality, just as it is, without requiring any love in return, leads to McCullers' version of cosmic consciousness.

Her simplest expression of the Spinozan principle is in the short story, "A Tree, A Rock, A Cloud." Here the Spinozan visionary, whose namelessness helps underscore his escape from his separate identity, had originally unified his being around an erotic passion. "Then I met this woman. . . . I met her at a filling station and we were married within three days. And do you know what it was like? . . . All I had ever felt was gathered together around this woman. Nothing lay around loose in me any more but was finished up by her." With the failure—inevitable in McCullers—of the personal relationship (the man's wife left him for another man), her protagonist descends into the sick soul state preparatory to receiving the unifying, reconciling insight. "I was a sick mortal. . . . I boozed. I fornicated. . . . When I recall that period it is all curdles in my mind, it was so terrible." What rescues McCullers' sick soul, converting him into the twice-born state, is the gradual growth of his "science of love"—the word *science* indicating the intellectual discipline necessary for acquiring this kind of love.

The mind's union with the whole of nature in this short story begins with the state of passivity that James identified (p. 293) in all forms of mystic experience: "Peace. A queer and beautiful blankness. It was spring in Portland and the rain came every afternoon. All evening I just stayed there on my bed in the dark. And that is how the science came to me." In this case the rain appears to be a psychedelic agent illustrating James's perception that "Certain aspects of nature seem to have a peculiar power of awakening such mystical moods" (p. 302). The full fruition of this cosmic consciousness in the McCullers story is a love that radiates out from the lover without any love, or even knowledge of his existence, returning from the loved objects: "For six years now I have . . . built up my science. And now I am a master, Son. I can love anything . . . a street full of people . . . a bird in the sky . . . a traveler on the road. Everything, Son. And anybody. All stranger and all loved!" Something greatly similar to this experience occurs in one of James's testimonies, whose author likewise participated in the whole of nature without requiring any cognizance of his own being in return: " . . . the moments of which I speak did not hold the consciousness of a personality, but something in myself made me feel myself a part of something bigger than I. . . . I felt myself one with the grass, the trees, birds, insects, everything in Nature. I exulted in the mere fact of existence, of being a part of it all—the drizzling rain, the shadows of the clouds, the tree-trunks . . ." (p. 303).

The importance of Biff Brannon, McCullers' finest portrayal of the Spinozan insight, in *The Heart Is a Lonely Hunter*, her finest novel, is implied in the book's organization: Brannon's vision "of the endless fluid passage of humanity through endless time" occupies the closing pages, transmitting the book's final wisdom. Two allusive figures shadow the text, Christ and Spinoza. Both are related to John Singer, who serves as a personal Savior to the book's lonely people, whose death occurs at the appropriately Christlike age of thirty-three, and who has "something gentle and Jewish" in his face, reminding Dr. Copeland of his beloved philosopher Spinoza. But it is actually Biff Brannon, and not Singer, who deserves the allusive analogies. It is his kindly sympathy for all the others, not Singer's bewilderment, that exemplifies Alice's Sunday School lesson, "And the text is, 'All men seek for Thee.' " In this context, Biff's cruciform position—indicating vicarious suffering—and his sun-caused halo outweigh Singer's claim as a Christ-figure: "Biff stretched both of his arms outward and crossed his naked feet. . . . with the closed, shrunken eyelids and the heavy, iron-like beard on his cheeks and jaw. . . . The hard, yellow rays of the sun came in through the window so that . . . Biff turned wearily and covered his eyes with his hands." And it is Biff who is actually Jewish, "an eighth part Jew," and whose great-grandfather "was a Jew from Amsterdam" (Spinoza's city).

The two Spinozan tenets as related to Biff require the whole novel for development. First, although freed from Eros by his impotence, Biff must overcome his inclination to settle his love on a single person: "And Mick. The one who in the last months had lived so strangely in his heart. Was that love done with too? Yes. It was finished." And secondly, he must convert that singular love into a science of love like that in "A Tree, A Rock, A Cloud": "But who would he be loving now? No one person. Anybody decent who came in out of the street to sit for an hour and have a drink. But no one person."

As in the short story, the novel portrays the attainment

of cosmic consciousness as requiring years of disciplined spiritual growth, attested in Biff's case by milestones of passage: his broadening range of love objects, including "freaks"; his escape from Eros into androgyny, as evidenced in his having a heavy, dark beard while also using perfume and hair rinse; his assumption of responsibility for others, in managing Singer's funeral and assisting Jake's getaway, though Jake has despised Biff as a capitalist cafe-owner; and his twenty-year newspaper collection, "docketed and outlined and complete," again managed like a "science" to show his "mind's union" with the larger human community.

And in the end he is vouchsafed the moment of mystic insight, irrupting into the dead silence and solitude of night when "Loneliness gripped him so that his breath quickened." Replacing the "dead feelings" and "cold beliefs" of his past loves, Alice and Mick, is a new "hot place" in Biff's consciousness:

> The silence in the room was deep as the night itself. . . . Then suddenly he felt a quickening in him. His heart turned. . . For in a swift radiance of illumination he saw a glimpse of human struggle and of valor. Of the endless fluid passage of humanity through endless time. And of those who labor and those who—one word— love. His soul expanded.

After this, as T. S. Eliot said, our exile. Biff's vision lasts "for a moment only," followed by "a shaft of terror" that leaves him "suspended between radiance and darkness. Between bitter irony and faith." He has arrived, in short, at the concept of tragedy as a universal experience that gives community to all men. But brief as it is, that glimpse of "the endless fluid passage of humanity through endless time" suffices to subsume "The riddle. The question that had taken root in him and would not let him rest. The puzzle of Singer and the rest of them. . . . —something like an ugly joke." Like Eliot's convert who is advised from the *Bhagavad Gita* to do his job unques-

164

tioningly, "Which shall fructify in the lives of others," Biff resumes his role as priest offering communion in his True Church, the New York Cafe, fortified by his vision: "Somehow he remembered that the awning had not yet been raised. . . . And when at last he was inside again, he composed himself to await the morning sun."

Carson McCullers' other "big" novel, *Clock Without Hands* (1961), was not received with the kind of acclaim that greeted her earlier work; one cannot doubt that her deteriorating health seriously undermined McCullers' creative powers over her last two decades. But *Clock Without Hands* does render, as its primary purpose I believe, a final portrayal of psychic conversion through cosmic consciousness. In this case, the recipient of mystic insight is J. T. Malone, afflicted with cancer (the clock without hands) but able to accept his dying by grace of the conversion experience. Malone's life, like those portrayed in all McCullers' other books, had been profoundly afflicted in youth by the trauma of alienation from his own innermost self, caused in his case by a marriage without passion.

> And ever afterward there was no particular time when he regretted marrying Martha, but regret, or disappointment was certainly there. There was no particular time when he asked "Is this all there is of life?" but as he grew older he asked it wordlessly. No, he had not lost an arm, or a leg, or any particular five dollars, but little by little he had lost his own self.

Like McCullers' other personae, Malone first tries to alleviate his emptiness with an erotic interlude, a summer affair with a secretary, but in the end he too finds his peace in an irruption of cosmic consciousness:

> Yes the earth had revolved its seasons and spring had come again. But there was no longer a revulsion against nature, against things. A strange lightness had come upon his soul and he exalted. He looked at nature now and it was part of himself. He was no longer a man watching a clock without hands. He was not alone, he did not

rebel, he did not suffer. He did not even think of death these days. He was not a man dying . . . nobody died, everybody died.

Just before his death, Malone displays the "science of love" by investing his emotions in strangers who know nothing of him: "Yet the last flush of life was with him. His spirit was strangely raw that day. In the *Milan Courier* he read that a man had saved a child from burning and had lost his own life. Although Malone did not know the child or the man, he began to cry, and kept on crying. . . . he was possessed by a strange euphoria."

Like Robert Penn Warren, Carson McCullers evidently attempted through her more philosophical personae to resolve the dilemma that William James described as "the final question of philosophy," that of the "monistic-pluralistic alternative," or the One and the Many. Like Warren, McCullers maintains both alternatives, seeing reality as having both one collective identity and many separate identities simultaneously. Toward the end of *Clock Without Hands*, the rider in an airplane may glimpse the Spinozan monistic perspective:

> Looking downward from an altitude of two thousand feet, the earth assumes order. A town . . . is symmetrical, exact as a small gray honeycomb, complete. The surrounding terrain seems designed by a law more just and mathematical than the laws of property and bigotry: a dark parallelogram of pine woods, square fields, rectangles of sward. . . . From this height you do not see man and the details of his humiliation. The earth from a great distance is perfect and whole.

But McCullers would not be an artist if she were to rest solely at that distance from individual human beings. The detachment that might serve the philosopher becomes untenable for the philosophical novelist, whose double vision—of the One and the Many—here represents a qualification, though not, I believe, a repudiation, of her Spinozan-style cosmic consciousness:

> Gliding downward, low over the town and countryside, the whole

breaks up into a multiplicity of impressions. . . . As you circle inward, the town itself becomes crazy and complex. . . . Gray fences, factories, the flat main street. From the air men are shrunken and they have an automatic look, like wound-up dolls. They seem to move mechanically among haphazard miseries. You do not see their eyes. And finally this is intolerable. The whole earth from a great distance means less than one long look into a pair of human eyes.

7.

Among other expressions of mystic consciousness in the South, one might mention the poetry of Archie Ammons and the fiction of Reynolds Price, whose vision of his parents returning from death (in *Love and Work*) actually exceeds anything in William James's range of assertion.[7] (In his Postscript to the *Varieties*, James said, "Facts, I think, are yet lacking to prove 'spirit-return' "—p. 395). By way of transition to our greatest exponent of mysticism, the non-Southerner Hart Crane, we might also glance at a few mystical fragments in John Updike's writing.

Part of Updike's support for his belief in a spiritual universe rests on what James referred to as "medical materialism" in his chapter on "Religion and Neurology": "for aught we know to the contrary, 103° or 104° Fahrenheit might be a much more favorable temperature for truths to sprout in, than the more ordinary blood-heat of 97 or 98 degrees". In "Fever" (a poem in *Verse*), Updike reports on a psychedelic experience greatly similar to those we shall see brought on by alcohol or ether in Hart Crane's poetry:

> I have brought back a good message from the land of 102°:
> God exists.

---

[7] *Love and Work* (New York: 1968), pp. 142–3. Also cited is *The Centaur* (New York: Fawcett, 1963), p. 127.

I had seriously doubted it before;
but the bedposts spoke of it with utmost confidence,
the threads in my blanket took it for granted,
the tree outside the window dismissed all complaints,
and I have not slept so justly for years.
It is hard, now to convey
how emblematically things sat
upon the membranes of my consciousness. . . .

Something similarly mystical happens to Peter Caldwell in *The Centaur* when, falling asleep, he experiences cosmic consciousness while passing the border between consciousness and unconsciousness: "as the dissolution of drowsiness crept toward me, a sensation . . . of enormity entered my cells, and I seemed a giant who included in his fingernails all the galaxies that are. This sensation operated not only in space but in time." Metaphysical intuitions like these, deriving from sources outside of ordinary consciousness, are peripheral to Updike's religious thought, perhaps to some degree because of his willful commitment to established Christian dogma. For Hart Crane, however, direct and immediate immersion in the "higher consciousness" of mystical perception was the sole function of poetry.

8.

In the end, we must judge the success of Hart Crane's verse in Jamesian terms; the failure of his life in Freudian terms. Before going into our Jamesian analysis, we might admit a few Freudian insights by way of a context. Topping the list, the struggle for sexual identity no doubt loomed foremost in Crane's final, fatal torments, a struggle that had Crane on one day paying lavish tribute to Peggy Cowley for rescuing him from homosexuality—"I am very happy because I have discovered I am not a homosexual"—while on another day he might revert to his old ways categorically: "She thinks she can reform me, does she? I'll show her! Why, God damn her, I'd rather sleep with a man any day than with her!"[8] That struggle in turn clearly stems from his unhappy relationship with his parents, both of whom seemed to typify classic homosexual background influences. Of the elder Cranes, the cold and aloof father was trouble enough for the estranged poet, who at times felt wholly abandoned: "CA's silence can mean only one thing to me now—an absolute denial and confession of complete indifference—if not enmity." The possessive and domineering mother, however, was much the greater burden—a woman capable even after her son's tragic suicide of rendering the following remarkable analysis:

> All my life I have devoted myself to his interests and ambitions, have sacrificed anything to help him. . . . Hart's disintegration began when he let go of me—and he went straight to Hell, from then. . . . His life was wholly selfish—consequently destructive to his career and happiness. If he had done as he should, showed me consideration and respect, I am sure he would be alive today. . . .

Compounding these sources of pain was that ultimate despair of any artist, the sense of failing creativity. Just a few weeks before his immolation, he wrote in humiliation—his publisher's advance money by now completely dissipated—" Of the 'Epic' [a poem about the Spanish Conquest he had gone to Mexico to write]—I haven't yet written a line." And crowning it all, by 1932 the country of Crane's prophetic vision seemed darkening into a Spenglerian decline contradicting not only his mystic utterances in *The Bridge*, but his fundamental feeling that "any true expression must rest on faith in

---

[8] John Unterecker, *Voyager: A Life of Hart Crane* (New York: 1969), pp. 739, 736. Other quotations are cited from this book, pp. 353, 756, 741, 187, 355–6; Philip Horton, *Hart Crane* (New York: 1937), pp. 131, 144, 126–7, 146, 167, 84, 122; Allen Tate, *Collected Essays* (Denver: 1959), p. 288; *The Complete Poems and Selected Letters and Prose of Hart Crane*, ed. Brom Weber (New York: 1966), pp. 231–2, 221–2, 235; Malcolm Cowley, *Exile's Return* (New York: 1951), p. 228; Carl Gustav Jung, *The Undiscovered Self* (New York: 1959), p. 110; and Robert Penn Warren (see "osmosis of being" in Note 5 above).

something": "With all the world going to hell—what can one gather together with any confidence these days anyway?"

It all adds up to a profound case of the Jamesian sick soul condition, a state wherefrom a man whose life has lost its meaning must become "born again" or "converted" in order to be happy. Indeed, Allen Tate, in his Crane Obituary, felt that something like a Jamesian Second Birth had been Crane's only hope for survival: "Suicide was the sole act of will left to him short of a profound alteration of character." Such an alteration, unhappily, was not to be forthcoming, yet—in fairness to Crane's life and art—it seems better to let William James rather than Freud have the main say. As a rational atheist, Freud dismissed both art and religion as "Illusions," and hence enemies of his "science," whereas James, with his unbiased curiosity toward all psychic phenomena, has much to say about the central feature of Crane's poetic vision, his mysticism. And Crane in his turn drew solid satisfaction from his readings in James's *Varieties* for its "corroboration of several experiences in consciousness that I have had."

Although Crane left these "corroborations" unspecified, we may identify two elements in James's study as holding special relevance to Crane's life as an artist. These would be James's validation of the mystic's resort to psychedelic stimuli, and his clarification of several phases of mystic consciousness. Concerning the origin of the "higher mystical flights," James thought it most reasonable (p. 327) "to ascribe them to inroads from the subconscious life," thereby marking a milestone of sorts towards Jung's conclusion that "the unconscious is the only accessible source of religious experience." In some of his cases, James noted that mystic perception occurred without the mediation of psychedelic agents. James Russell Lowell enjoyed an unsolicited revelation of God, as cited in James's chapter on "The Reality of the Unseen": ". . . last Friday evening . . . I was at Mary's, and happening to say something of the presence of spirits, . . . the whole system rose up before

170

me. . . . I never before so clearly felt the Spirit of God in me and around me. The whole room seemed to me full of God . . ." (p. 67). Another example, closer to Crane's experience, is provided by Lord Tennyson's reminiscence of a mystic trance wherein the poet's "individuality itself seemed to dissolve and fade away into boundless being . . .—the loss of personality (if so it were) seeming no extinction, but the only true life" (p. 295).

Unlike Lowell's and Tennyson's spontaneous visions, Crane's were heavily reliant on psychedelic agents. As attested by the poet's own words, we might classify five mind-expanders in particular as having outstanding potency and importance, each of them leading to that "consciousness of illumination" that James identified as "the essential mark of the 'mystical' state" (p. 313n):

1. GAS: "At times, dear Gorham, I feel an enormous power in me—that seems almost supernatural. . . . Did I tell you of that thrilling experience this last winter in the dentist's chair when under the influence of ether and amnesia my mind spiralled to a kind of seventh heaven of consciousness and . . . a voice kept saying to me—'You have the higher consciousness—you have the higher consciousness.' . . . O Gorham, I have known moments in eternity."

2. LIQUOR: "[My] subconscious [comes] out through gates that only alcohol has the power to open." "If I could afford wine *every* evening, I might do more. . . . However, today I have made a good start on the first part of 'Faustus and Helen.' "

3. MUSIC. "Modern music almost drives me crazy! . . . My hair [has] stood on end at its revelations."

4. LOVE: "I have seen the Word made Flesh. I mean nothing less, . . . where a purity of joy was reached that included tears. . . . And I have [had] . . . the ecstasy of walking hand in hand across the most beautiful bridge in the world, the cables enclosing us and pulling us upward in such a dance as I

171

have never walked and can never walk with another."

5. THE SEA: "I think the sea has thrown itself upon me and
been answered, at least in part, and I believe I am a little
changed . . . changed and transubstantiated. . . . And my
eyes have been kissed with a speech that is beyond words
entirely."

In assessing the validity of Hart Crane's poetry, it is
significant for us that James's book endorses each one of these
psychedelic agents as perfectly legitimate and efficacious in
inducing mystical consciousness. James's endorsement of
these pathways to mystic awareness is precise and absolute.
Concerning gas, he observed that "Nitrous oxide and ether
. . . stimulate the mystical consciousness in an extraordinary
degree. Depth beyond depth of truth seems revealed to the
inhaler," and he further went on to report that "Some years
ago I myself made some observations on this aspect of nitrous
oxide intoxication. . . . One conclusion was forced upon my
mind at that time, and my impression of its truth has ever since
remained unshaken. It is that our normal waking consciousness, rational consciousness as we call it, is but one special
type of consciousness, whilst all about it, parted from it by the
filmiest of screens, there lie potential forms of consciousness
entirely different. . . . No account of the universe in its totality
can be final which leaves these other forms of consciousness
quite disregarded" (p. 298). A likely example of the "corroboration of several experiences in consciousness I have had"—to
quote Crane's letter about James's *Varieties*—would be the
testimony of the English poet J. A. Symonds while under
chloroform: "After the choking and stifling had passed away
. . . , I thought that I was near death; when, suddenly, my
soul became aware of God, who was manifestly dealing with
me, handling me, so to speak, in an intense personal present
reality. I felt him streaming in like light upon me. . . . I cannot
describe the ecstasy I felt" (pp. 300–1).

About alcohol, James drew much the same conclusions:

"The sway of alcohol over mankind is unquestionably due to its power to stimulate the mystical faculties of human nature, usually crushed to earth by the cold facts and dry criticisms of the sober hour. Sobriety diminishes, discriminates, and says no; drunkenness expands, unites, and says yes. It is in fact the great exciter of the *Yes* function in man. It brings its votary from the chill periphery of things to the radiant core. It makes him for the moment one with truth. . . . The drunken consciousness is one bit of the mystic consciousness . . ." (p. 297). Crane admitted in "The Wine Menagerie" that mere booze was often his path to the higher vision, with the result that when "wine redeems the sight" he might be able to glimpse "New thresholds, new anatomies!" or feel "August meadows somewhere clasp his brow"; unlike James, with his narrower experience of these matters, Crane also renders the sad terminus of the alcoholic revelation, the charm of those August meadows lapsing back into ordinary reality ("the treason of the snow") and thence—even worse—into delirium tremens, with Holofernes' and John the Baptist's severed heads floating by.

In addition to gas, alcohol, and other drugs, James attributed the "sense of deeper significance" to such natural agencies as "effects of light on land and sea, odors and musical sounds" (p. 294), this latter agent being especially potent psychedelically: "not conceptual speech, but music rather, is the element through which we are best spoken to by mystical truth. . . . Music gives us ontological messages which nonmusical criticism is unable to contradict" (pp. 322–323). Impressive testimony supports James on this point, including Schopenhauer's definition of music as the only art that looks *directly* into the cosmic Will, Whitman's perception of "the puzzle of puzzles,/And that we call Being" in his catalogue on music in Section 26 of *Song of Myself*, and T. S. Eliot's response to "music heard so deeply/That it is not heard at all, but you are the music/While the music lasts" in *Four Quartets*. Crane's best known tribute to what music can do is the jazz party on the roof in "For the Marriage of Helen and Faustus"—"O I have known metallic paradises" (the horns playing) "Above the deft catastrophes of drums"—but better yet was music in combination with another psychedelic agent, which taken in tandem might liberate not only Crane's mystic but his creative consciousness. Malcolm Cowley's reminiscence of the artist at work, after some serious drinking at a party, points up these complementary stimulations: ". . . a little later he disappeared . . . we would hear a new hubbub through the walls of his room—the phonograph playing a Cuban rumba, the typewriter clacking simultaneously; then . . . the typewriter [would] stop while Hart changed the record, . . . perhaps to Ravel's *Bolero*."

Above all, any sights or sounds connected with the sea could fix Crane's vision upon what James called "the vivified face of the world, as it may appear to converts after their waking" (p. 361). Thus the breaking surf on a calm day creates thunder and lightning for Crane's heightened sense at the outset of *Voyages*: "The sun beats lightning on the waves,/The waves fold thunder on the sand." And "Repose of Rivers" describes Crane's first such mystic moment, with the delta seascape totally absorbing the poet into its sights and sounds amid a Wordsworthian hush of willows, an epiphany so intense that he "would have bartered" his Ohio childhood's best memories for it. When his love affairs were going well, the sea additionally served as the only serviceable symbol of his passion's magnitude; thus, his love for Emil Oppfer attains oceanic boundlessness in *Voyages III*, which deems the ocean currents of smaller magnitude than the "stream of love advancing now/ . . . , singing, . . ./Through clay aflow immortally to you." But these heights of joy could be overmatched by the depths of anguish that followed upon the loved one's infidelity or departure, as we see in *Voyages*, and then the sea

174

proved to be Crane's ultimate and truest soul-mate, the visible, audible, and palpable symbol not only of his rimless passions but of the Absolute towards which he yearned like a lover.

Whatever its genesis, the mystic consciousness that is produced anaesthetically always involves "a monistic insight," in James's phraseology (p. 299), a passage "as from a smallness into a vastness" and into "reconciling, unifying states" (p. 319). A typical instance of such monistic absorption in the *Varieties* is that of a German woman, Malwida von Meysenburg, who, after years of being unable to pray, was suddenly smitten at seaside much like Crane in "Repose of Rivers": "I was impelled to kneel down, this time before the illimitable ocean, symbol of the Infinite. I felt that I prayed as I had never prayed before, and knew now what prayer really is: to return from the solitude of individuation into the consciousness of unity with all that is. . . . Earth, heaven, and sea resounded as in one vast world-encircling harmony" (p. 304). Crane's experience of some such monistic insight is evident in his declaration that "the true idea of God is the only thing that can give happiness—and that is the identification of yourself with *all of life*" (emphasis Crane's). In saying this, Crane bears out James's conclusion in his "Postscript" to the *Varieties* that through religious experience "we can experience union with *something* larger than ourselves and in that union find our greatest peace" (p. 395).

As to what that *something* is, James further concludes that "All that the facts require is that the power should be both other and larger than our conscious selves" (p. 396). When such a connection to something "other and larger than our conscious selves" reaches the extent of Crane's "identification of yourself with *all of life*," we are witness to the phenomenon that James calls "cosmic consciousness," a state of mind repeatedly evidenced in the documents James analyzes in his chapter on "Mysticism." As one who could see "All hours clapped dense into a single stride" ("Recitative"), who worshipped the sea for the "Infinite consanguinity it bears" (*Voyages III*), and who devoted his imagination to making a bridge from "us lowliest . . . to God" ("To Brooklyn Bridge" in *The Bridge*), Hart Crane obviously falls under James's definition of the mystic as one who sees the world's "various forms . . . absorbed into the One" (p. 299). "This overcoming of all the usual barriers between the individual and the Absolute is the great mystic achievement," James went on to say, calling it "the everlasting and triumphant mystical tradition, hardly altered by differences in clime or creed," the same in "Hinduism, in Neoplatonism, in Sufism, in Christian mysticism, in Whitmanism . . ." (p. 321).

In joining the poet to "*all of life*," Crane's mysticism displays all four of the characteristics that James identified as typical of the phenomenon—ineffability (a trait that renders some of Crane's verse unintelligible), noetic quality, transiency, and passivity. Of these, the trait of passivity seems most significant in Crane's case, enabling him to feel—in James's words—"as if his own will were in abeyance, and indeed sometimes as if he were grapsed and held by a superior power" (p. 293). Crane's best moments in poetry, those immensely passionate compressions of vision and feeling, resulted from the poet's seizure by some such superior power; by "the imaged Word" in *Voyages*, the "Hand of Fire" in *The Bridge*, the "volcano [that] burst" in "Emblems of Conduct." "Possessions"—Crane's master poem on the creative impulse—shows the poet waiting like Ben Franklin in the storm, hoping to attract the divine lightning to his "key, ready to hand," his passivity attested by his "sifting/Through a thousand nights . . . for bolts that linger/Hidden" and the transiency of the experience attested by his hope to "Accumulate such moments to an hour." Later in the poem Crane compares himself to Moses on Sinai, again encompassed to the horizon by a fierce storm and waiting for the deific lightning to strike the "stone" he carries—Crane's verse, like Moses' tablets, being "writ by the finger of God":

> The pure possession, the inclusive cloud
> Whose heart is fire shall come,—the white wind rase
> All but bright stones wherein our smiling plays.

In the light of the Jamesian system, two somewhat contradictory aspects of mysticism stand out in this poem. First, Crane's description of his poetry as "bright" and "smiling" on the last line above sustains James's contention that "the mystic range of consciousness . . . *is on the whole . . . optimistic, or at least the opposite of pessimistic*" (emphasis his, p. 323). Given his sense of mission, Crane was normally unable to write a line except in affirmation, so much so that in a letter to Waldo Frank he worried about his readings in Spengler and Eliot possibly aborting *The Bridge*, then in composition. On the other hand, "Possessions" illustrates most vividly mysticism's greatest peril, the possible annihilation of the ego—a natural enough concomitant of cosmic consciousness. In this connection, the "stone" in stanza one becomes transmuted via Crane's "logic of metaphor" into a sacrificial altar, the poet himself becoming immolated on the altar's horns ("Tossed on these horns, who bleeding dies") following his "one moment in sacrifice (the direst)" under the sky-bolt. Crane himself said that "A poem like 'Possessions' really cannot be technically explained" but I think a few analogies from James's book can be illuminating. In the *Varieties*, three accounts of "possessions" in particular—all couched in terms similar to Crane's imagery of fire and electricity—display an interesting pattern with respect to the risk of annihilation. The mildest of these experiences, happily devoid of annihilative overtones, occurred when that which Crane called "the inclusive cloud/Whose heart is fire" fell upon Walt Whitman's Canadian friend, Dr. R. M. Bucke (pp. 306–7):

All at once, without warning of any kind, I found myself wrapped in a flame-colored cloud. For an instant I thought of fire, an immense conflagration somewhere close by in that great city; the next, I knew that the fire was within myself. Directly afterward there came upon me a sense of exultation, of immense joyousness accompanied or immediately followed by an intellectual illumination impossible to describe. Among other things, . . . I saw that the universe is . . . a living Presence. . . .

Another who felt the "Hand of Fire"—but with markedly more danger of annihilation—was Charles G. Finney, the nineteenth century evangelist whose baptism in the Holy Spirit assumed a nearly unbearable intensity (p. 204):

As I turned and was about to take a seat by the fire, I received a mighty baptism in the Holy Ghost. Without any expectation of it, without ever having the thought in my mind that there was any such thing for me, . . . the Holy Spirit descended upon me in a manner that seemed to go through me, body and soul. I could feel the impression, like a wave of electricity, going through me and through me. Indeed, it seemed to come in waves and waves of liquid love. . . . These waves came over me, and over me, and over me, one after the other, until I recollect I cried out, "I shall die if these waves continue to pass over me." I said, "Lord, I cannot bear any more. . . ."

Our final analogue, involving a woman under ether for surgery, describes the divine presence in imagery remarkably parallel to that of Crane's outcry to the "Hand of Fire" in *The Bridge*—"Eloihim, still I hear thy sounding heel" ("Ave Maria") (pp. 301–302n):

A great Being or Power was traveling through the sky, his foot was on a kind of lightning as a wheel is on a rail, it was his pathway. The lightning was made entirely of the spirits of innumerable people close to one another, and I was one of them. He moved in a straight line, and each part of the streak or flash came into its short conscious existence only that he might travel. I seemed to be directly under the foot of God. . . . I was the means of his achieving and revealing something, I know not what or to whom. . . .

Passages like these from James's *Varieties* can clarify and validate the most crucial aspect of Crane's mysticism in poetry, his hope for "conquest of consciousness" through promulgating "certain spiritual illuminations, shining with a morality essentialized from experience directly, and not from previous precepts or preconceptions." Such passages further clarify the sense of spiritual risk and sacrifice inherent in so much of Crane's work: the moth bending toward "the still/Imploring flame" in "Legend"; the "One moment in sacrifice (the direst)" in "Possessions"; the submission to the heel of Eloihim in *The Bridge*; and the "Kiss of our agony" offered to the gathering "Hand of Fire" in "The Tunnel."

It is curious how Crane's tone calms when his absorption into the All occurs in the context of water rather than fire. Once past the warning note of *Voyages I*, "The bottom of the sea is cruel," we find the actual absorption in and annihilation by the sea to yield a wholly desirable state, a union with the Absolute devoutly to be wished (*Voyages III*):

> Light wrestling there incessantly with light,
> Star kissing star through wave on wave unto
> Your body rocking!
>   and where death, if shed,
> Presumes no carnage, but this single change,—
> Upon the steep floor flung from dawn to dawn
> The silken skilled transmemberment of song. . . .

We may never know whether some such siren's song as this lured Crane to his final leap overboard, or whether he was impelled by the darker forces—as previously noted—gathering behind him, his alcoholism, his sense of failing talent, and his inability to sustain the heterosexual life style that his elopement with Peggy Cowley (Malcolm Cowley's first wife) implied. Here, in any case, James's *The Varieties of Religious Experience* ceases to apply, the relevant analogues being found rather in the mood captured by other artists: Walt Whitman "Lost in the loving floating ocean of thee/Laved in the flood of thy bliss O death" in "Lilacs"; Faulkner's suicide "in the caverns and grottoes of the sea tumbling peacefully" in *The*

179

Sound and the Fury; Robert Penn Warren's drowning victim "Tumbling and turning, hushed in the end,/With hair afloat in waters that gently bend" in *Kentucky Mountain Farm* (III); and T. S. Eliot's Phlebas the Phoenician finding in his death by water a serenity ("A current under sea/Picked his bones in whispers. . . .") similar to that of Crane's undersea figure, though in other respects Crane took Eliot and his *Waste Land* "as a point of departure towards an almost complete reversal of direction."

On the personal level, James's *Varieties* presents no parallels to these intimations of watery annihilation, but on the scale of human history at large, we may draw out from James and Crane one last correlation. One of Crane's most moving passages in poetry occurs at the end of the section of *The Bridge* called "The River," where the Mississippi's absorption into the ocean depths symbolizes the flow of time and history finding its terminus in eternity:

> . . . Ahead
> No embrace opens but the stinging sea
> The River lifts itself from its long bed,
>
> Poised wholly on its dream, a mustard glow
> Tortured with history, its one will—flow!
> —The Passion spreads in wide tongues, choked and slow,
> Meeting the Gulf, hosannas silently below.

Here, in appropriately religious language, Crane attests his purpose as a mystic poet, one whose "monistic insight" (in James's phrase) suffices to unify otherwise contradictory realities—life and death, time and eternity—into a final sacramental whole. Concerning such monistic insights, James observed that "the keynote . . . is invariably a reconciliation. It is as if the opposites of the world, whose contradictoriness and conflict make all our difficulties and troubles, were melted into unity" (p. 298). Other revelations of unity stud Crane's poems, and none more inspired than those in "Atlantis," which, although the final section of *The Bridge*, was written at the outset of composition when the poet's creative force was most intense. Here Crane speaks of the divine Cognizance "Within whose lariat sweep encinctured sing/In single chrysalis the many twain," and whose "multitudinous Verb" might link "tomorrows into yesteryear."

In images like these we may see the ultimate significance of Crane's statement that "the bridge is a symbol of all such poetry as I am interested in writing." To the extent that he succeeds in bridging the span between the finite self and ultimate reality, Crane may lead his readers into the "reconciling, unifying states" James spoke of (p. 319), thereby enabling them to "still love the world," as Crane put it in "Chaplinesque"—just as the poet of *The Waste Land* was enabled by his conversion to say, "I rejoice that things are as they are" in *Ash-Wednesday* (I), and Robert Penn Warren was able to apprehend "a mystic osmosis of being" that merges "the ugly with the beautiful, the slayer with the slain . . . [until] the world which once provoked . . . fear and disgust may now be totally loved." Such are the fruits of the monistic insight for Crane and others.

To conclude, then, our study shows that with respect to many important features of Crane's poems—their relation to psychedelic stimuli, their fire and water imagery, their mood of mingled fear and welcome towards annihilation of the ego, and above all, their striving to express monistic insight— William James's *The Varieties of Religious Experience* is an important and neglected source of understanding. Concerning Crane's tragic end as well as his poems, James provides further vindication, if we may apply what he says about conversions and backslidings with equal logic to the flights and crash landings of mysticism (p. 205):

> One word, before I close this lecture, on the question of the transiency or permanence of these abrupt conversions. Some of you, I feel sure, knowing that numerous backslidings and relapses take place, . . . dismiss it [the whole experience] with a pitying smile as so much "hysterics." Psychologically, as well as religiously, this is shallow. It misses the point of serious interest, which is . . . [that] it

181

reveals new flights and reaches of ideality while it lasts. . . . That it [conversion] should for even a short time show a human being what the highwater mark of his spiritual capacity is, this is what constitutes its importance. . . .

9.

To conclude this discussion of Mysticism, it seems appropriate to remark that our visionary poets and novelists have sometimes found surprising support within the scientific community. A less "mystical" writer than Charles Darwin would be hard to identify, yet Loren Eiseley terminates his book, *Darwin's Century*, with the great naturalist's version of the monistic insight:

> *"If we choose to let conjecture run wild, then animals, our fellow brethren in pain, disease, suffering and famine . . . may partake of our origin in one common ancestor—we may be all melted together."*
> Darwin was twenty-eight when he jotted down this paragraph in his notebook. If he had never conceived of natural selection, if he had never written the *Origin*, it would still stand as a statement of almost clairvoyant perception. . . . "We are all one— all melted together." It is for this, as much as for the difficult, concise reasoning of the *Origin*, that Darwin's shadow will run a long way forward into the future.[9]

It is well to think that art and science may fuse their ultimate perceptions, such that Darwin's shadow may in fact be perceptible in the visionary literature we have been considering— in Robert Penn Warren's assertion that "we are all one Flesh," for example. Interestingly, Mr. Warren has himself spoken of artists and scientists as "brother symbolists with merely a different kind of net for snaring 'reality.'"

---

[9] Loren Eiseley, *Darwin's Century* (New York: 1961), p. 352. Also cited are Robert Penn Warren's Lyric 3 of "Ballad of a Sweet Dream of Peace" in *Promises: Poems 1954–1956* and *Democracy and Poetry* (Cambridge: 1975), p. 51.

Whatever its source, however—whether derived from subconscious intuition or cultural stimuli or from studies in religion or science—the expression of mystic consciousness persists as a paramount impulse in literature. Concerning its value to the literary audience, we will leave it to William James himself to draw forth the largest extension of his meaning (p. 295):

> . . . lyric poetry and music are alive and significant only in proportion as they fetch these vague vistas of a life continuous with our own. . . . We are alive or dead to the eternal inner message of the arts according as we have kept or lost this mystic susceptibility.

Chapter VI

Saintliness

Of all the effects of religious consciousness, good behavior is undoubtedly the dullest. Virtuous character has ever been a most difficult thing for the literary artist to make credible and interesting, and even writers as pietistic as Dante and Milton wrote their most compelling verse about inhabitants of the infernal regions. Yet, for all its fascination with evil, serious literature has never departed radically from the heroic view of life which gave literature its birth in the epics and sacred writ of antiquity. Which is to say that after three millennia of gradually changing mores, inclination and duty remain the axis and circumference of the human squirrel cage, to cite a metaphor of Faulkner's.[1]

If anything, the deepening skepticism of our age, its sense of life as tragic or absurd, has only hastened the fulfillment of Matthew Arnold's prophecy that artists would be the priesthood of the coming era, as "more and more mankind will discover that we have to turn to poetry to interpret life for us."

---

[1] *Mosquitoes* (New York: 1953), p. 201. Also cited is Matthew Arnold, from C. F. Harrold and W. D. Templeman, *English Prose of the Victorian Period* (New York: 1938), p. 1248.

William James saw the religious function of literature as particularly efficacious in the area of the moral imagination: "Mankind is susceptible and suggestible in opposite directions, and the rivalry of influences is unsleeping. The saintly and the worldly ideal pursue their feud in literature as much as in real life" (p. 287). So people look now as in Homer's time to literature (including films) as well as to history, both sacred and secular, for characters to emulate and ideals to live by. They find, as James put it in his opening paragraph on "Saintliness," "a succession of such examples as . . . only in the readng of them, is to feel encouraged and uplifted and washed in better moral air" (p. 207).

1.

In our time, the literary climate of sophistication demands that those examples be presented subtly enough to avoid didacticism. Perhaps our last great didacticist among major American authors was Emerson (last because he outlived Thoreau), who in the Divinity School Address counted the greatest achievement of the Christian faith to be the institution of preaching (its other great achievement, the institution of the Sabbath, hearkens far back into Judaic history). So Emerson wrote essays, not fiction, preaching mainly on the value of saintliness, we may say, if we accept William James's broad definition of that concept (p. 215–216):

> The collective name for the ripe fruits of religion in a character is Saintliness. . . . and there is a certain composite photograph of universal saintliness, the same in all religions, of which the features can easily be traced.
> They are these:—
> 1. A feeling of being in a wider life than that of this world's selfish little interests; and a conviction, not merely intellectual, but as it were sensible of the existence of an Ideal Power. In Christian saintliness this power is always personified as God; but abstract moral ideals, civic or patriotic utopias, or inner visions of holiness

or right may also be felt as the true lords and enlargers of our life. . . .

2. A sense of the friendly continuity of the ideal power with our own life, and a willing self-surrender to its control.

3. An immense elation and freedom, as the outlines of confining selfhood melt down.

4. A shifting of the emotional centre towards loving and harmonious affections, towards "yes, yes," and away from "no," where the claims of the non-ego are concerned.

That Emerson propagated the first three of these doctrines is obvious to anyone familiar with Emerson's writings on the Oversoul. "Man is conscious of a universal soul within or behind his individual life," Emerson proclaimed in "Nature," and thereafter he defined what James would call the "saint" in terms of his service to that cosmic spirit. "His duties . . . may all be comprised in self-trust," Emerson says of the American Scholar; "He is the world's eye. He is the world's heart. . . . He then learns that in going down into the secrets of his own mind he has descended into the secrets of all minds."[2]

As supporting evidence for his "composite photograph" of saintliness, William James cites a book by Dr. W. R. Inge which practically sums up the essence of Emerson's preaching. "It will be found," says Dr. Inge (p. 216), "that men of preeminent saintliness agree very closely in what they tell us. They tell us that they have arrived at an unshakable conviction, not based on inference but on immediate experience, that God is a spirit with whom the human spirit can hold intercourse; that in him they meet all that they can imagine of goodness, truth, and beauty; that they can see his footprints everywhere in nature, and feel his presence within them as the very life of their life, so that in proportion as they come to

---

[2] *Selections from Ralph Waldo Emerson*, ed. Stephen E. Whicher (Boston: 1957), pp. 32, 72–74. Other quotations are cited from this book, pp. 104, 108, 154–5, 206, 173, 67, 109; William James, *Principles of Psychology*, Volume I, (New York: 1890), pp. 315–316; and Henry James, *The Art of the Novel* (New York: 1962), p. 111.

themselves they come to him. They tell us what separates us from him and from happiness is, first, self-seeking in all its forms; and, secondly, sensuality in all its forms. . . ." Needless to say, this passage also sums up the essence of Thoreau—whose communion with the Oversoul prompted James to quote *Walden* while discussing Saintliness (p. 218). But since Emerson preaches the same sermon, a few final excerpts from his writings may complete our view of saintliness from the didacticist's perspective.

From the universal soul, Emerson's "saint"—his American Scholar, Preacher (in "The Divinity School Address"), or Representative Men (The Poet, The Mystic, The Sceptic, etc)—brings messages about life's significance. "Life is comic or pitiful as soon as the high ends of being fade out of sight," says "The Divinity School Address"; but "The man on whom the soul descends, through whom the soul speaks, alone can teach. Courage, piety, love, wisdom, can teach; and every man can open his door to these angels, and they shall bring him the gift of tongues." In "Self-Reliance" Emerson specifies a few saints of his calendar under the thesis that "all history resolves itself very easily into the biography of a few stout and earnest persons": "A man Caesar is born, and for ages after we have a Roman Empire. Christ is born, and millions of minds so grow and cleave to his genius that he is confounded with virtue and the possible of man. An institution is the lengthened shadow of one man; as Monachism, of the Hermit Antony; the Reformation, of Luther; Quakerism, of Fox; Methodism, of Wesley; Abolition, of Clarkson." So finally, in "The Transcendentalist," "the path which the hero travels alone is the highway of health and benefit to mankind."

William James's agreement with Emerson on this point is essential enough to form the basis of his concept of saintliness. "A genuine firsthand religious experience," he says, "is bound to be a heterodoxy to its witnesses, the prophet appearing a mere lonely madman" (p. 263). But if, after being pronounced a heresy, the prophet's new doctrine "prove contagious enough to triumph over persecution, it becomes itself an orthodoxy; and when a religion has become an orthodoxy, its day of inwardness is over: the spring is dry; the faithful live at second hand and stone the prophets in their turn." For James, then, the orthodox definition of saintliness is supplanted by the imperatives of modern pragmatism. "According to the empirical philosophy, all ideals are a matter of relation," he says (p. 288); and what he calls "the empirical method" puts a limitation on his subject that accords perfectly with the stance of modern literature (pp. 256–7):

> We cannot divide man sharply into an animal and a rational part. We cannot distinguish natural from supernatural effects; nor among the latter know which are favors of God, and which are counterfeit operations of the demon. We have merely to collect things together without any *a priori* theological system, and out of an aggregate of piecemeal judgments as to the value of this and that experience—judgments in which our general philosophic prejudices, our instincts, and our common sense are our only guides—decide that *on the whole* one type of religion is approved by its fruits, and another type condemned.

To our writers about saintliness, then, we may apply the Jamesian precept that we earlier applied to Emerson, that "Nothing is more striking than the secular alteration that goes on in the moral and religious tone of men, as their insight into nature and their social relationships progressively develop." For James and for religious thinkers at large, the other-worldly fixation of medieval sainthood has lost relevance to the need for social responsibility in this world: "To-day, rightly or wrongly, helpfulness in general human affairs is, in consequence of one of those secular mutations in moral sentiment of which I spoke, deemed an essential element of worth in character; and to be of some public or private use is also reckoned as a species of divine service" (p. 275).

For Emerson, then, as he declared in "Circles," "The use of literature is to afford us a platform whence we may com-

188

mand a view of our present life, a purchase by which we may move it. . . . Therefore we value the poet." If later writers felt moved by the same purpose, they seldom used literature as a preaching-pulpit quite so blatantly, preferring to insinuate their view of life more persuasively through what Henry James called "the coercive charm of form." Yet even so, a great deal of direct preaching of the artist's "truth" comes across in the editorial statements of writers like Hawthorne and Dreiser, and even those writers clever enough to adopt a persona are far from convincing in their claim to aesthetic distance. When one thinks of Melville and his Ishmael, Twain and his Huck Finn, Frost and his Job in *A Masque of Reason*, Hemingway and his Nick Adams, Bellow and his Herzog, and even that god indifferently paring his fingernails, James Joyce and his Stephen Dedalus, the pose of authorial detachment seems a pretense concerning which one must willingly suspend disbelief.

Certainly we will allow the author his artistic revisions in his process of transmuting life into truth, to use Emerson's noble phrase. But the identity of these characters with their maker is far more significant than the discrepancies, and so far as our theme of saintliness is concerned, we may say that these and many other artistic personae, despite the gentle irony that often touches them, represent in many ways the Jamesian ideal self. By way of proceeding to our specific portraits of saintliness, it might be well to quote, from William James's chapter on "The Self" in *Principles of Psychology*, his profile of the saintly person:

> When for motives of honor and conscience I brave the condemnation of my own family, club, and "set," . . . the emotion that beckons me on is indubitably the pursuit of an ideal social self, of a self that is at least *worthy* of approving recognition by the highest *possible* judging companion, if such companion there be. . . .
>
> All progress in the social self is the substitution of higher tribunals for lower; this ideal tribune is the highest; and most men . . . carry a reference to it in their breast. . . . This sense of an ideal spectator . . . is a much more essential part of the conscious-

189

ness of some men than of others. Those who have the most of it are possibly the most *religious* men.

In what remains of this chapter, this definition of saint-liness shall affect our analysis, which shall focus chiefly on four exemplars of the concept. Drawn from writers whose careers represent intervals of about one and a half generations, our series of portraits begins with Melville's Billy Budd; then moves to the other genius in the James family, for Henry James's Isabel Archer; to Faulkner's "Christian hero" (a composite of characters); and to Updike's George Caldwell, the Centaur. All of these authors notably use Christ-symbolism to enhance their characters' saintliness—since Henry James's protagonist is female, he uses Madonna imagery—and in doing so, all four show, as William James put it, how "After an interval of a few generations the mental climate proves un-favorable to notions of the deity which at an earlier date were perfectly satisfactory" (p. 257). That the figure of Christ has changed, in these writers' religious imaginations, from a metaphysical presence into an ethical symbol is a symptom of the great crisis of belief that spanned, in particular, Herman Melville's lifetime.

2.

Melville, indeed, may be America's only major author to write of the Savior in both the old and new fashions. Back in *Mardi* (1849), he had allegorized Christ as Alma, the traditional savior of souls to whom Babbalanja became an orthodox con-vert. In *Billy Budd*, published after the writer's death in 1891, we find the first major instance in American fiction of a Christ figure employed to appeal to our myth-making capacities. Emily Dickinson's self-portrait as the "Empress of Calvary," and even Twain's Nigger Jim, for his Christlike virtues, could be considered forerunners to Melville's portrait of Billy, but neither is so modern as Melville's usage. Since Melville's time, a considerable roll call of Christ figures have answered their author's summons: Crane's Jim Conklin, the martyred soldier (connected with the red wafer pasted in the sky) in *The Red Badge of Courage*; Eliot's Hanged Man, portentously missing from the Tarot Pack in *The Waste Land* (he reappears in Part V on the Road to Emmaus); Hemingway's Santiago in *The Old Man and the Sea* staggering up the beach with "nailed" hands holding the mast after his Friday-to-Sunday absence from his young disciple; West's Miss Lonelyhearts, with the desire but not the power to save his supplicants; Carson McCullers' Biff Brannon, who lay with bare, crossed feet and arms outstretched while the sun lit his dark beard and hair with a halo;[3] Steinbeck's Jim Casey, who joins the twelve Joads as their spiritual leader and eventual martyr; and of course the various Christ figures of Faulkner, about which more shortly. Of all these, Billy Budd is a prototype, though not necessarily a direct influence owing to Melville's long-lasting obscurity.

Billy's Christlike role as a scapegoat, a blameless man sacrificed to save his mates from their own perversity, derives from the crisis in culture in which the book is grounded, the clash between "Christendom" and the French Revolution. Ultimately, this conflict of ideologies produced one of Melville's most profound generalizations, the theme statement formulated in Chapter 28 (H-S 27): "With mankind . . . forms, measured forms, are everything; and that is the import couched in the story of Orpheus with his lyre spell-binding the wild denizens of the wood." As elaborated by the narrative, on

---

[3] Biff Brannon's cruciform posture occurs at the end of Chapter 2 of *The Heart Is a Lonely Hunter*. Because *Billy Budd* consists mostly of short chapters, I am using chapter numbers rather than page references in this discussion, noting the variants of the Hayford-Sealts edition in parenthesis (H-S).

one side of the struggle are aligned the "measured forms" which defend civilization, forms such as church and state, religion and law, which impose moral and legal disciplines so that men will not act too bestially toward one another. Billy, enacting the Christian ritual of self-sacrifice, and Vere, upholding the king's law even against his private conscience, support the measured forms and thereby prevent mutiny, enabling the *Indomitable* to vanquish the *Atheiste*—the enemy of all forms, all order—in the final battle. Aligned against the measured forms that uphold civilization are the French Revolution and the Great Mutiny, two uprisings which seem initially justified but which, given the defects of human nature, develop only into continuing holocaust. Once men have flung aside all law and religion—as the French Directory did with its capricious guillotines and its official atheism—the emancipated natural man will find himself not in a primeval Golden Age but in a state of primitive savagery. The spell cast by Orpheus' lyre once broken—the measured forms of civilization once cast aside—the wild denizens of the wood revert to their natural bestiality.

Like Edmund Burke (whom he cites in the novel), Herman Melville viewed violent revolution with a sympathy changing rapidly to alarm. Thus in the "Preface" to *Billy Budd*, Melville admits that the French Revolution aimed at "rectification of the Old World's hereditary wrongs," but adds: "Straightway the Revolution itself became a wrongdoer, one more oppressive than the kings." And likewise, The Great Mutiny which the French Revolution fostered "emboldened the man-of-war's men to rise against real abuses, longstanding ones, and afterwards at the Nore to make inordinate and aggressive demands." Again, in Chapter 3, Melville repeats his revulsion against the Revolution in even stronger tones of disapproval:

> To the British Empire the Nore Mutiny was what a strike in the fire-brigade would be to London threatened by general arson

192

. . . . the bluejackets, to be numbered by the thousands, ran up with huzzas the British colors with the union and cross wiped out; by that cancellation transmuting the flag of founded law and freedom defined into the enemy's red meteor of unbridled and unbounded revolt. Reasonable discontent growing out of practical grievances in the fleet had been ignited into irrational combustion as by live cinders blown across the Channel from France in flames.

So there we have it again: measured forms versus chaos, the "union and cross," the "flag of founded law and freedom defined," aligned against the "red meteor of unbridled and unbounded revolt," "irrational combustion," "live cinders . . . from France in flames." Given this kind of backdrop, it seems clear that it is not a defect in his character that causes Billy to hang, nor a defect in Captain Vere's, but rather a defect on the part of the crew. Having already tasted success in earlier mutinies, they might all too readily interpret Billy's slaying of an officer, if unpunished, as a sign of authoritarian breakdown inviting mutiny. Thus, in the crucial Chapter 28 (H-S 27), where the ship's crew is ominously described as resembling "mobs ashore," incipient mutiny is put down only by resort to a series of traditional measured forms, beginning with such "mechanisms of descipline" as the Boatswains' whistles, a drum-beat ("the drum-beat dissolved the multitude"), and "the customary salute," and culminating with the measured forms of religion: "all proceeded as at the regular hour. The band on deck played a sacred air. After which the Chaplain went through the customary morning service. That done, the drum beat the retreat, and toned by music and religious rites . . . the men in their wonted, orderly manner dispersed to the places allotted them."

The efficacy of Billy's and Vere's sacrifice—and certainly Vere's sacrifice of his private conscience to save his crew is greater than Ahab's sacrifice of his crew to suit his private conscience—is seen in the Christian imagery at the end of the novel. First, Vere's ship does overcome the *Atheiste* in an action that gives Vere the chance to die heroically (Chapter 29,

H-S 28) but not before having a beatific vision of Billy: "Not long before death . . . he was heard to murmur words inexplicable to his attendant—'Billy Budd, Billy Budd.' That these were not the accents of remorse would seem clear." Next we have the official record of Billy's death—naming Claggart the hero and Billy the "criminal of the episode"—ironically set off against the folk literature wherein Billy is explicitly compared to Christ. The spar from which Billy was hanged is regarded like "the Cross" by Billy's fellow sailors, one of whom composes a crude ditty containing eucharist symbols: "They'll give me a nibble—bit o' biscuit ere I go./Sure, a messmate will reach me the last parting cup."

Because *Billy Budd* has been—and continues to be—Melville's most controversial book, a final corroborating piece of evidence, drawn from one of Melville's poems, is in order. This poem, "The House Top," subtitled "A Night Piece" and dated "July, 1863," was occasioned by a mob action similar to those Melville deplores in *Billy Budd*, as the afternote to the poem tells us: "Note: 'I dare not write the horrible and inconceivable atrocities committed,' says Froissart, in alluding to the remarkable sedition in France during his time. The like may be hinted of some proceedings of the draft rioters."[4]

The backdrop for this poem, then, is exactly the same as the backdrop for *Billy Budd* set forth in that novel's Preface: a revulsion against "the horrible and inconceivable atrocities committed" by people asserting the Rights of Man. In the case

---

[4] According to the *Encyclopedia Americana*, Melville's deep revulsion toward the draft-rioters was altogether well founded:

. . . the necessity of drafting men for army service resulted in one of the most sanguinary riots New York had ever known. On Saturday, July 11, 1863, a mob of thousands of frenzied laborers and idlers attacked and destroyed one of the enrollment centers. . . . Drunk with their first success, they attacked other buildings. For three days and nights, the rioters raged through the town, robbing stores and sacking and burning buildings, including the Colored Orphan Asylum. . . . Negroes were the special object of their savagery. Many unfortunate Negroes, including women and chil-

of the New York City draft riots, the bloodiest in the city's history, the Rights of Man are aligned against America's need to suppress the war against the Union. To be drafted, of course, means to surrender one's Constitutional Rights in favor of assuring the survival of one's society. Billy Budd made this sacrifice cheerfully, as we remember, when he said, upon being transferred from the merchant vessel to warship, "And good-bye to you too, old *Rights of Man.*" The New York draft rioters, however, are rather less than cheerful about this sacrifice of their Rights, as Melville's "House-Top" overview of their rioting makes clear:

> No sleep. The sultriness pervades the air
> And binds the brain. . . .
>   All is hushed near by,
> Yet fitfully from far breaks a mixed surf
> Of muffled sound, the Atheist roar of riot.
> Yonder where parching Sirius set in drought,
> Balefully glares red Arson—there—and there.
> The town is taken by its rats—ship rats
> And rats of the wharves. All civil charms
> And priestly spiels which late held hearts in awe—
> Fear-bound, subjected to a better sway
> Than sway of self; these like a dream dissolve,
> And man rebounds whole aeons back in nature.
> . . . .
> Wise Draco comes, deep in the midnight roll
> Of black artillery; he comes, though late;
> In code corroborating Calvin's creed. . .
> He comes, nor parlies; and the Town, redeemed,
> Gives thanks devout; nor being thankful, heeds
> The grimy slur on the Republic's faith implied,
> Which holds that Man is naturally good,
> And—more—Is Nature's Roman, never to be scourged.

---

dren, were caught and hanged on the nearest lamp posts. . . . Meanwhile, the vastly outnumbered police and the few military units in the city fought heroically. Not until Thursday did the 7th Regiment, followed by other troops also summoned from the front, enter the city. . . . The veteran guardsmen gave the rioters short shrift. That day saw the end of the worst phase.

(1961 Edition: Volume 20, p. 232)

The above lines clearly contain an exact foreshadowing of the ideas at the center of *Billy Budd*: there is Melville's abhorrence of "the Atheist roar of riot" and the "red Arson" in which the draft resisters have indulged; there is the skepticism towards the presumption of man's innate goodness—this mob "rebounds whole aeons back in nature" to become not "upright barbarians" (like Billy, a unique type) but the most savage and destructive of all animals: "the town is taken by its rats"; there is the idea of civilization as a "charm" which restrains these "rats" from their innate evil through the use of laws ("civil charms") and ethics ("priestly spiels"); there is the comparison of the Northern army coming to suppress this riot to "Wise Draco," an Athenian archon who laid down a severe set of laws; and finally, as in *Billy Budd*, there is the observation that the need for such a Draco, once "civil charms" and "priestly spiels" have "like a dream dissolved," corroborates "Calvin's creed" concerning the innate depravity of man and refutes "the Republic's faith . . . Which hold that Man is naturally good,/And—more—is Nature's Roman, never to be scourged."

In *Moby Dick* Melville had dramatized the handful of elementary virtues that make Ishmael worthy of survival: an open, searching mind; personal loyalty and affection; freedom from malice; humility. He had also dramatized, in Captain Ahab, the supreme virtue—courage—allied with what he elsewhere called the only sin, malice. In *Billy Budd*, Melville rendered his ethical judgment more clearly, assigning that only sin to Claggart and the role of saintliness to Vere and Billy. So as to avoid the melodrama of a morality play, he converted the portrait of Claggart into a masterful profile of a psychopath, and he invested Billy and Vere with the mythical aura of the Christian Passion. As we have noted, Christian symbolism abounds in the book; even Claggart's death is rendered in terms of Christian prophecy. God's promise to Eve that her seed would bruise the serpent's head (Genesis

3:15) is borne out in two details of Melville's Chapter 20 (H-S Chapter 19): Claggart dies of a cracked skull ("thick black blood was now oozing from nostril and ear"), and carrying away his body is "like handling a dead snake." And Melville's theme reposes at last on the Christian example of martyr-like suffering for the sins of others, in a freely chosen gesture of sacrifice. Billy's "God bless Captain Vere" just before his hanging is Melville's final answer not only to Claggart's irrational malice but also to Ahab's epic effort to avenge the heaped-up sufferings of the world.

Melville's moral philosophy thus appears to have rested in the end on a reinterpretation of holy writ, much in the vein of William James's observation about "the secular alteration that goes on in the moral and religious tone of men, as their insight into nature and their social arrangements progressively develop" (p. 257). That reinterpretation has both a conservative and a radical dimension. On the conservative side, Melville reconceived Original Sin to comport with his essentially Burkeian vision of human society. The following comment by Edmund Burke, in a letter written in 1791, correlates perfectly with Melville's perspective in *Billy Budd*:

> Men are qualified for civil liberty in exact proportion to their disposition to put moral chains upon their own appetites; in proportion as their love of justice is above their rapacity; in proportion as their soundness and sobriety of understanding is above their vanity and presumption. . . . Society cannot exist unless a controlling power upon will and appetite be placed somewhere, and the less of it there is within, the more there must be without. It is ordained in the eternal constitution of things, that men of intemperate minds cannot be free. Their passions forge their fetters.[5]

On the radical side, Melville remythologized the Christian story of sacrifice and redemption to make it relevant for a

---

[5] *The Writings and Speeches of the Right Honorable Edmund Burke*, Volume Four (Boston: 1901), pp. 51–52.

secular age. In so doing Melville seems to answer affirmatively William James's question: "At bottom the whole concern of both morality and religion is with the manner of our acceptance of the universe. . . . Shall our protests against certain things in it be radical and unforgiving [cp. Captain Ahab], or shall we think that, even with evil, there are ways of living that must lead to good?" (p. 49). Although both James and Melville greatly doubted the supernatural claims of Christianity, with respect to their ethical thinking we are justified in calling them Christian writers. (James was fond of addressing his audience in the Gifford lectures, later published as *The Varieties of Religious Experience*, as "we Christians.") And so far as the Christian ideology of *Billy Budd* is concerned, we might say that Melville's religious sensibility comprises an early version of Jamesian pragmatism, vindicated by the efficacy of Vere's and Billy's saintliness.

3.

By way of linking up his chapter on Conversion with the subsequent chapter on Saintliness, William James asks a question: "What may the practical fruits for life have been, of such movingly happy conversions as those we heard of? With this question the really important part of our task opens" (p. 207). And in the following paragraph, he anticipates that to answer the question "ought to be the pleasantest portion of our business in these lectures . . . because the best fruits of religious experience are the best things that history has to show." Merely to read about them, he adds, "is to feel encouraged and uplifted and washed in better moral air." If this statement has any literary application at all, it surely applies to William's brother, Henry James, and most notably to his master portrait of a saint, *The Portrait of a Lady*. "Be kind, be kind, be kind" was Henry James's answer to the question of moral philosophy,[6] and in books like *The American* and *The Wings of the Dove* he attempted and largely mastered the terribly difficult problem of making goodness both interesting and psychologically credible. But *The Portrait of a Lady* is doubly interesting for us because it treats the two phenomena of conversion and saintliness, so intriguing to William James the religious psychologist, with the skill and depth peculiar to Henry James the literary genius.

To begin, *The Portrait of a Lady* gives us two portraits or conceptions of a lady. One of them is the result of Isabel's deliberate and splendid artifice in emulating her model of Europeanized ladyhood, Madame Merle; the other—and more important—conception results from the development of Isabel's essential character in facing a series of harsh and unexpected crises. One portrait, that is to say, is Isabel's creation of an identity, and the other is her discovery of what her true identity has been all along, underneath the glamorous surface she has so assiduously been cultivating. It is this double pattern of developing conceptions and especially the conflict between them that gives James's masterpiece much of its structure.

Isabel Archer, at the beginning, is an unknown quantity whom even the clairvoyant Ralph Touchett regards as a lovely but inscrutable mystery. For this reason he compares her personality to a mansion with locked doors: "He surveyed the edifice from the outside and admired it greatly; he looked in at the windows and received an impression of proportions

---

[6] Jason Epstein, in his review of Volume V of Leon Edel's biography of Henry James, *The Master*, drew my attention to this comment. When William James's son, Billy, came to visit his uncle Henry James in 1902, Henry James told him: "Three things in human life are important. The first is to be kind. The second is to be kind. And the third is to be kind." Epstein's review, entitled "The Biography of the Century," appeared in *Book World*, February 6, 1972. Because I quote so widely from *Portrait of a Lady* (Boston: 1963), I am including page references to it within my main text.

equally fair. But he felt that he saw it only by glimpses and that he had not yet stood under the roof. The door was fastened, and though he had keys in his pocket he had a conviction that none of them would fit" (p. 63).

What is more significant is that Isabel is equally a mystery to herself. In her highest moments of crisis, when she rejects her two ardent suitors, she herself doesn't understand why she would do such a thing, and her prevailing mood is one of fear and bewilderment as to what sort of a person she must be to have acted so perversely. When Lord Warburton asked to visit her, for example, "she made answer to his declaration, coldly enough, 'Just as you please.' And her coldness was not the calculation of her effect . . . It came from a certain fear" (p. 77).

The fear, it becomes evident, is fear of herself, of her intrinsic identity, for after rejecting Warburton's proposal of marriage a bit later (p. 101) "she was wondering if she were not a cold, hard, priggish person, and . . . felt, as she had said to her friend, really frightened at herself." Later, after rejecting Caspar Goodwood, she would similarly drop to her knees before her bed and hide her face in her arms—"not praying . . . [but] trembling all over" for a good ten minutes of uncontrollable psychic turmoil.

Her problem, then, is the ageless one of finding or establishing a satisfactory role and identity, something to justify her irrational behavior: "Who was she, what was she, that she should hold herself superior? What view of life, what design upon fate, what conception of happiness, had she that pretended to be larger than these large, these fabulous occasions?" (p. 101).

As though bestowed by the hand of Providence, Madame Merle makes her superb entrance almost in answer to Isabel's question. Born in the Brooklyn navy yard, Madame Merle shows everything Europe can do for the American woman of true cultural potentiality. A musician, painter, artist of the needle, master of several languages, Madame Merle is so endowed with all the arts and graces as to pass for European aristocracy—"a Frenchwoman," Isabel thinks, or "a German of high degree, perhaps an Austrian, a baroness, a countess, a princess. It would never have been supposed she had come into the world in Brooklyn" (p. 152). And so our title theme gets underway, Isabel's search for identity having found its perfect objective correlative in her new friend's magnificent bearing: "she had yet to Isabel's imagination a sort of greatness. To be so cultivated and civilized, so wise and so easy, and still make so light of it—that was really to be a great lady . . ." (p. 164).

To become a Madame Merle in her own right is now Isabel's manifest destiny, the new purpose of her existence, the "design upon fate" by which she would justify her rejection of an English lord and an American millionaire. Thus "she wandered, as by the wrong side of the wall of a private garden, round the enclosed talents, accomplishments, aptitudes, of Madame Merle. She found herself desiring to emulate them, and in twenty such ways this lady presented herself as a model. 'I should like awfully to be so!' Isabel secretly exclaimed" (p. 163).

So there develops before our eyes one portrait of a lady, the glamorous, graceful, Europeanized creature who fulfills half of the meaning of James's title. For a start, in pursuing the cultural fullness of her model, Isabel ingests all she can of Europe, taking in the Pyramids, the Acropolis, Constantinople, and so forth, "like a thirsty person draining cup after cup" (p. 268), and as a result she feels "as if she were 'worth more' for it, like some curious piece in an antiquary's collection" (p. 270)—which is exactly how Gilbert Osmond would regard her, perceiving "a new attraction in the idea of taking to himself a young lady who had qualified herself to figure in his collection of choice objects" (p. 253).

The culmination of this Europeanization of Isabel is seen

in the splendid full-length portrait that we encounter, through Edward Rosier's eyes, as Isabel stands framed in the doorway at the outset of Chapter 37: "He . . . met Mrs. Osmond coming out of the deep doorway. She was dressed in black velvet; she looked high and splendid. . . . The years had touched her only to enrich her; the flower of her youth had not faded, it only hung more quietly on its stem. . . . Now, at all events, framed in the gilded doorway, she struck our young man as the picture of a gracious lady" (p. 303). So Isabel Archer has achieved her secret ambition; she has become, to all appearances, an even finer version of Madame Merle.

But this development, impressively as it strikes the eye, has sinister implications. In fitting herself to the portrait of a European lady, Isabel has become tainted with the European duplicity. Like her model, she has become a social actress, a careful and willing performer in the play that is staged and directed by Gilbert Osmond. It is not so bad that she lies to Lord Warburton about her marriage, telling him "Fortunately, I'm very happy" (p. 317), but it does become unconscionable that she maintains her act in Ralph's presence, thus causing a tragic deterioration in her relationship with the man who has so loved and befriended her.

In place of her original identity, all she will permit him to see now is a mask, the synthetic self which the European code requires from the leaders of its social hierarchy. This, alas, is not the portrait of a genuine lady: "He should see nothing, he should learn nothing; for him she would always wear a mask . . . if she wore a mask it completely covered her face. There was something fixed and mechanical in the serenity painted on it; this was not an expression, Ralph said—it was a representation, it was even an advertisement" (p. 323).

Being a generous spirit, Ralph does not blame Isabel for this perversity, but rather looks to its source, the stagecraft of Gilbert Osmond—"Ralph, in all this, recognized the hand of the master; for he knew that Isabel had no faculty for producing studied impression" (p. 323). Nevertheless, Isabel's aloofness from him is deeply wounding, and provokes the most profound moral crisis of the book until its resolution in the next to the last chapter. Until then, Isabel's synthetic identity as a fine lady is, for Ralph, far from satisfactory: "Poor human-hearted Isabel, what perversity had bitten her? . . . The free, keen girl had become quite another person; what he saw was the fine lady who was supposed to represent something. What did Isabel represent? Ralph asked himself; and he could only answer by saying that she represented Gilbert Osmond" (p. 324).

So Ralph must wait, perforce, until the final crisis of his deathbed to see Isabel's true identity re-emerge at last—the warm, spontaneous creature he had known earlier. And right up until that final crisis, neither he nor Isabel knows her true identity well enough to predict what her behavior will be (p. 469):

> "It was very good of you to come," he went on. "I thought you would; but I wasn't sure."
> "I was not sure either till I came," said Isabel.

Until this final epiphany, poor Ralph is doomed to play out his lonely waiting game, uncertain whether Isabel's stubborn facade has become so fixed that this is all he will ever see of her: "What kept Ralph alive was simply the fact that he had not yet seen enough of the person in the world in whom he was most interested; he was not yet satisfied. . . . This was only the first act of the drama, and he was determined to sit out the performance" (p. 326).

Originally, however, Isabel Archer was not given to making performances. On the contrary, before her metamorphosis into the European lady had ever presented itself as an object of her desiring, she had determined that "she would appear what she was" (p. 54). "It was wrong to be mean, to be jealous, to be false, to be cruel," she had decided, and "the chance of inflicting a sensible injury upon another person

. . . struck her as the worst thing that could happen to her" (p. 53). This, as we have seen, is exactly what does "happen" to her, the injury being inflicted upon not just "another person" but upon her kindly benefactor who loved her "as if he had been her brother" (p. 357).

To be sure, she rationalized her mask as a kindness to Ralph, which calls forth a wry editorial intrusion from the author: "Women find their religion sometimes in strange exercises, and Isabel, at present, in playing a part before her cousin, had an idea that she was doing him a kindness. It would have been a kindness perhaps if he had been for a single instant a dupe. As it was, the kindness consisted mainly in trying to make him believe that he had once wounded her greatly [in warning her not to marry Osmond] and that the event had put him to shame, but that, as she was very generous and he was so ill, she bore him no grudge" (p. 357). In Ralph's deathbed scene, she admits that this "kindness" had been a rationalization all along (p. 470):

> ". . . I always tried to keep you from understanding; but it's all over."
> "I always understood," said Ralph.
> "I thought you did, and I didn't like it. . . ."

Prior to this last-minute confession, as time wears on and Ralph's illness worsens, the falsity of Isabel's pose parallels the deterioration of his health as an aggravation of his suffering, such that the smallest glimpse through her mask is, to him, pathetically exciting (p. 381):

> "Ah, Ralph, you give me no help!" she cried abruptly and passionately.
> It was the first time she had alluded to the need for help, and the words shook her cousin with their violence. He gave a long murmur of relief, of pity, of tenderness; it seemed to him that at last the gulf between them had been bridged. It was this that made him exclaim in a moment, "How unhappy you must be!"
> He had no sooner spoken than she recovered her self-possession and the first use she made of it was to pretend she had not heard him.

So the gulf is not bridged; the moment of real warmth and honesty is supplanted quickly by the synthetic portrait so important to Isabel's pride as a woman. "Her mask had dropped for an instant, but she had put it on again, to Ralph's infinite disappointment" (p. 382). He "had caught a glimpse of her natural face," but now the public portrait would be all he would see until his dying hour.

So much, then, for this portrait of a lady, the beautiful actress who must at all costs preserve her splendid public image, her dearly bought artificial identity. But this is only half the portrait. In counterpoint with the story of Isabel's creation of an identity is the theme of self-discovery, Isabel's search for whatever true identity underlies the pose of a gracious and happily married woman. This, of course, is James's real portrait of a lady, for it is only in ethical character, not in the acquired glamor of Europe, that one's bedrock identity may be found. Madame Merle demonstrates the obverse of this truism, for in lacking an ethical character she must remain "a public performer, condemned to emerge only in character and costume" (p. 269); too perfect an actress, she simply does not have an off-stage identity, and so must return to America after her exposure a hopeless, hollow woman. In place of Isabel's garden of the soul, Madame Merle has cultivated only a weed patch, a "Dusky pestiferous tract . . . planted thick with ugliness and misery" (p. 55). Her story is thus more tragic than Isabel's.

As in actual life, Isabel's ethical character can be defined and clarified only in action, in the unpredictable contingencies of whatever crisis happens to be looming at hand. This is why her emulation of Madame Merle turns out to be unsatisfactory; the identity it can give is only for the outer world, while within her inner psyche she must still confront the sense of fear as to who and what she really is. Thus the anxiety which had followed her rejection of Goodwood and Warburton follows her to the end, as she admits in her conversation with Ralph just before his final journey home from Rome (p. 412):

> ". . . I'm afraid," said Isabel. After a pause she repeated, as if to make herself, rather than him, hear the words: "I'm afraid."
> Ralph could hardly tell what her tone meant . . . "Afraid of your husband?"
> "Afraid of myself!" she said.

What she fears, it turns out, is that her ethical character will be found lacking. It is a fear that is finally resolved only in the last two chapters, when Isabel at last flings aside her pride and her mask to claim Ralph as her "brother" and then proceeds to fight off the two supreme temptations of the concluding pages. But although Isabel herself cannot be sure of how strong her character will be under pressure, there is no doubt that James laid a subtle and careful groundwork to prepare for and justify Isabel's victory of character in the closing pages.

That ground work begins in the first chapter when old Touchett, voicing the American ethic, tells Warburton, "you young men are too idle. You think too much of your pleasure" (p. 22). His antidote for Warburton's boredom is the exhortation to "take hold of something," a bit of advice which Henrietta Stackpole, that spirit of pure Americanism, later repeats verbatim to Ralph ("Take right hold of something"—p. 84.) Ralph, of course, does take hold of something, taking his cousin Isabel under his benevolent wing, while Isabel at this time appears interested only in taking hold of the aesthetics of Europe, under her program of emulating Madame Merle's spectacular cultural metamorphosis. Isabel's propensity to take hold of something more important than Europe's cultural feast lies dormant and waiting, however, for "Deep in her soul—it was the deepest thing there—lay a belief that if a certain light could dawn she could give herself completely" (p. 55).

Isabel's clear-sighted aunt sees this element in Isabel's

nature with prophetic accuracy some time later (but before Isabel has decided to marry Osmond), when she complains that "we shall have my niece arriving at the conviction that her mission in life's to prove that a stepmother may sacrifice her-self—and that, to prove it, she must first become one" (p. 232).

Such an awareness of her true nature dawns more slowly on Isabel herself, as she senses that something is wrong with the splendid surface portrait she has so successfully been cultivating—that perhaps her real identity is not found in that picture: "The desire for unlimited expansion had been suc-ceeded in her soul by the sense that life was vacant without some private duty that might gather one's energies to a point" (p. 291). What that private duty will be emerges slowly into clarity in fragmentary intuitions such as the following pre-monition that little Pansy will stand in need of a friend and protector: " 'My good little Pansy,' said Isabel gently, 'I shall be ever so kind to you.' A vague, inconsequent vision of her coming in some odd way to need it had intervened with the effect of a chill" (p. 293).

As Isabel's awareness grows continually keener, Pansy looms larger and clearer as the object of her search for "some private duty" to fill the inner vacancy. Led by "her tenderness for things that were pure and weak," Isabel comes to think of Pansy as her personal responsibility, something to take hold of: ". . . the girl's dependence was more than a pleasure; it operated as a definite reason when motives threatened to fail her. She had said to herself that we must take our duty where we find it, and that we must look for it as much as possible" (p. 334). From here it is but a short step to give her commitment a religious sanction: "not to neglect Pansy, not under any provocation to neglect her—this she had made an article of religion" (p. 334).

"Not under any provocation" is strong language, and put to the severest imaginable test in the twin temptations of the final chapter, but Isabel does live up to this "religion" of sacrifice and renunciation. She does bear out her promise, "I won't desert you" (p. 455), at whatever cost to herself, and so merits the full tribute of James's title.

That title assumes its positive meaning only in this second portrait, then, not in the portrait of a beautiful lady dressed in black velvet whom Edward Rosier saw framed in the gilded doorway and whom Ralph Touchett saw cruelly hidden behind a mask. The one portrait derives from her setting in Italy, Catholic and aesthetic ("a land in which a love of the beautiful might be comforted by endless knowledge"— p. 190), while the other comes from Isabel's origins in America, Protestant and ethical in its insistence on one's private duty.

This Catholic-Protestant discrepancy is nowhere more intolerable than in Isabel's observation of Pansy's incarceration in the convent-prison—where Osmond is walling her away from Rosier's ardent courtship. Isabel sees clearly the sinister function of the convent—"It produced today more than before the impression of a well-appointed prison; for it was not possible to pretend that Pansy was free to leave it" (p. 448)—but Osmond is happy to use this venerable institution as a doubly safe extension of his wax museum: "Convents are very quiet, very convenient, very salutary. I like to think of her there . . . among those tranquil virtuous women" (p. 434).

So Isabel's Protestant conscience asserts its latent authority: "The old Protestant tradition had never faded from Isabel's imagination, and . . . poor little Pansy became the heroine of a tragedy. Osmond wished it to be known that he shrank from nothing, and his wife found it hard to pretend to eat her dinner" (p. 435). Isabel's behavior in the book's closing paragraphs is anything but the gratuitous impulse it appears, then, for her character has been shaped and nurtured towards just such a gesture of sacrifice.

Rounding out this spiritual portrait of a lady are two other notable virtues evidenced in her attitudes toward the

208

two co-conspirators who have ruined her life. Her sacrifice for Pansy is supplemented by fidelity toward Pansy's father and by charity toward Pansy's mother. Osmond may think himself sincere when he says "I think we should accept the consequences of our actions, and what I value most in life is the honour of a thing" (p. 438), but for him, after all, the "consequences of his actions" is the rather pleasant fact of being married to a woman of great wealth, and the "honour of a thing" is for him the integrity of the surface facade so important to his status in European society. He has no more appreciation of those fine phrases than he had when he spoke of "my wilful renunciation" (p. 253) during their courtship. It remains for Isabel to give meaningful content to his "observance of a magnificent form" (p. 439).

Isabel's charity toward Madame Merle is also remarkable; although Isabel herself had been ready to apply "the great historical epithet of *wicked*" to her arch-deceiver (p. 424), she will not allow Pansy to speak ill of her—"You must never say that—that you don't like Madame Merle" (p. 455). In her last encounter with Madame Merle, Isabel does not even allow herself the modest comfort of verbal retaliation, though for a moment she veers close to it (p. 451):

> She saw . . . the dry staring fact that she had been an applied handled hung-up tool, as senseless and convenient as mere shaped wood and iron. All the bitterness of this knowledge surged into her soul again. . . . There was a moment during which, if she had turned and spoken, she would have said something that would hiss like a lash. But she closed her eyes, and then the hideous vision dropped . . . Isabel's only revenge was to be silent still.

For all her vague, uncertain fears as to her interior identity, then, Isabel's character through test after test proves to be strong and attractive, marked by an uncommon charitableness, fidelity, and self-sacrifice. Even while her surface portrait is leading to the deterioration of her relationship with Ralph, her interior character portrait is building steadily towards the ultimate revelation of her spiritual ladyhood, hither-to an uncertain matter to herself, to Ralph, to Pansy, and to all involved in the story. Out of this carefully etched complex of motivations, Isabel arrives at the concluding scenes strongly armored against the final supreme temptations, the escapism of a death wish beckoning from one side of the path and that of Caspar Goodwood's "life force" calling from the other.

Of these two climactic temptations, the death-wish is the most difficult to resist: "She envied Ralph his dying, for if one were thinking of rest that was the most perfect of all. To cease utterly, to give it all up and not know anything more—this idea was as sweet as the vision of a cool bath in a marble tank, in a darkened chamber, in a hot land" (p. 457). But Caspar's enor-mously powerful and logical appeal is almost as tempting, as her American suitor nearly wins her over: "she believed just then that to let him take her in his arms would be the next best thing to her dying" (p. 481). And when he does take her in his arms, with a kiss "like white lightning" and with a passion that made "each thing in his hard manhood that had least pleased her . . . justified of its intense identity," she is saved from yielding only by an ethical character that James had subtly and carefully threaded through all his previous chapters.

So, in response to the kiss, "she darted from the spot. . . . She had not known where to turn; but she knew now. There was a very straight path" (p. 482). The Biblical echo in this phrase about a straight path is not an accident, for this final portrait of a lady, the lady of ethical character, is estab-lished upon the Christian paradoxes concerning sacrifice and renunciation: he who would save his life must lose it, and she who loses her life will save it. In this way, Isabel has safely survived her identity crisis. That gnawing fear of herself, of a failure in her character, has proved unfounded in the crucible of actual experience.

Perhaps in keeping with the Christian paradoxes, the culminating imagery of Isabel's character is that of angel and

Madonna to the two people who mean the most to her. For Ralph she becomes "an angel beside my bed" because she has finally achieved the necessary humility to lay down her social mask, the artificial portrait, so as to bridge the gulf between them: "She had lost all her shame, all wish to hide things. Now he must know; she wished him to know, for it brought them supremely together" (p. 469).

Likewise, she has become comparable not just to a painting of a Madonna, which Mrs. Touchett had compared her to ("She has looked as solemn, these three days, as a Cimabue Madonna"—p. 179), but to the spiritual status of a Madonna, as Pansy would have it: " 'I wish you would try to find one [a way to help Rosier's courtship of Pansy],' the girl exclaimed as if she were praying to the Madonna" (p. 385). In her final sacrifice, Isabel has indeed become Ralph's angel and Pansy's Madonna. There can be no finer portrait of a lady than this, no better discovery of identity.

Concerning the religious phenomena of conversion and saintliness that Henry James has melded in his portrait of Isabel, some concluding quotations from his brother William appear powerfully relevant. First, as to the psychology of conversion, Isabel Archer obviously demonstrates in the conflict between her two concepts of a lady William James's contention that "The psychological basis of the twice-born character seems to be a certain discordancy or heterogeneity in the native temperament of the subject, an incompletely unified moral and intellectual constitution" (p. 141). In her inner shift from one ideal of a lady to the other we further see exemplified William James's comment that "there are dead feelings, dead ideas, and cold beliefs, and there are hot and live ones; and when one grows hot and alive within us, everything has to re-crystallize about it" (p. 162). Furthermore,

Isabel falls into the latter category of William James's "two forms of mental occurrence in human beings, which lead to a striking difference in the conversion process. . . . There is thus a voluntary way and an involuntary and unconscious way in which mental results may get accomplished . . . the *volitional type* and the *type by self-surrender*" (p. 169). In that closing scene between Isabel and Goodwood, Henry James appears to have anticipated by five years the date—1886— when his brother claimed the subconscious mind was discovered. Turning from her suitor's kiss into the "straight path"—"She had not known where to turn; but she knew now"—Isabel comprises an instance of "the shifting of men's centres of personal energy within them . . . partly due to explicitly conscious processes of thought and will, but . . . due largely also to the subconscious incubation and maturing of motives deposited by the experiences of life. When ripe, the results hatch out, or burst into flower" (p. 186). Poor Goodwood, and many a reader as well, might find Isabel's final action inexplicable, but William James would have understood it perfectly in terms of a largely subconscious conversion towards saintliness: "Even in the most voluntarily built-up sort of regeneration there are passages of partial self-surrender interposed; and in the great majority of all cases, when the will has done its uttermost towards bringing one close to the complete unification aspired after, it seems that the very last step must be left to other [i.e., subconscious] forces and performed without the help of its activity. In other words, . . . 'The personal will . . . must be given up' " (p. 170–171).

As a result of the shift in her center of energy, Isabel may achieve something else that must seem, to the uninitiated, inexplicable. Because she has felt "a force that re-infuses the positive willingness to live, even in full presence of the evil perceptions that erewhile made life seem unbearable" (p. 155), she may return with equanimity to live with her tormentor, Gilbert Osmond. To Isabel Archer as to few other personae in

American literature we may relate William James's insight that, through conversion, "what is attained is often an altogether new level of spiritual vitality, a realitively heroic level, in which impossible things have become possible, and new energies and endurances are shown. The personality is changed, the man *is* born anew" (p. 194). Almost as though they had collaborated—regrettably, they seemed to understand one another's work rather poorly—the brothers James give us in *The Portrait of a Lady* and *The Varieties of Religious Experience* a consummate profile of the saint for our time. William James could have been speaking of Henry's Isabel in correlating the phenomena of conversion and saintliness: "The real witness of the spirit to the second birth is to be found only in the disposition of the genuine child of God, the permanently patient heart, the love of self eradicated" (p. 192).

4.

Though Faulkner did not much care for Henry James, calling him the "nicest little old lady I ever met," he propagated with almost didactic openness the broadly Christian ideals such as Henry James had advocated. "No one is without Christianity, if we agree on what we mean by the word," Faulkner told Jean Stein in his *Paris Review* interview of 1956. "It is every individual's code of behavior by means of which he makes himself a better human being than his nature wants to be, if he followed his nature only."[7] Essentially, this war between "Christianity" and one's "nature" produced the two

[7] *Writers at Work: The Paris Review Interviews* (New York: 1959), p. 132. Other quotations are cited from *Flags in the Dust* (New York: 1974), p. 433, 330; Joseph Blotner, *Faulkner: A Biography*, pp. 531, 1002, 1034–35, 1094; *The Sound and the Fury*, pp. 282, 303–4, 332; *Go Down, Moses*, pp. 258, 257, 260, 299, 284, 296–7; *Sanctuary* (New York: 1958), pp. 11–12, 16; *Requiem for a Nun* (New York: 1975), p. 237; Allen Tate, "Faulkner: An Obituary," *The (continued on page 214)

213

central topics of Faulkner's work according to his Nobel Prize Address, the "heart in conflict with itself" ("the only thing worth writing about") and "the old verities of the heart." This latter theme in particular, which Faulkner restated emphatically in his Foreword to *The Faulkner Reader* in 1953, links Faulkner to William James's concept of saintliness, for it defines Faulkner's purpose in literature as the old heroic one of uplifting man's heart. "The poet's, the writer's, duty . . . is to help man endure by lifting his heart, by reminding him of the courage and honor and hope and pride and compassion and pity and sacrifice which have been the glory of his past."

Faulkner's earlier critics had fair reason for failing to grasp his heroic purpose. His first book was an elegaic exhalation of poems in a Keatsian tone and a French Symbolist manner; hence his title, *The Marble Faun*, after Mallarmé's *L'après-midi d'un faune*. His first important fiction, coming like a cosmic big bang in the later 1920's, dealt on one side with the collapse of the Old South and on the other with the rise of the Snopeses—neither theme evincing any ostensible heroic possibilities. But the heroic spirit *was* there, if you knew where to look for it. Faulkner learned very early where not to look for it, in the proud but decaying aristocratic lineage of the Sartorises and Benbows and Compsons. Doomed and emasculate, self-pitying and self-absorbed, these old families had dwindled to a shadow of their former splendor, leaving the true verities to reside in the opposite end of the social spectrum: in poor whites, Negroes, old maids, criminals, and outcasts of every description. Faulkner even extended this principle into the animal kingdom, elevating a little mongrel fyce to heroic status in *The Bear* and rendering an epic digression in *Sartoris* (or *Flags in the Dust*) on behalf of the noble mule.

(continued from page 213) Sewanee Review (Winter, 1963); William James, *Talks to Teachers on Psychology: and to Students on Some of Life's Ideals* (New York: 1929), pp. 274–278, 299; *The Wild Palms* (New York: 1966), p. 324.

But before Faulkner could present his myriad exponents of courage both physical and moral, it was necessary for him to stop—in William James's words—"steeping myself in pure ancestral blindness." That is to say, the lingering hold of romantic nihilism had to be exorcised so as to clear the eyes for a new perception. For Faulkner, the exorcism occurs in the closing paragraphs of *Sartoris* (or *Flags in the Dust*), which describes the aristocratic tradition as "a game outmoded and played with pawns shaped too late and to an old dead pattern." Yet the hold of the Sartoris legend (based on Faulkner family history) is strong with "a glamorous fatality, like silver pennons downrushing at sunset, or a dying fall of horns along the road to Roncevaux," and the Blotner biography confirms the elegaic mood of this early novel—a mood that carried over into *The Sound and the Fury*: ". . . nothing served but that I try by main strength to recreate between the covers of a book the world . . . I was already preparing to lose and regret. . . ." What happened to Faulkner, turning him from the aristocracies to the likes of Wash Jones as an exemplar of the old verities, was a sort of revelation surprisingly parallel to that which William James attested in "What Makes a Life Significant":

> I perceived, by a flash of insight, that I had been steeping myself in pure ancestral blindness. . . . Wishing for heroism and the spectacle of human nature on the rack, I had never noticed the great fields of heroism lying round about me, I had failed to see it present and alive. I could only think of it as dead and embalmed, labelled and costumed, as it is in the pages of romance. And yet there it was before me in the daily lives of the laboring classes. . . .

By way of expanding upon this insight, James in effect envisioned the literary program that Faulkner's whole canon of fiction would some day realize:

> Divinity lies all about us, and culture is too hide-bound to even suspect the fact. . . . And there I rested on that day, with a sense of widening of vision, and with what is surely fair to call an increase of religious insight into life. In God's eyes the differences of social

position, of intellect, of culture, of cleanliness, of dress, which different men exhibit, and . . . on which they pin their pride, must be so small as practically quite to vanish; and all that should remain is the common fact that here we are, a countless multitude of vessels of life, each of us pent in peculiar difficulties, with which we must struggle by using whatever of fortitude and goodness we can summon up. The exercise of the courage, patience, and kindness, must be the significant portion of the whole business. . . . At this rate, the deepest human life is everywhere, is eternal.

A better paraphrase of Faulkner's Nobel Prize speech, and of the fiction which the speech tried to crystallize, can hardly be attempted; nor can a clearer picture of either Faulkner's or James's concept of saintliness. The result, in both cases, is an inversion of the social order, so that the last shall be first; the lowest, highest; and vice-cersa. "Thus," James puts it—but it could as well be Faulkner—"are men's lives levelled up as well as levelled down,—levelled up in their common inner meaning, levelled down in their outer gloriousness and show."

To verify this James-Faulkner correlation, let us consider a roll-call of Faulknerian heroes. A few of them, like Horace Benbow in *Sanctuary* and Hightower in *Light in August*, are from the upper classes, but their heroism consists mainly in wanting to live by the code of a Christian gentleman; because they lack the crucial virtue, fortitude, they are ineffectual, like Quentin Compson and his father. If a few of their class are effectual, like Miss Jenny in *Sartoris* and Ike McCaslin in *The Bear*, that is because these characters have renounced James's "ancestral blindness" in judging their patrician legacy.

Meanwhile, Faulkner invested his low-life people with royal dignity, on a broad scale. There is Dilsey in *The Sound and the Fury*, the illiterate Negro cook whose figure looks ". . . as though muscle and tissue had been courage or fortitude which the days or the years had consumed until only the indomitable skeleton was left rising like a ruin or a landmark above the somnolent and impervious guts." (Dilsey's real-life prototype, Mammy Caroline Barr, was eulogized in the dedication of *Go*

Down, Moses in terms straight out of William James's above rumination: "Who was born in slavery and who gave to my family a fidelity without stint or calculation of recompense and to my childhood an immeasurable devotion and love.") In Faulkner's bitterest novel, *Sanctuary*, the moral putrefaction of conventional society is set off against the nobility of its criminal heroes, the prostitute Ruby Lamar and the murderer-moonshiner-ex-convict Lee Goodwin. Faulkner's stage-managing of Goodwin's first entrance into the novel is a minor masterpiece in the mode of moral vignette:

> As she was doing that [Ruby is setting the table], Goodwin entered. . . . He was leading by the arm an old man with a long white beard stained about the mouth. Benbow watched Goodwin seat the old man in a chair, where he sat obediently with that tentative and abject eagerness of a man who has but one pleasure left and whom the world can reach only through one sense, for he was both blind and deaf: a short man with a bald skull and a round, full-fleshed, rosy face in which his cataracted eyes looked like two clots of phlegm. Benbow watched him take a filthy rag from his pocket and regurgitate into the rag an almost colorless wad of what had once been chewing tobacco. . . . Then Benbow quit looking. When the meal was over, Goodwin led the old man out again. Benbow watched the two of them pass out the door and heard them go up the hall.

That this sort of care "without stint or calculation of recompense" is a measure of saintliness is evident from Faulkner's repetition of the motif, but his major manifestation of the theme is reserved for his recurring set of Christ figures. This long series of characters, from the idiot Benjy to the private in *A Fable*, may be seen as having two essential functions. One is the role of scapegoat, in the style of the messianic profile of 53rd Isaiah—he was wounded for our transgressions, he was bruised for our iniquities. Characters like Benjy and Charles Bon and Joe Christmas serve that role powerfully enough to verify Faulkner's role as prophet, thundering damnation upon a godless society. But the other role, perhaps having an even deeper power, is the Jamesian one of affirming

217

the efficacy and vicariousness of all suffering. No definition of saintliness, however orthodox or secular, can have more importance than this "dark truth," as one of the most unforgettable testimonies reported to William James describes it (p. 302n):

> I realized that in that half hour under ether I had served God more distinctly and purely than I had ever done in my life before. . . . I was the means of his achieving and revealing something, I know not what or to whom, and that, to the exact extent of my capacity for suffering.
>
> While regaining consciousness, I wondered why, since I had gone so deep, I had seen nothing of what the saints call the *love* of God, nothing but his relentlessness. And then I heard an answer, which I could just catch, saying, "Knowledge and Love are One, and the *measure* is suffering"—I give the words as they came to me. . . . If I had to formulate a few of the things I then caught a glimpse of, they would run somewhat as follows:—
>
> The eternal necessity of suffering and its eternal vicariousness. The veiled and incommunicable nature of the worst sufferings; . . . finally, the excess of what the suffering 'seer' or genius pays over what his generation gains. . . .

The relevance of this passage to our other figures of saintliness—Billy Budd and Captain Vere, Isabel Archer, Updike's centaur—must seem obvious. The passage also evokes echoes of other artists we have studied. One thinks, for example, of T. S. Eliot's thesis in *Murder in the Cathedral*, that suffering is action. And one thinks also of poor Hart Crane, scorched by the deific Fire—"Kiss of our agony Thou gatherest,/O Hand of Fire/gatherest—."

For Faulkner the vicariousness of suffering is indicated in the first and lowliest of all his Christ figures, the idiot Benjy whose wail "might have been all time and injustice and sorrow become vocal for an instant by a conjunction of planets." Or again, Benjy as the Man of Sorrows "bellowed slowly, abjectly, without tears; the grave hopeless sound of all voiceless misery under the sun." Such suffering may have seemed minimally efficacious in Faulkner's earlier fiction, especially that produced during his black mood of the early 1930's wherein the scapegoats—Joe Christmas and Charles Bon—predominated. But Faulkner's later Christ figures represent a quantum leap into the higher ranges of saintliness such that suffering becomes both vicarious and redemptive. Three figures in particular—Ike McCaslin in *The Bear*, Nancy Mannigoe in *Requiem for a Nun*, and the corporal in *A Fable*—evince a kind of religious psychology that harkens back to James and Melville. Despite the apparent futility of their sacrifice, they represent an avant garde of the human conscience, willing to suffer ignominy as fool or criminal in their own time so as to remedy the future.

Nancy Mannigoe, as the simplest and most orthodox Christian of these portrayals, accepts her suffering—as "nigger, dopefiend, whore" and condemned murderess—with blind faith:

> Stevens: The salvation of the world is in man's suffering. Is that It?
> Nancy: Yes, sir.
> Stevens: How?
> Nancy: I don't know.

Her assertions in the execution chamber, "I believes" and "Trust in Him," reflect William James's observation that the "abandonment of self-responsibility seems to be the fundamental act in specifically religious, as distinguished from moral practice . . . Christians who have it . . . are never anxious about the future, nor worry about the outcome of the day" (p. 229).

About the corporal in *A Fable* two Jamesian statements may apply. First, James observes in "The Value of Saintliness" that "history shows us that, as a rule, religious geniuses attract disciples, and produce groups of sympathizers" (p. 261): enough sympathizers in Faulkner's novel to shut down the entire French war machine during the great mutiny of 1917. The other statement, rendered world-famous now by the bloodshed of this turbulent century, is James's comment in the same chapter that "What we now need to discover in the social realm is the moral equivalent of war" (p. 284).

In the pacifism of the corporal, Faulkner portrays not only the moral equivalent but the negation of war, a negation made necessary in Faulkner's judgment from the moment the news reached home about Hiroshima. (In his Nobel Prize Speech, Faulkner complained that the question of "When will I be blown up?" had displaced the old verities of the heart; yet, *A Fable* was written largely in the light of that question.) But in view of the general disappointment with *A Fable*—Allen Tate described it as its author's only failure—perhaps Faulkner's best conceived moral equivalent of war is that which William James himself went on to identify just after introducing the phrase (p. 284):

> I have often thought that in the old monkish poverty-worship . . . there might be something like that moral equivalent of war which we are seeking. . . . and when one sees the way in which wealth-getting enters as an ideal into the very bone and marrow of our generation, one wonders whether a revival of the belief that poverty is a worthy religious vocation may not be "the transformation of military courage," and the spiritual reform which our time stands most in need of.

For Faulkner, Ike McCaslin became that Jamesian monk of poverty, renouncing his title to the ancestral estate in favor of a "communal anonymity of brotherhood" with respect to all land ownership. To his cousin who tries to persuade him of the folly of this move (and, later, to Ike's bride, who reacts much as Tolstoy's wife did on a similar occasion), Ike McCaslin already fits James's initial definition of sainthood: "These devotees have often laid their course so differently from other men that, judging them by worldly law, we might be tempted to call them monstrous aberrations from the path of nature" (p. 208).

Ike's vision of human history as a series of dispossessions—from Eden to Canaan to Rome to the barbarians who "snarled . . . over the old world's gnawed bones, blasphemous in His name"—parallels James's view that "the desire to

220

gain wealth and the fear to lose it are our chief breeders of cowardice and propagators of corruption" (p. 285). Writing *The Bear* in the early years of World War II, Faulkner had more reason than James did to conceive this view of all human history as a bloody struggle over control of land, and all the more reason therefore to espouse Ike McCaslin's ideal of poverty. But James must have had some similar presentiment in saying "it is certain that the prevalent fear of poverty among the educated classes is the worst moral disease from which our civilization suffers" (p. 285).

So James's moral equivalent of war is a freely chosen life of poverty. "Poverty," he says, is "felt at all times and under all creeds as one adornment of a saintly life. . . . Hindu fakirs, Buddhist monks, and Mohammedan dervishes unite with Jesuits and Franciscans in idealizing poverty as the loftiest individual state" (pp. 247, 249). Neither Faulkner nor James, however, had any practical interest in these orthodox traditions concerning poverty. As pragmatists, their faces are set toward the future; and Ike McCaslin thereby serves as another model for the Jamesian principle of the changing of the gods. James's statement, we may remember, was that "Nothing is more striking than the secular alteration that goes on in the moral and religious tone of men, as their insight into nature and their social arrangements progressively develop. After an interval . . . the mental climate proves unfavorable to notions of the deity which at an earlier date were perfectly satisfactory" (p. 257). For Ike McCaslin, this interior alchemy eventually required him to revise Holy Writ so as to counteract the Bible's endorsement of landowning ("the tedious and shabby chronicle of His chosen sprung from Abraham") and of black slavery ("The sons of Ham. You who quote the Book: the sons of Ham"): "There are some things He said in the Book, and some things reported of Him that He did not say."

There remains one final affinity between Faulkner's Ike McCaslin and William James's profile of saintliness. In "The

221

Value of Saintliness" James refers to the saints as "torch-bearers, . . . the tip of the wedge, the clearers of the darkness." "The world is not yet with them," James says, "so they often seem in the midst of the world's affairs to be preposterous." Yet, he continues, "the general function of his charity in social evolution is vital and essential. If things are ever to move upward, some one must be ready to take the first step, and assume the risk of it. . . . This practical proof that worldly wisdom may be safely transcended is the saint's magic gift to mankind. . . . He is an effective fermenter of goodness, a slow transmuter of the earthly into a more heavenly order" (pp. 277–278). While this statement could be applied to almost any saintly portrait, Ike McCaslin would have to be its prime exemplar in the Faulknerian canon. In his debate with his cousin, Ike himself appears to conceive of his mission in this way: [the cousin speaks first] " 'Chosen, I suppose (I will concede it) out of all your time by Him. . . . And it took you fourteen years to reach that point. . . . And you are just one. How long, then? How long?' and he [Ike] 'It will be long. I have never said otherwise. But it will be all right because they will endure. . . .' "

Among Faulkner's other books, one might cite many a figure we have slighted—Cash Bundren for his endurance of pain in *As I Lay Dying*, Bayard Sartoris for breaking the revenge cycle in *The Unvanquished*, Mink Snopes for his tenacity in the Snopes trilogy—but our final Faulknerian portrait in saintliness will be yet another figure with Biblical overtones, Harry Wilbourne in *The Wild Palms*. The Biblical reference in this instance is to the title—perhaps Faulkner's finest ever—which his editor forced Faulkner to discard on the grounds that it might stir up anti-Semitic feelings. That title, *If I Forget Thee O, Jerusalem*, refers to one of the most passionate of all the Psalms, number 137, composed during the Hebrews' captivity in Babylon. So far as any of the Israelites knew, Jerusalem had been sacked and laid waste forever; none of them in any case could ever hope to see it again. In the circumstances, to remember Jerusalem was to be suffused in grief and despair; as the psalmist says, "we wept, when we remembered Zion." This experience of memory as the most painful of tortures had led Horace Benbow to want to be dipped in Lethe every ten years; but as Horace admits in *Sanctuary*: "I lack courage: that was left out of me."

Harry Wilbourne, we might say, is Horace's opposite number. So, like the psalmist in Babylon, Harry in his prison cell chooses to remember Jerusalem—that fair time when he and his sweetheart lived their idyll together. Sentenced to fifty years at hard labor for performing the abortion that killed her, he rejects both the proffered escape—because there is no place he can escape her memory—and suicide, because in oblivion he would no longer remember Jerusalem: "*when she became not then half of memory became not and if I become not then all of memory will cease to be.*" The psalmist's will to suffer, to remember his paradise lost, and even to "prefer Jerusalem above my chief joy," now becomes transmuted into one of Faulkner's most profound theme statements: "*Yes*, he thought, *between grief and nothing I will take grief.*" Because every investment of love—in a parent, child, friend, sweetheart, pet, or whatever—must involve loss and grief eventually, this emotional stance must be the most universally applicable among all of Faulkner's heroic profiles, excepting only the person of total emotional independence such as Jason Compson.

To conclude, one of the unifying elements of Faulkner's artistic career was his deepening commitment to the Jamesian ideals of saintliness. Illuminating that theme and the wide spectrum of figures who embody it is a final Jamesian assertion: "The solid meaning of life is always the same eternal thing,—the marriage, namely, of some unhabitual ideal, however special [Ike McCaslin's ideal of poverty, Harry Wilbourne remembering Jerusalem], with some fidelity, courage, and endurance."

5.

Unlike Faulkner, John Updike portrays saintliness as a thing of the past, displaced now by the totally selfish hedonism that has come to prevail in contemporary mores. Novels about contemporary life such as the Rabbit books, *Couples*, *A Month of Sundays*, and *Marry Me* carry not a trace of the Christian goodness that Updike had eulogized in his earlier fiction, particularly in *The Poorhouse Fair* and *The Centaur*. It is as though the later books were designed to bear out the prophecy of John Hook, the 94-year-old Christian hero of *The Poorhouse Fair*: "When you get to be my age . . . you shall know this: There is no goodness, without belief. There is only busy-ness."[8] What might be a mere generation gap for some writers thus widens for Updike into a chasm separating the millennia, with Christian civilization expiring on one side— "Protestant goodness going down with all guns firing"— while on the other side a horde of neo-pagan hedonists assumes sovereignty.

The goodness Updike speaks of in *The Centaur* is what theologians call *agape*, that love which St. Paul placed at the top of his famous triad in I Corinthians 13; and though we see very little faith and not much hope in *The Centaur*, we do see an abundance of love in George Caldwell, love which in the

---

[8] *The Poorhouse Fair* (New York: 1958), p. 81. Other quotations are cited from this book, p. 127; TIME (April 26, 1968), p. 74; Karl Barth, *Church Dogmatics* (New York: 1962), pp. 188, 190; *The Centaur* (New York: 1963), pp. 65, 67, 24, 221, 73, 133, 81; *Couples* (New York: 1968), p. 158; *The Paris Review*, 45 (Spring, 1969), pp. 93–94.

224

Pauline phrases "suffreth long, and is kind, . . . seeketh not her own, is not easily provoked, thinketh no evil." Here perhaps a few words from Updike's religious mentor, Karl Barth, will focus Caldwell's role more clearly: "In *agape*-love a man gives himself to the other with no expectation of a return, in a pure vventure, even at the risk of ingratitude. . . ." Or again: "In his love there takes place the encounter of I and Thou, the open perception of the other and self-disclosure to him, conversation with him, the offering and receiving of assistance, and all with joy". Caldwell's encounter with the queer hitchhiker appears consciously designed to bear out these Barthian precepts. A "reservoir of slime" to the centaur's teen-age son (at whom he makes a pass), the stranger attests his vile personality in every word he utters—"What a fucking day. Freeze your sucking balls off"; "That's right, buddy. That's what the fucking sucker did"—and he ungratefully steals Caldwell's gloves. But Caldwell opens his life to him in conversation, and calls out in parting, "I've enjoyed talking to you."

As the last Christian in a world that has otherwise reverted back to pagan hedonism— this is the meaning of the novel's Olympic framework—Chiron-Caldwell here manifests the "fruits of the spirit" that James catalogues in his chapter on "Saintliness." Among these fruits, which make up a "composite photograph of universal saintliness, the same in all religions," James particularly remarks "an increase of charity, tenderness for fellow creatures," in such a magnitude that "the saint . . . treats loathsome beggars as his brothers" (pp. 216–218). There would be other "Christians" in Updike's oeuvre, for nearly all his protagonists—like Updike himself— are professors of the faith, but George Caldwell is Updike's last Christian who may be known by his fruits of saintliness, as the episode of the queer hitchhiker makes manifest. Updike's later "Christians" profess the faith solely as a stay against death. So far as the fruits of the spirit are concerned, they are indistinguishable from the atheistic hedonists that surround them. Unlike the centaur, these "Christians" thus become eligible—though Updike would probably not approve of this—for a strong dose of the dry Jamesian irony (pp. 191–192):

> Well, how is it with these fruits? . . . Were it true that a suddenly converted man as such is, as Edwards says, of an entirely different kind from a natural man, partaking as he does directly of Christ's substance, there surely ought to be some exquisite class-mark, some distinctive radiance attaching even to the lowliest specimen of this genus. . . . But notoriously there is no such radiance. Converted men are indistinguishable as a class from natural men . . . .

It is this lack of "radiance" among ordinary Christians that permits Chiron-Caldwell to assume his true vocation as teacher. In his ostensible vocation, as a high school science teacher, he is—and deems himself—an utter failure, much in the style of James's "Sick Soul" personality: "Failure, then, failure! so the world stamps us at every turn. We strew it with our blunders, our misdeeds, our lost opportunities, with all the memorials of our inadequacy to our vocation. . . . The subtlest forms of suffering known to man are connected with the poisonous humiliations incidental to these results" (p. 119). But as every parent learns, teaching is not a matter of words, in the classroom or elsewhere. For young people, the only meaningful teaching is that done by example—in Chiron's case, the example of saintliness. By the Jamesian definition—and Updike *would* approve of this—the centaur is a magnificent teacher of Christianity: "The real witness of the spirit to the second birth is to be found only in the disposition of the genuine child of God, the permanently patient heart, the love of self eradicated" (p. 192). It is in this character that Chiron, more than any of Updike's "Christians," effects a stay against death.

This stay against death relates to Updike's oft-stated belief in "dualism," a belief that is objectified in this novel by the centaur's bodily form: above the waist, men are spiritual beings, capable of love and sacrifice and loyalty; below the waist, they are dung- and semen-spewing animals, which is the meaning of Chiron's inadvertent defecation by the trophy cases. In resisting Venus's advances, Chiron affirms his above-the-waist identity ("From the waist up, I am told, I am fully human") at the expense of "his nether half" which—"imperfect servant of his will"—stomps and prances in unsatisfied desire. Unlike the adulterous pleasure-seekers in most Updike novels, Chiron accepts—in the words of Updike's *Paris Review* interview—"the suppressed pain, . . . the sacrifice I suppose that middle-class life demands, and by that I guess I mean civilized life." Thereby he becomes the subject of the novel's final litany: *"What is a hero? A hero is a king sacrificed to Hera."*

Hera, the patron goddess of the family; Caldwell, a king sacrificed: the religious meaning of this situation is developed in James's discussion of sacrifice. The nature of the universe, he says, is such that everyone is "drawn and pressed" into "sacrifices and surrenders of some sort" as "permanent positions of repose." "Now in those states of mind which fall short of religion," he observes "the surrender is submitted to as an imposition of necessity. . . . In the religious life, on the contrary, surrender and sacrifice are positively espoused." Religion thus "becomes an essential organ of our life" from a practical viewpoint, "performing a function which no other portion of our nature can so successfully fulfill" (p. 56). Or, as John Hook put it in *The Poorhouse Fair*, "There is no goodness without belief." There may be sacrifice without belief, but sacrifice grudgingly rendered is not goodness.

Man's dualism, as portrayed in Venus' enticement of Chiron, is discussed in James's "Conclusions" about religious experience, where he observes that though "the warring gods and formulas of the various religions do indeed cancel each other, . . . there is a certain uniform deliverance in which religions all appear to meet. It consists of two parts" (and the two parts correspond to the centaur's self-division): "(1) . . . a sense that there is *something wrong about us* as we naturally stand. (2) . . . a sense that *we are saved from the wrongness* by making proper connections with the higher powers" (p. 383). These terms, James feels, "allow for the divided self and the struggle" and "involve the change of personal centre and the surrender of the lower self" (p. 384). Because "he suffers from his wrongness and criticizes it," James goes on to explain, the religious individual is (pp. 383–4):

> in at least possible touch with something higher, if anything higher exist. Along with the wrong part there is thus a better part of him. . . . When stage 2 (the stage of solution or salvation) arrives, the man identifies his real being with the germinal higher part of himself, and does so in the following way. *He becomes conscious that this higher part is conterminous and continuous with a MORE of the same quality, which is operative in the universe outside of him, and which he can . . . in a fashion get on board of and save himself when all his lower being has gone to pieces in the wreck.*

I have quoted this passage at length because I think it is crucial to understanding the full meaning of Updike's belief that "Only goodness lives. But it does live." As against the dread of death, James had stated in "The Sick Soul," "We need . . . a kind of good that will not perish, a good in fact that flies beyond the Goods of nature" (p. 121). The centaur's effort to suppress his horse's body in favor of his above-the-waist humanity is precisely Updike's correlative to these Jamesian formulations, his finding "a good that will not perish" which he can "get on board of and save himself when all his lower being has gone to pieces in the wreck."

The "wreck" in Updike's writing involves death for the animal self and entropy for the physical universe, but because of his intuition of duality, Updike envisions a spiritual counterpart to the physical universe that is free from death and entropy. The sole but sufficient proof we have of such a spiritual universe is agape love. As against the dread of death that hovers almost palpably over most of Updike's fiction, the immortality of agape gathers paramount importance. "Only goodness lives. But it does live" is in effect Updike's version of Karl Barth's assertion that "love, *agape*, never fails (I Cor. 13:8). . . . It is imperishable even in the midst of a world which perishes."

For his "countless, nameless acts of charity and good will"—as his obituary puts it—George Caldwell is spared the last despair of his dying father, the minister, over the prospect of being "eternally forgotten," committed without a trace to the geological eons. For George Caldwell, the good is not interred but lives on after him. The statement in his obituary, "What endures, perhaps, most indelibly in the minds of his ex-students (of whom this present writer counts himself one) was his more-than-human selflessness," is borne out by ex-student Diefendorf's statement fourteen years later: "a great man, your Dad. Did you know that?" All the testimony of Caldwell's life is such as to bear out the theme, stated only ironically in *Couples*, that "we're all put here to humanize each other." On achieving this purpose, Caldwell also solves the mystery that Updike had left unclarified in his closing lines of *The Poorhouse Fair*: "[Hook's] encounter with Conner had commenced to trouble him. . . . A small word would perhaps set things right. . . . He stood motionless, half in moonlight, groping after the fitful shadow of the advice he must impart to Conner, as a bond between them and a testament to endure his dying in the world. What was it?" The small word was agape.

6.

Saintliness, like Conversion, is an almost infinitely expandable topic in its relation to literature. Apart from expressly anti-moralistic writers like Poe and Nabokov, most writers do feel moved to impart some wisdom concerning the conduct of life, and their work is likely to reflect the author's

229

ethical aspirations. "The study of literature is hero-worship," remarked Ezra Pound in *The Spirit of Romance*, and though his own search for heroes turned up some motley specimens like Hitler and Mussolini, his remark is psychologically sound.[9] Hemingway's code heroes, like Jake Barnes and Count Greffi; Eliot's persona bringing the thunder of Mosaic Law—Give, Sympathize, Control—into the Waste Land; Faulkner's stalwart exemplars of the Old Verities of the Heart; Scott Fitzgerald's "fundamental decencies" in *The Great Gatsby*—these and many other models of an ideal self have handsomely survived even the great skepticism of the modern age.

Saul Bellow, winner of the 1976 Nobel Prize for Literature, has extended this tradition right through the Viet Nam and Watergate era, giving us a Jewish counterpart to the Centaur in his Mr. Sammler, for example. At the time he published *Herzog*, Bellow declared it his favorite creation not only because "Its scale is larger. The mind of the hero is more complete," but because Herzog "believes in certain virtues which have nearly disappeared. Goodness, duty, courage"— concerning which virtues, Bellow adds: "I think they're just in hiding everywhere." To disclose where they are hiding has been the collective function of our figures of Saintliness, providing for our age that Jamesian "succession of such examples as . . . only in the reading of them, is to feel encouraged and uplifted and washed in better moral air."

---

[9] *The Spirit of Romance* (New York: 1968), p. 5. Also cited is Saul Bellow, SHOW (September, 1964), pp. 36–38.

Chapter VII

Postscript

As a philosopher, William James is identified with the chief (and perhaps only) important ideology America has contributed to world philosophy, the concept of Pragmatism. *Pragmatism*, the book of essays published in 1907; *A Pluralistic Universe*, published in 1909; and his two books published posthumously, *Some Problems in Philosophy* (1911) and *Essays in Radical Empiricism* (1912)—these works appear solid enough some three generations later to have ensured the permanence of James's high status as a philosophical thinker. Likewise, James's status as a great psychologist now appears permanently rescued from the neglect that resulted from the meteoric rise, earlier in this century, of the modern analytic and archetypal schools of psychology. In the closing pages of his biography of James, Gay Wilson Allen noted the re-emergence of James from under Freud's shadow, citing some distinguished voices in psychology for evidence. For one example, Gordon W. Allport, of Harvard, brought out a reprint of James's

Psychology in 1961 with the comment, "now that we have recovered from the irreverent shocks administered by Freud, Pavlov, Watson, we begin to perceive that the psychological insights of James have the steadiness of a polar star."[1] And Ashley Montagu, introducing a more recent reprint of the *Psychology*, observed that "nothing which has developed during that period [since James's book] or is likely to happen will ever render this book out-of-date." More recently still, in *Love and Will*, the existentialist psychologist Rollo May speaks of "William James, the psychologist-philosopher American-man-of-genius," as a "redoubtable crusader who was far ahead of his time."

The Varieties of Religious Experience, representing a confluence of William James's psychological and philosophical insights, may never have fallen into the unjust neglect that for a time affected the *Principles of Psychology*. On the other hand, neither has it evoked in Academe the keen interest accorded the *Psychology* during its high-crest periods of acclaim, both former and latter-day. Evidently the problem with *The Varieties* has been its seeming irrelevance to its prospectively divided reading audience: to the skeptical scientific eye, the book must seem questionably subjective in its substance, and hence feebly unrealistic; with respect to traditional religious thought, meanwhile, this work may well appear theologically unsound, if not vacuous. So we have sought to resolve the question of scientific/theological relevance by appealing to a third world of human sensibility, the realm of art.

Having now considered some thirty major American writers in light of the Jamesian religious psychology, and having made passing reference to at least that many more, we must surely regard the relevance of James's *Varieties* to

---

[1] Gay Wilson Allen, *William James: A Biography* (New York: 1969), pp. 517, 518. Also cited is Rollo May, *Love and Will* (New York: 1969), pp. 218, 39.

American literature as large and significant. (That any number of literary figures not included in this study might also have demonstrated James's relevance must also be taken into account; one can only repeat Herman Melville's apology for his Hawthorne criticism, based on the observation that all subjects are infinite.) As we glance back over our literary personalities for one last time, a number of especially illuminating Jamesian insights may crowd our memory. One may think of Emily Dickinson's valiant struggle to perserve her innate healthy-mindedness in the face of her Calvinist social environment, for example; or of the fine distinction defining Wallace Stevens' strongly willed affirmations—the "voluntary" form of healthy-mindedness, James called it—as against William Carlos Williams' "involuntary" version of that temperament. Then, too, there is the roll call of so many sensitive spirits—Melville, Twain, Stephen Crane, Nathanael West and other black humorist thinkers—trapped harrowingly in the Jamesian sick soul state owing to the rise of naturalistic beliefs about the world. The literary record of escapes from this chilling view of life, recorded by artists as disparate as Poe, T. S. Eliot, Nabokov, and Bellow, makes manifest the permanent relevance of William James concerning the psychology of Conversion. So, too, James's open-minded investigation of Mysticism must surely remain an unrivalled source of insight concerning writers as various as Thomas Wolfe, James Baldwin, and Hart Crane. And finally, William James's psychology of saintliness—a reconceptualization of virtue that finds parallels in brother Henry's portrait of a Madonna, in Melville's and Updike's Christ figures, in Faulkner's monk of poverty— shows that ancient human aspiration to be more resilient and enduring than might have seemed possible in this secular age.

Let us terminate our reflections upon *The Varieties of Religious Experience* with a slight revision of something William James said about it. "In a general way," James said, "our testing of religion by practical common sense and the empirical method leaves it in possession of its towering place in history" (p. 290). Of James himself we are now prepared to say that, in a general way, our correlation between American literature and James's religious psychology leaves this admirable man more securely in possession of *his* towering place in American literary history.

Index of Names

(Parentheses indicate the citing of a writer without using his name.)

studia humanitatis

PUBLISHED VOLUMES

GENARO J. PÉREZ, *Formalist Elements in the Novels of Juan Goytisolo.* xii–216 pp. US $12.50.

SARA MARIA ADLER, *Calvino: The Writer as Fablemaker.* xviii–164 pp. US $11.50.

LOPE DE VEGA, *El amor enamorado,* critical edition of John B. Wooldridge, Jr. xvi–236 pp. US $13.00.

NANCY DERSOFI, *Arcadia and the Stage: A Study of the Theater of Angelo Beolco* (called *Ruzante*). xii–180 pp. US $10.00

JOHN A. FREY, *The Aesthetics of the* ROUGON-MACQUART. xvi–356 pp. US $20.00.

CHESTER W. OBUCHOWSKI, *Mars on Trial: War as Seen by French Writers of the Twentieth Century.* xiv–320 pp. US $20.00.

JEREMY T. MEDINA, *Spanish Realism: Theory and Practice of a Concept in the Nineteenth Century.* xviii–374 pp. US $17.50.

MAUDA BREGOLI-RUSSO, *Boiardo Lirico.* viii–204 pp. US $11.00.

ROBERT H. MILLER, ed. *Sir John Harington: A Supplie or Addicion to the Catalogue of Bishops to the Yeare 1608.* xii–214 pp. US $13.50.

NICOLÁS E. ÁLVAREZ, *La obra literaria de Jorge Mañach.* vii–279 pp. US $13.00.

MARIO ASTE, *La narrativa di Luigi Pirandello: Dalle novelle al romanzo Uno, Nessuno, e Centomila.* xvi–200 pp. US $11.00.

MECHTHILD CRANSTON, *Orion Resurgent: René Char, Poet of Presence.* xxiv–376 pp. U.S. $22.50.

FRANK A. DOMÍNGUEZ, *The Medieval Argonautica.* viii–122 pp. US $10.50.

EVERETT HESSE, *New Perspectives on Comedia Criticism.* xix–174 pp. US $14.00.

ANTHONY A. CICCONE, *The Comedy of Language: Four Farces by Molière.* xii–144 $12.00.

ANTONIO PLANELLS, *Cortázar: Metafísica y erotismo.* xvi–220 pp. US $10.00.

MARY LEE BRETZ, *La evolución novelística de Pío Baroja.* viii–476 pp. US $22.50.

Romance Literary Studies: Homage to Harvey L. Johnson, ed. Marie A. Wellington and Martha O'Nan. xxxvii–185 pp. US $15.00.

GEORGE E. MCSPADDEN, *Don Quijote and the Spanish Prologues,* volume I. vi–114 pp. US $17.00.

Studies in Honor of Gerald E. Wade, edited by Sylvia Bowman, Bruno M. Damiani, Janet W. Díaz, E. Michael Gerli, Everett Hesse, John E. Keller, Luis Leal and Russell P. Sebold. xii–244 pp. U.S. $20.00.

LOIS ANN RUSSELL, *Robert Challe: A Utopian Voice in the Early Enlightenment.* xiii–164 pp. U.S. $12.50.

CRAIG WALLACE BARROW, *Montage in James Joyce's* ULYSSES. xiii–218 pp. US $16.50.

MARIA ELISA CIAVARELLI, *La fuerza de la sangre en la literatura del Siglo de Oro.* xii–274 pp. US $17.00.

JUAN MARÍA COROMINAS, *Castiglione y La Araucana: Estudio de una Influencia.* viii–139 pp. US $14.00.

KENNETH BROWN, *Anastasio Pantaleón de Ribera (1600 1629) Ingenioso Miembro de la República Literaria Española.* xix–420 pp. US $18.50.

JOHN STEVEN GEARY, *Formulaic Diction in the* Poema de Fernán González *and the* Mocedades de Rodrigo. xv–180 pp. US $15.50.

HARRIET K. GREIF, *Historia de nacimientos: The Poetry of Emilio Prados.* xi–399 pp. U.S. $18.00.

El cancionero del Bachiller Jhoan López, edición crítica de Rosalind Gabin. lvi–362 pp. US $30.00

VICTOR STRANDBERG, *Religious Psychology in American Literature.* xi–237 pp. US $17.50

FORTHCOMING PUBLICATIONS

HELMUT HATZFELD, *Essais sur la littérature flamboyante.*

JOSEPH BARBARINO, *The Latin Intervocalic Stops: A Quantitative and Comparative Study.*

NANCY D'ANTUONO, *Boccaccio's novelle in Lope's theatre.*

Novelistas femeninas de la postguerra española, ed. Janet W. Díaz.

La Discontenta and La Pythia, edition with introduction and notes by Nicholas A. De Mara.

PERO LÓPEZ DE AYALA, *Crónica del Rey Don Pedro I,* edición crítica de Heanon y Constance Wilkins.

ALBERT H. LE MAY, *The Experimental Verse Theater of Valle-Inclán.*

DENNIS M. KRATZ, *Mocking Epic.*

CALDERÓN DE LA BARCA, *The Prodigal Magician,* translated and edited by Bruce W. Wardropper.

241